£49.95

D0275680

UNDERSTANDING
HEALTHCARE
INFORMATION

UNDERSTANDING
HEALTHCARE
INFORMATION

Lyn Robinson

facet publishing

Published by Facet Publishing
7 Ridgmount Street, London WC1E 7AE
www.facetpublishing.co.uk

Facet Publishing is wholly owned by CILIP: the Chartered
Institute of Library and Information Professionals.

British Library Cataloguing in Publication Data
A catalogue record for this book is available
from the British Library.

ISBN 978–1-85604–662–6

First published 2010

Mixed Sources
Product group from well-managed
forests and other controlled sources
www.fsc.org Cert no. SA-COC-1565
© 1996 Forest Stewardship Council

Text printed on FSC accredited material.

Typeset from author's files in 11/13pt American Garamond and
Function by Facet Publishing.
Printed and made in Great Britain by MPG Books Group, UK.

Contents

Acronyms and abbreviations

AACR	Anglo-American Cataloguing Rules
AAMC	Association of American Medical Colleges
ABPI	Association of the British Pharmaceutical Industry
AMA	American Medical Association
AMED	Allied and Complementary Medicine Database
ASSIA	Applied Social Sciences Index and Abstracts
BBC	British Broadcasting Corporation
Biosis	a biomedical database, formerly Biological Abstracts
BL	British Library
BMA	British Medical Association
BMC	BioMed Central
BMJ	British Medical Journal
BNF	British National Formulary
BS	British Standard
BUBL	Bulletin Board for Libraries [an internet resource directory]
BUPA	a UK-based health insurer
CD-ROM	Compact Disk – Read Only Memory
CHILL	Consortium of Independent Health Information Libraries in London
CILIP	Chartered Institute of Library and Information Professionals (UK)
CINAHL	Cumulative Index to Nursing and Allied Health Literature
CISMeF	French health information portal

COSTART	Coding Symbols for a Thesaurus of Adverse Reaction Terms
CTCAE	Common Terminology Criteria for Adverse Events
DDC	Dewey Decimal Classification
Dialog	an online host system
DIMDI	German Institute of Medical Documentation and Information – an online host system
DTI	Department of Trade and Industry (UK) [now defunct]
EAHIL	European Association for Health Information and Libraries
EMBASE	a biomedical database, formerly Excerpta Medica
eMC	electronic Medicines Compendium
EMEA	European Medicines Agency
Entrez	a bioinformatics database system
EU	European Union
FADE	grey literature service for the North-West region of the UK NHS
FDA	Food and Drug Administration (US)
GCP	Good Clinical Practice
GLP	Good Laboratory Practice
GMC	General Medical Council (UK)
GP	general practitioner (family doctor – UK usage)
HES	Hospital Episodes Statistics (UK)
HHMI	Howard Hughes Medical Institute
HILJ	Health Libraries and Information Journal
HON	Health on the Net
HONcode	quality denotation of web resources, from the HON Foundation
HR	human resources
HRG	Healthcare Resources Groups (UK categorization)
IARC	International Agency for Research on Cancer
ICD	International Classification of Diseases
ICF	International Classification of Functioning, Disability and Health
ICHI	International Classification of Health Interventions
ICPC	International Classification of Primary Care
ICECI	International Classification of External Causes of Injury
ICT	Information and Communication Technology
IDdb	Investigational Drugs database
IEEE	Institute of Electrical and Electronics Engineers

IFLA	International Federation of Library Associations
IHTSDO	International Health Terminology Standards Development Organization
Intute	UK-based internet resource directories
IPSV	Integrated Public Sector Vocabulary (UK)
ISO	International Standards Organization
IT	information technology
JISC	Joint Information Systems Committee (UK)
JMLA	Journal of the Medical Library Association
KM	knowledge management
LCC	Library of Congress Classification
LibQual	library survey tool
LIS-MEDICAL	UK-based discussion list for health librarians
LOM	learning object metadata
MARC	MAchine Readable Cataloguing
MCH	Maternal and Child Health (thesaurus)
MEDLINE	a biomedical database, formerly Index Medicus
MedDRA	Medical Dictionary for Regulatory Affairs
MeSH	Medical Subject Headings
MIT	Massachusetts Institute of Technology
MIUA	Medical Image Understanding and Analysis (UK internet forum)
MLA	Medical Library Association (US)
NeLH	National electronic Library for Health (UK) [now succeeded by NHS Evidence]
NHS	National Health Service (UK)
NICE	National Institute for Heath and Clinical Excellence (UK)
NIH	National Institutes of Health (USA)
NIOSH	National Institute for Occupational Safety and Health (USA)
NLH	National Library for Health (UK) [now succeeded by NHS Evidence]
NLM	National Library of Medicine (US); also the classification of that name
NTIS	National Technical Information Service (US)
OCLC	Online Computer Library Center
OMNI	Organizing Medical Networked Information
OPCS	Office of Population, Censuses and Surveys (US); also the classification of that name

OPS	Operationen und Przeduernschlüssel classification (Germany)
Ovid	an online host system
PC	personal computer
PDA	Personal Digital Assistant
Pharmline	a pharmacy database
PHL	Public Health Language
PIF	Patient Information Forum
Pinakes	listing of internet resource directories
PsychInfo	a psychology / psychiatry database
PubMed	an implementation of the MEDLINE bibliographic database
QAA	Quality Assurance Agency (for Higher Education, UK)
RCN	Royal College of Nursing (UK)
RCP	Royal College of Physicians (London)
RCS	Royal College of Surgeons (London)
Ringdoc	a pharmaceutical database
RSM	Royal Society of Medicine (London)
RTECS	Registry of Toxic Effects of Chemical Substances
RxNorm	a medicines nomenclature
SCONUL	Society of College, National and University Libraries (UK)
SERVPERF	a library survey tool
SNOMED	Systematized Nomenclature of Medicine
SNOMED/CT	Systematized Nomenclature of Medicine/Clinical Terms
Toxline	a toxicology database
ToxTown	interactive tutorial (US NLM)
UDC	Universal Decimal Classification
UK	United Kingdom
UMLS	Unified Medical Language System
US(A)	United States (of America)
WHO	World Health Organization
WHOART	World Health Organization Adverse Reaction Terminology
WHOSIS	World Health Organization Statistical Information System

Introduction

The aim of this book is to embody the substance of what an information specialist or librarian in healthcare needs to know although, in our information society, an interest in healthcare information is of course no longer restricted to information professionals, and all of us, at some time in our lives, are likely to encounter a need or desire to interact with information within this field. Hence, this work is of value to a wider audience than those practising as healthcare information or knowledge workers. The increase of 'consumer' health information is one obvious factor driving the rising popularity of healthcare information, and this is discussed further throughout the text.

The book attempts to explain healthcare information in an age of internet resource guides, which by their very nature are outdated before they are published. In an effort to counter the ephemeral nature of network resource listings, rather than focusing on internet resources alone, the book examines the field of healthcare information in its entirety, offering an exposition of how resources are created, disseminated, handled within organizations and institutions, indexed and retrieved, and ultimately used. This passage of information between author and user is known as the 'information communication chain' (Figure I.1).

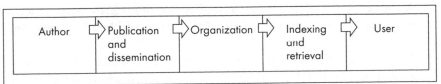

Figure I.1 The information communication chain

The healthcare information audience

An understanding of healthcare information is important for several groups of people:

- For healthcare professionals and practitioners: because greater emphasis is placed on evidence-based working, for all practitioners, not just doctors, and the increasingly strong requirements for them to make effective use of information and knowledge resources.
- For the general public: because health is an important issue for everyone, and health information is among the most commonly sought. Consumers cannot be expected to become health information specialists; but at a time when databases like Medline are offered on consumer health portals, and when there is emphasis on patients becoming 'informed' or even 'expert', some understanding of the world of healthcare information is vital.
- For healthcare information specialists: because such an understanding is obviously essential for their work. There is a diversity of roles, duties and subject interests in healthcare information work, but there is also a strong commonality, and each speciality has much to tell the others. It may be difficult to obtain an understanding of the whole area; a genomics data specialist in a research institute and a public librarian assisting with health promotion, a medical information officer in a pharmaceutical company and a librarian in a medical school, may have come to their roles through very different pathways of training and experience. An overview, of the kind promoted by this book, is essential. Particularly so, if information specialists in the area are to go on to the kind of 'value adding' activities mentioned throughout this book, such as compiling systematic reviews, evaluating information sources and constructing taxonomies and thesauri.
- For library/information practitioners generally: precisely because health is important to everyone, and there may be needs and demands for healthcare information in any environment. And also because the healthcare information area has so often been the leader in innovation of sources, services and techniques, and an exemplar for good practice for the rest of the library/information professions: in evidence-based practice, for example, and in the assessment of the impact of library/information services.
- For library/information educators: because it is a domain to which all students of librarianship and information science should be introduced; not just as a potential area for employment, but as an exemplar –

arguably *the* exemplar – of an innovative and information-rich domain. It is also, pragmatically speaking, a source of many good principles and examples for teaching (Smith, 2006).

It is the author's hope that this book, and the way of understanding the healthcare information domain which it promotes, will prove useful to all these groups.

Information science and domain analysis

The book does not attempt to detail specific practical skills such as the writing of abstracts and reviews, or the searching of databases. The approach is to aid an understanding of what is meant by 'healthcare information', so that the reader is equipped to answer personal or professional queries irrespective of current technology or the design of individual resources. The term 'information' is used broadly, and whilst this can certainly include data such as patient information, the book does not focus on systems and procedures of healthcare management and governance.

The text is written from the perspective of information science, and so should satisfy readers of an academic bent, as well as those with a practical, vocational or personal interest. Whilst there is no single, agreed definition for 'information science' within the literature, Robinson's (2009) simple conceptual model is the foundation for the approach taken in this book. In this model information science takes the information communication chain (see Figure I.1) as its focus and studies it using techniques known as domain analysis (Hjørland, 2002). Thus, the work of the information scientist or specialist is in understanding and facilitating the communication of information from author to user. The workings of, and factors affecting, elements of the communication chain are what anyone wishing to understand healthcare information needs to know.

Domain analysis

Hjørland (2002) defined domain analysis, as practised by the information specialist, as comprising eleven distinct approaches, any of which may be used to gain an understanding of information within a domain. These approaches are:

- production of literature guides and subject gateways
- production of special classifications and thesauri
- research on indexing and retrieval in specialist subjects
- empirical user studies
- bibliometric studies
- historical studies
- studies of documents and 'genres'
- epistemological and critical studies
- studies of terminology and special languages, discourse studies
- studies of structures and organizations in the communication of information
- studies in cognition, computing and artificial intelligence.

This is not to suggest that these 11 approaches provide a 'complete' understanding of any given domain. Other authors have suggested additional components for domain analysis, but these will not be discussed here and the interested reader is directed towards references in the section on further reading at the end of this introduction. Nor is it implied that any domain analysis must consider all of the 11 aspects. Subjects may be described using only those aspects considered appropriate for the intended audience.

Some of the 11 approaches are clearly concerned with specific aspects of the communication chain. For example, 'research on indexing and retrieval in specialist subjects' is clearly concerned with the 'indexing and retrieval' element of the chain, while 'empirical user studies' looks at the 'usage' element. Other aspects, however, such as 'historical studies' may be used to look at any element, or indeed at all the elements of the chain.

The question now is how a domain analysis of healthcare information should be undertaken in order to furnish readers of this book with a sound grasp of the field. The approach taken here is not to address each part of the chain in isolation, nor to employ all the 11 aspects of analysis in turn. Rather, the approach is to draw a picture of healthcare information that encompasses all five elements of the communication chain, elucidated by the relevant domain analytic techniques as described below.

Outline of the book

The book is divided into six chapters. Chapter 1, The healthcare information domain, examines the nature of healthcare and its associated disciplines and professions. Consideration is given to the epistemology of healthcare knowledge, the sorts of documents encountered, the size and nature of the knowledge base, relevant structures and organizations, and drivers for change.

Chapter 2 examines the history of healthcare and its information environment. The prevention and treatment of disease is one of the oldest recognizable 'practical disciplines' and among the first to be recorded in documents. In order to understand healthcare information today, we need to appreciate the kinds of recorded information which have been created to support it at various times, and so the historical development of healthcare is considered in conjunction with associated media and new technologies.

The producers and users of healthcare information are the subject of Chapter 3. Studies of the production and use of information are of clear, practical importance. For information providers, it is essential to know who your users are, what their needs are and how well their needs are met. The drivers for change noted in Chapter 1 have changed the nature of information production and use; there is now a wider range of both producers and users of healthcare information, and a greater diversity of resources for communication between them. This chapter aims to provide readers with a good understanding of the changing roles of producers and users in our environment today.

Chapter 4 looks at the organization of healthcare information. Information and knowledge in the healthcare domain involve a series of detailed and specific technical terminologies and a variety of classifications and nomenclatures. All are based around the hierarchical structure of healthcare knowledge. In practice, healthcare information is organized by a variety of alternative and generally overlapping controlled vocabularies, and this set of information organization tools is the subject of this chapter. General issues in the organization of healthcare information are considered first, followed by a more detailed examination of four forms of controlled vocabularies of importance for healthcare information: dictionaries and glossaries; classifications and taxonomies; subject headings and thesauri; and meta-vocabularies. The chapter concludes with a look at abstracting and indexing in the healthcare context.

Readers interested primarily in examples of resources can jump straight in to Chapter 5, which deals with healthcare information sources, services and retrieval. Healthcare information resources are diverse and very numerous, so it is not possible to give anything approaching a complete list. Nor is it feasible, at least in a printed book, to produce a list of the 'best' resources, since healthcare is a dynamic domain and its resources change over time. Rather, this book focuses on an explanation of the types of resources available and their purpose, value and significance, with examples of each.

The chapter uses a four-fold framework to categorize resources, loosely based on Robinson (2000), according to type and purpose of material. Resources are denoted as:

- primary: the 'original information'
- secondary: value-added information, from some organization of primary material
- tertiary: materials pointing to, and aiding the use of, primary and secondary materials
- quaternary: giving access to resource listings at a higher level, essentially, 'lists of lists'.

Chapter 6, on healthcare information and knowledge management, considers some issues in the management of information and knowledge, including the management of collections, records and archives, as they relate specifically to healthcare information. All of these topics have a very large general (i.e. non-healthcare) literature, which cannot be reviewed, still less repeated here. The focus will be on the specifics of the healthcare domain – either where the problems and solutions are specific, or at least particularly pressing, or where the healthcare domain has been an innovator and a leader for the rest of the information sector.

This book references many resources of various kinds, and whilst most of the web resources will be stable over time, it is inevitable that some sources will develop, undergo redesign or simply vanish. However, this approach to understanding healthcare information as a domain is intended to provide a longer view, so that, while individual resources change according to contemporary driving factors, the reader will have a firm grasp of how to identify, evaluate and utilize appropriate healthcare information resources and how to understand their context and value. This, in turn, will provide a basis for successful practice as a healthcare information specialist. As successful practice implies reflective practice, the text cites the literature extensively. This is done in two ways: firstly, sources and evidence are referenced within the text; secondly, a smaller number of selected resources are suggested for further reading, for those who wish to gain a deeper understanding.

References

Hjørland, B. (2002) Domain analysis in information science: eleven approaches – traditional as well as innovative, *Journal of Documentation*, 58 (2), 22–462.

Robinson, L. (2000) A strategic approach to research using internet tools and resources, *Aslib Proceedings*, 52 (1), 11–19.

Robinson, L. (2009) Information science: communication chain and domain analysis, *Journal of Documentation*, 65 (4), 578–91.

Smith, C. A. (2006) I am not a Specialist: why we all need to be worrying about medical information, *Journal of Education for Library and Information Science*, 47 (2), 96–105.

Further reading

Hartel, J. (2003) The serious leisure frontier in library and information science: hobby domains, *Knowledge Organisation*, 30 (3/4), 228–38.

Hjørland, B. and Hartel, J. (2003) Afterword: ontological, epistemological and sociological dimensions of domains, *Knowledge Organisation*, 25 (4), 162–201.

Sundin, O. (2003) Towards an understanding of symbolic aspects of professional information: an analysis of the nursing domain, *Knowledge Organisation*, 30 (3/4), 170–81.

Tennis, J. T. (2003) Two axes of domains for domain analysis, *Knowledge Organisation*, 30 (3/4), 191–5.

Our website

This book has a companion blog,

http://understandinghealthcareinformation.com,

which is used to provide updates and commentaries on new aspects of healthcare information as they arise. Please drop by.

1

The healthcare information domain

Introduction

This chapter deals with the nature of healthcare itself – one of the largest, oldest and most important of the information domains – and of its associated disciplines and professions. The analysis is necessary in order to set the context for later discussion of information users, resources, etc., and involves several domain analysis approaches, particularly:

- consideration of the kind of documents encountered in the discipline
- epistemological consideration of the nature of healthcare knowledge
- structures and organizations that are important for healthcare and its knowledge base
- bibliometrics, to illustrate the size and nature of the healthcare knowledge base.

Each of these has a historical perspective, which will be considered in Chapter 2.

Because a discipline is defined in large measure by its knowledge base, generally expressed as information in documents, this chapter focuses on the 'creation' stage of the information chain. The topics discussed here have extensive literatures in themselves, so this treatment will be tightly focused and very selective in its quotation of references and resources, which will usually be used simply as examples.

Nature of the discipline

In order to understand the healthcare domain in information terms, it is necessary first to understand something of the disciplines and professions within it. Before that, the idea of 'healthcare', and indeed of 'health' itself, must be clarified.

Health and healthcare

According to the World Health Organization (WHO), *health* is 'a state of complete physical, mental and social well-being and not merely the absence of disease or infirmity'. This definition was established in the WHO constitution, written in 1946, and has not been modified since (World Health Organization, 1946).

This ambitious definition is a broad one, unusually so for the time when it was originated, insisting that health includes social, as well as mental and physical well-being, and also in promoting a positive 'well-being' view of health. This is in contrast to a more negative viewpoint, which has influenced much medical practice: that health is simply the absence of disease (a diagnosed biological malfunction) or illness (the personal experience of the consequences of disease). These two views of health persist side by side (Baggott, 2004).

Healthcare has a similar dual aspect. The Oxford English Dictionary defines it very broadly as 'care for the general health of a person, community etc., especially that provided by an organized health service'. Another broad definition, seemingly following from the WHO concept but emphasizing that healthcare is the business of professionals, is offered, without attribution, by Wikipedia and several other websites: 'the prevention, treatment and management of illness and the preservation of mental and physical well-being through the services offered by the medical, nursing and allied health professions'. Merriam Webster's Medical Dictionary, by contrast, uses the narrower concept: 'the maintaining and restoration of health by the treatment and prevention of disease especially by trained and licensed professionals (as in medicine, dentistry, clinical psychology, and public health)'.

Taken together, the organized provision of professional services for maintaining and restoring health constitutes a *healthcare system*. Such systems are structured in various ways in different countries. In the United Kingdom (UK), services are divided into prevention, primary care, secondary care and tertiary care (Baggott, 2004; Talbot-Smith and Pollock, 2006). Preventive services include screening and immunization, as well as activities sometimes characterized as health promotion, such as campaigns against cigarette smoking, or in favour of exercise. Primary care encompasses community services (including prevention and promotion) involving general practitioners (family doctors), district nurses, health visitors and a variety of other paramedical and social care services. Secondary care includes more specialist services, usually provided in hospitals, including in-patient and out-patient treatment and laboratory testing. Tertiary care involves highly specialized care for less common problems, usually provided in larger hospitals. There are also services, such as public health and various support functions, which cut across these 'tiers of care'.

Services are organized differently in other countries, with less emphasis in some cases, for example, on the primary care offered by the generalist family doctor. In any situation, the structure is likely to alter over time as, for example, procedures which once required admission to hospital are carried out in a local clinic. Nonetheless, this outline gives an idea of the complexity of healthcare systems, and the variety of professions involved.

Healthcare professions

A more detailed idea of the variety of professions involved in healthcare provision may be gained by considering the taxonomy of careers in the National Health Service (NHS) in England, provided on its website in late 2009 (www.nhscareers.nhs.uk). These are categorized alphabetically in ten main sections, with two levels of subdivision. For clarity, and to keep the long list within bounds, the top levels are shown below, with part or all of the second and third levels where this provides clarity and/or example.

Allied health professionals

Arts therapy
    Art therapy
    Drama therapy
    Music therapy
Chiropody and podiatry [foot problems]
Dietetics
Operating department practice
Orthoptics [eye problems]
Occupational therapy

Physiotherapy
Prosthetics and orthotics
Psychology
    Clinical psychology
    Health psychology
    Counselling psychology
    Forensic psychology
Psychotherapy
Radiography
    Diagnostic radiography
    Therapeutic radiography
    etc.
Speech and language therapy
Ambulance
    Ambulance technician
    Call handler
    Paramedic
    etc.
Dental
    Dentists
    Dental nurses
    Dental hygienists
    Dental therapists
    Dental technicians
Doctors
    Medical specialities
        Cardiology
        Dermatology
        Occupational medicine
        Pharmaceutical medicine
        etc.
    Surgical specialities
        Cardiothoracic surgery
        Ear, nose and throat surgery
        Plastic surgery
        etc.
    Psychiatry
        Forensic psychiatry
        Learning disability
        etc.

General practice
Paediatrics and child health
    Obstetrics and gynaecology
Pathology
    Chemical pathology
    Haematology
    Histopathology
    Immunology
    etc.
Radiology
Anaesthetics
Ophthalmology
Healthcare science
Pharmacy
    Hospital pharmacy
    Community pharmacy
    etc.
Life Sciences
    Clinical embryology
    Phlebotomy
    Clinical biochemistry
    Clinical microbiology
    etc.
Physiological sciences
    Audiology
    Cardiography
    Gastroenterology
    Respiratory physiology
    etc.
Clinical engineering and physical sciences
    Clinical engineering
    Medical physics
    Medical illustration
Health informatics
Information and communication technology
Knowledge management
Information management
Clinical informatics
Management
General management

Practice management
Financial management
Clinical management
etc.
Midwifery
Nursing
Adult nursing
Mental health nursing
School nursing
etc.
Wider healthcare team
Administration
Medical records
etc.
Estates (property maintenance)
Corporate services
Architecture
Surveying
Human resources
etc.
Clinical support services
Social work
Counselling
Complementary and alternative medicine
etc.
Domestic services
Catering
Housekeeping
etc.
Support services
Driving
Storekeeping
etc.

This emphasizes the complexity of health service provision and the very varied roles required. At the risk of over-simplification, these can be represented as two groups:

Healthcare professions and roles
>   Doctors, nursing, midwifery, dentists, allied healthcare professions, healthcare science, ambulance.

Ancillary functions and roles
>   Health informatics, management, wider healthcare team.

The first group comprises those activities which are essentially healthcare related. The second comprises more general activities (information technology (IT) management, librarianship, financial management, counselling, etc.) which happen to be carried out in a healthcare setting. However, some functions which appear here as ancillary are in fact healthcare specific: complementary and alternative medicine, clinical management and clinical informatics, for example. Conversely, an ambulance-call handler might be said to be practising a general role in a healthcare context. Nonetheless, in a general sense two distinct groupings within healthcare services can be seen, both of which will be producers and users of information.

The disciplinary background

The analysis above covers professions and roles in the practice of healthcare provision. In considering the nature of healthcare, however, its basis in more fundamental disciplines must be considered.

It is self-evident that the work of doctors, nurses and the other healthcare professions is based upon an understanding of the biomedical sciences, and the education and training of all healthcare professionals includes such sciences. Indeed, the practical expression of these sciences can be seen above, in pathology, clinical biochemistry and microbiology, and so on. Again, from the above, the application of chemistry, physics and engineering can be seen.

If the 'negative' understanding of health – an absence of disease – is taken, then healthcare will be a matter of preventing, diagnosing and treating disease. This is a rather traditional model of healthcare, with doctors and the profession of medicine taking the main role, supported by other healthcare professions. Healthcare in this sense is firmly based on biomedical sciences, the 'basic sciences' which traditionally made up the first years of medical education. There is no definitive understanding of exactly which sciences these are. Recent explanations include:

- 'such as anatomy, pharmacology and pathology' [British Medical Association] (British Medical Association, 2005)

- 'basic sciences – anatomy, biochemistry and physiology' [European medical school survey] (Jippes and Majoor, 2008)
- 'traditional disciplines of anatomy, biochemistry, microbiology, pharmacology and physiology' [USA medical school survey] (Mallon, Biebuyck and Jones, 2003)
- 'basic sciences [of] neuroscience, gross anatomy, cell biology, physiology, biochemistry, behavioural and social science, embryology, pharmacology, genetics, and neurology' [United States (US) medical school curriculum] (Clough, Shea, Hamilton, Estavillo, Rupp, Browning and Lal, 2004)
- anatomy, physiology, pathology, immunology, microbiology [Canadian nursing curriculum] (Thompson Rivers University, 2009)
- anatomy, physiology, microbiology, lifespan development, chemistry [US nursing curriculum] (University of North Carolina Greensboro, 2009)
- chemistry, biology, physics, microbiology, anatomy, physiology, pharmacology, toxicology [US pharmacy curriculum] (Purdue University, 2009)
- anatomy, biology, chemistry, mathematics, statistics, physics [US radiology curriculum] (Ohio State University, 2009)
- anatomy, biochemistry, cell biology, genetics, immunology, microbiology, molecular biology, nutrition, pathology, pharmacology and physiology (General Medical Council, 2009)

A recent trend, in line with general educational practice, has been to specify this background knowledge in terms of competencies, rather than of disciplines and courses. An example of this is a report on scientific foundations for future physicians from the US Howard Hughes Medical Institute and Association of American Medical Colleges (AAMC-HHMI 2009). This expresses the scientific knowledge needed by doctors in terms of general scientific competencies, illustrated by medical examples. For instance, a doctor should be able to:

- Explain how the regulation of major biochemical energy production pathways and the synthesis/degration of macromolecules function to maintain health and identify major forms of dysregulation in disease.
- Explain how lack of insulin results in the metabolic consequences of diabetes mellitus, such as hyperglycemia and ketoacidosis.
- Explain how urea metabolism and its abnormal regulation in renal and hepatic disease can result in uremia.

Although this competencies-based specification may be more helpful in promoting understanding of what doctors should know, and why, it does not alter the general perspective of the breadth of sciences relevant to healthcare.

It is clear that, although expressed differently and with varying emphasis in different environments, the whole spectrum of biomedical science, and much of other sciences, is seen to be of relevance as the underlying basis for healthcare education. As healthcare education and training have changed, there has been a trend towards merging these subjects more closely with clinical training (see, for example, Clough, Shea, Hamilton, Estavillo, Rupp, Browning and Lal, 2004; Jippes and Majoor, 2008), with consequent concerns that there may be a damaging loss of foundational knowledge (see, for example, British Medical Association, 2005). There have been similar concerns about an emphasis on interpersonal issues in nurse training, at the expense of scientific knowledge (Sturgeon, 2008). Furthermore, changes in the way biomedical science itself is carried out, with consequent restructuring and renaming of departments and institutions, affects the issue (see, for example, Mallon, Biebuyck and Jones, 2003 for a survey of basic science departments in American medical schools).

Behavioural and social sciences were mentioned in one of the examples of basic sciences above. As the broader and more holistic understanding of health – well-being, including the social context – comes to the fore, so the healthcare system will necessarily rely on a greater range of 'non-scientific' disciplines. The British Medical Association (2005), for example, recommends that undergraduate medical education should include 'important social issues, such as homelessness and care of the elderly [and] ... factors influencing health and healthcare . . . including political, socioeconomic, cultural and religious factors'. De Gooijer (2002) similarly suggests that healthcare in Western Europe is 'constantly implementing new combinations of science, technology, organization, economics, politics, philosophy, opinions and fashion', and that consequently healthcare systems are complex, and difficult to compare across countries.

Taking these arguments even further, the relatively new discipline of 'health studies' uses the broadest feasible definition of health and its promotion, as a matter of the realization of human potential in all ways. The disciplines contributing to health studies include biomedicine, medical sciences and epidemiology – although these are by no means the central concepts – and also psychology, social policy, economics, organization and management, cultural studies, history, philosophy, sociology and education (Duncan, 2007). This interdisciplinary and multidisciplinary nature is emphasized by the UK's Quality Assurance Agency for Higher Education, which notes that health studies courses may rely upon 'the physical and social sciences and the humanities' (Quality Assurance Agency 2002).

The situation therefore seems to be one in which virtually any academic discipline may be seen as important in supporting the healthcare professions and healthcare systems. To help clarify matters, it is necessary to ask what sort of a discipline healthcare is – if indeed it is a discipline at all.

What kind of discipline?

The educational philosopher Paul Hirst argues that, since disciplines are closely associated with their knowledge base, we can understand a discipline by understanding its 'form of knowledge' (Hirst, 1974; Hirst and Peters, 1970; Walsh, 1993). Hirst identifies seven main domains or forms of knowledge, defined by the fundamental nature of the knowledge and concepts with which they deal: mathematics, physical sciences, human sciences, literature and the fine arts, morality, religion, and philosophy. Where a discipline equates to one of these forms, it is what would be regarded as a 'pure' academic subject. Hirst also recognizes 'practical disciplines', based on one of these forms, but oriented toward solving practical problems. Engineering, for example, would be a practical discipline based on the form of the physical sciences.

Many academic subjects, however, do not align neatly with any of the forms defined by Hirst. Rather, they are focused on a topic or subject of interest, using any of the forms which are useful in studying and understanding it. Hirst refers to these as 'fields of study'; they are typically, though not necessarily, multidisciplinary; he gives the example of women's studies. More recently, Bawden (2007) and Robinson (2009) have argued that the library and information sciences may be regarded as a field of study focused on information. It seems clear that adopting the broader meanings of healthcare, as outlined above, suggests that it is best understood as a field of study focusing on the broad concept of health and supporting a number of practical healthcare disciplines. If this view is taken, then there will be no expectation of any particular form of knowledge associated with the topic, and it will draw as required from the biological and social sciences, and beyond them to the physical sciences and humanities.

However, it is true to say that much of what is generally understood as healthcare takes the more restrictive view of health, and is viewed as the prevention, diagnosis and treatment of disease. In this concept healthcare is firmly based around medicine, itself relying almost entirely on biomedical sciences, though the model was criticized decades ago for ignoring the social and behavioural dimensions of illness (Engel, 1977). In Hirst's terms, medicine and related professions are generally thought of as practical disciplines based on the form of knowledge of the biological sciences. This 'embedding' of a scientifically based discipline into a broader field of study, with diverse forms of knowledge at its base, is the root cause of the complexity and differing views noted above. As will be seen later, this has very real and practical consequences for the kinds of healthcare knowledge that are created in the discipline's information chain.

An immediate example can be seen in the Medical Subject Headings (MeSH) vocabulary, widely used for indexing of healthcare subject matter. Of the 16 main headings in MeSH, 5 are mainly related to narrowly defined healthcare concepts (diseases; chemicals and drugs; analytical, diagnostic and therapeutic techniques and equipment; psychiatry and psychology; and healthcare), 4 to basic sciences (anatomy; organisms; biological sciences; and natural sciences), and 4 to wider disciplines [anthropology, education, sociology and social phenomena; technology, industry and agriculture; humanities; and information science]. (The remaining 3 deal with people, places and publications, rather than with subjects.) Even in this rather traditionally medically oriented vocabulary, the need to include other disciplines is evident.

These ideas may be used to consider the nature of healthcare knowledge, and its creation, in more detail.

Nature of healthcare knowledge

In this section we will consider in general terms what healthcare knowledge is like. We will first look at the kinds or forms of knowledge involved, and then in more detail at the nature of some of those forms. We will then consider how much healthcare knowledge there is, how that quantity is changing, and the kinds of documents which communicate it.

Forms of knowledge

It will be obvious from what has been said above that there is no such single entity as 'healthcare knowledge'; the topic is much too diverse for that. Furthermore, the nature of medical knowledge itself changes greatly over time. One of the main themes is that of the balance between the general and the particular, the focus on an abstract 'universal' or a general disease type, as against the focus on the specific and unique case being treated (see, for example, Nutton, 2004 on these issues in classical medicine, and Wear, 1995 on the conflict between these forms of medical knowledge in the Renaissance). The balance between, on the one hand, theory and philosophy expounded in the 'canon' of approved medical texts, and on the other the empirical evidence provided by examination of a patient, has not always taken the form it does today. And it is also the case that some forms of knowledge simply 'leave' the domain; who now has any insight into medical astrology, a major tool of the physician in medieval times and afterwards? (Nutton, 1995). We see the issue of 'what counts' as healthcare knowledge arising today in the contested status of some alternative forms of therapy. We should therefore be careful to acknowledge that the nature of healthcare knowledge – even in those aspects of it which are generally accepted today – has changed from the past, and may change again in the future.

Most obviously, the knowledge needed by the practitioner or provider of healthcare will differ from that needed by recipients, patients and carers. However, health information for lay people has been provided for hundreds of years, and this trend has been reinforced by late 20th century developments in consumer health information and the concept of the 'expert patient', so that this distinction is not so black and white as might be thought.

The idea of the 'practice knowledge' of the healthcare professional has received much attention since 1990 (see Higgs, Richardson and Dahlgren, 2004 for an overview). This has led to several typologies or categorizations of healthcare knowledge, in general terms. It has also led to a recognition that practitioners will often need to use, integrate and criticize different forms of knowledge, and not rely on a single form, whether this be an undue reliance only on data from rigorous clinical research or, at the other extreme, a sole reliance on personal professional experience. The ability to combine forms of knowledge appropriately has been termed 'practice wisdom' (Richardson, Higgs and Dahlgren, 2004); assisting practitioners to do this should be one of the aims of healthcare information specialists.

A common view in Western philosophy is that there are two main ways of 'knowing': propositional knowledge ('knowing that') and non-propositional, or tacit knowledge ('knowing how'). Propositional knowledge comes from rational enquiry and research, especially in the sciences. It has traditionally been given a higher status than tacit knowledge, which is gained by professional or life experience. In healthcare, as in other areas which have a scientific basis and also a practice 'craft' element, there is a tension between the views of what the knowledge base of such disciplines should be like (Higgs and Titchen, 2000; Higgs, Andresen and Fish, 2004). Some contend that it should, as far as possible, be objective and generalizable propositional knowledge, obtained from research and theory. Such a view underlies evidence-based medicine, with its reliance on published scientific and clinical research. An alternative view argues for the inclusion, or even the primacy, of subjective, interpretive and context-specific knowledge, largely derived from reflection on and interpretation of personal and professional experience. This attitude points to some limitations of reliance on evidence-based practice in offering the best care in a specific situation, and offers practitioners the freedom to use different forms of knowledge to achieve healthcare aims. Most commentators now agree on the need to integrate different forms of knowledge for best healthcare practice, including in particular the need to relate personal experience to the objective evidence of the literature (Higgs, Fish and Rothwell, 2004; Higgs, Jones, Edwards and Beeston, 2004; Richardson, Dahlgren and Higgs, 2004; see also Bawden, 2002 for an analysis of healthcare knowledge in terms of Karl Popper's somewhat similar epistemology).

A simple typology of healthcare knowledge, now generally accepted, divides non-propositional knowledge into two types: professional craft knowledge, derived from experience in practice, and personal knowledge, derived from personal life experience. This gives a threefold breakdown of healthcare knowledge (Higgs and Titchen, 2000):

- Propositional knowledge: publicly available, communicable, objective knowledge, of the kind typically generated by research, theory, observation and experiment. It is 'scientific' and 'technical' knowledge, using these terms in a general way. Most of the knowledge base of medicine and other science-based healthcare disciplines, and of the underlying sciences, is of this form.
- Practical craft knowledge: the kind of tacit knowledge gained by professional experience, which is difficult to communicate in an abstract general way. It is associated with the ideas of 'professional judgement', 'clinical intuition', etc. It is not incompatible with the use of formal propositional knowledge, and an expert practitioner is able to integrate the two.
- Personal knowledge: subjective knowledge, which individuals gain by reflecting on their experiences, not necessarily just in a professional context, and which is associated with attitudes and values and hence influences professional judgement. In a healthcare context, this is the kind of knowledge which allows a practitioner 'to appreciate the concerns, needs and frames of reference of their patients or clients, to learn to cope with pain, frailty and human endeavour, and to learn to

deal with ethical dilemmas within the clinical situation' (Higgs and Titchen, 2000, 29). It may also include cultural knowledge, important in the provision of healthcare in a multicultural setting (Henley and Twible, 2000).

Traditionally, propositional 'scientific' knowledge has always been given priority in healthcare generally, and in medicine specifically. Greater attention is now being given to the value of practical and personal knowledge as an essential complement for effective healthcare practice (see Figure 1.1). Objective, scientifically based knowledge still dominates the practice of

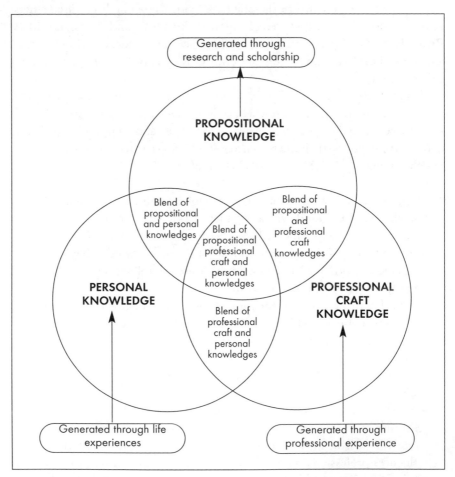

Figure 1.1 Forms and derivation of knowledge
Reproduced with permission from Higgs, J., Richardson, B. and Dahlgren, M. A. (eds), *Developing Practice Knowledge for Health Professionals*, Butterworth Heinemann, 2004

disciplines such as medicine and physiotherapy – albeit that such knowledge is not static, but potentially rapidly changing, requiring changes in practice – while more subjective and context-specific tacit practice knowledge is currently more accepted in disciplines such as nursing and occupational therapy (Higgs, Andreson and Fish, 2004; Fleming and Mattingly, 2000).

For effective practice, the three forms of knowledge should be used together. Titchen, McGinley and McCormack (2004) give a specific and detailed example of this, based on the work of a nurse caring for a particular patient, and combining technical knowledge, practical know-how and personal knowledge.

Healthcare knowledge viewed in this way is complicated and without very clear boundaries, and requires integration of sources beyond those of 'traditional' science and medicine. 'A broader notion of health professional knowledge is required that is derived from diverse sources of reflective, tacit and interpretive knowledge as much as it is from propositional knowledge. These together can contribute to a professional knowledge base that can underpin the range of skills needed by practitioners to achieve expertise in the heterogeneous health care settings of today' (Garbett, 2000, 169).

The knowledge of healthcare is therefore 'messy', in that the field of practice is one where problems may be ill defined and ill structured and it is not always possible to derive clear-cut solutions from abstract principles (Dahlgren, Richardson and Kalman, 2004; Patel and Kaufman, 2000). It is a field of knowledge of many dimensions, which does not fully comply with the forms of knowledge of the natural sciences (Richardson, Dahlgren and Higgs, 2004). And it is one where it is necessary to 'extract something from a messy, complicated, amorphous individual story [of the care of a patient] that is sufficiently clear and well-defined to serve as the raw material of scientific study' (Taylor, 2006, 11).

Implications for the communication chain

This perspective raises some immediate issues for the communication chain. The creation of knowledge since the 19th century has been largely left to biomedical scientists and leading practitioners working in a scientific paradigm. Most practitioners have been content to occupy a role as users of information. The emphasis on practical 'craft' knowledge and on personal knowledge as of equal importance suggests that there is an important role for the 'average' practitioner in the creation of disciplinary knowledge (Garbett, 2004; Richardson, Higgs and Dahlgren, 2004).

Moving on from creation to communication, it has traditionally been the formal, objective propositional knowledge that has been handled in the information chain, through books, journal articles, lecture notes and so on. Practical know-how and personal knowledge have sat uneasily in this environment and have usually been communicated directly or by example. The most obvious mechanism for this has been the 'apprenticeship' system for junior health professionals, involving ward rounds, case conferences and supervised practice. Other recommendations for sharing such knowledge generally revolve around discussions, 'critical conversations', peer review, appraisal of research findings, story-telling, etc. (Richardson, Dahlgren and Higgs, 2004; Titchen, McGinley and McCormack, 2004; Titchen and Higgs, 2000). The advent of the communications capabilities of the internet, and especially of Web 2.0, may tend to move these informal, face-to-face interactions into the realm of published information, with potentially dramatic results for the communication of this kind of knowledge.

Structure of healthcare knowledge

We can now examine in a little more detail the nature of the healthcare knowledge outlined above. It will be immediately obvious that the structure of formal, abstract propositional knowledge will be different from that of the less formal, tacit, personal and practical knowledge. These varied structures will determine, to a large extent, the ways in which such knowledge may be organized, disseminated and accessed. We will concentrate here on some main points of these structures, of particular importance for the communication of medical information.

Propositional knowledge

More attention has been paid to the structure of propositional knowledge, following from its traditionally greater status. This is what is generally regarded as 'medical knowledge', and it includes two aspects: the basic scientific knowledge of the underlying disciplines noted above, such as anatomy, biochemistry and physiology; and clinical knowledge, relating to diseases and their prevention and treatment. It has been conventional to believe that these form a single, integrated 'network of knowledge', in which the basic scientific knowledge 'feeds into' and supports clinical knowledge. This is the basis for regarding the healthcare disciplines as based on the form of knowledge of the biological sciences, noted earlier in this chapter. However, this view has been challenged on the grounds that clinical knowledge does not always seem, in practice, to be intertwined with basic science. Patel and Kaufman (2000, 42), for example, suggest that 'clinical medicine and the biomedical sciences constitute two distinct and not completely compatible worlds, with distinct modes of reasoning and quite different ways of structuring knowledge. . . . Clinical knowledge is based on a complex taxonomy, which relates disease symptoms to underlying pathology. In contrast, the biomedical sciences are based on general principles defining chains of causal mechanisms'.

Sir Arthur Conan Doyle, like the many medical students who followed the traditional model of first mastering the basic sciences before proceeding to clinical studies, would have agreed with this assessment of the difference between scientific and clinical knowledge, as he wrote that he found his medical studies at Edinburgh in the 1870s 'a long weary grind at botany, chemistry, anatomy, physiology, and a whole list of compulsory subjects, many of which have a very indirect bearing upon the art of healing' (Lellenberg, Stashower and Foley, 2007, 90).

Even in 'clinical' areas, the 'scientific research' view of knowledge may also pose problems for the communication of information: 'Many, if not most, [clinical research journal articles] are written as contributions to clinical research, rather than as attempts to help clinical decision making. This means that even when the information in the article is genuinely useful, it is often written up and presented in such a way that a practising clinician will struggle to find it' (Taylor, 2006, 56).

Patel and Kaufman (2000) suggest that the mismatch between scientific and clinical knowledge may differ in different parts of the knowledge base: clinical knowledge in specialities like dermatology and radiology is closely tied to, and dependent upon, basic anatomical models, while in specialities like cardiology and endocrinology the relation is more distant. Therefore, even within the area of scientific medicine, there is some variation in the exact nature of the knowledge structures. This has implications, for example, for the way in which information may best be indexed or coded. It has even greater implications for attempts to formalize clinical reasoning and hence create useful and cost-effective systems based on artificial intelligence in the medical domain, which has proved a more difficult task than anticipated.

Despite this variation, the extent and significance of which is debated, it is clear that this kind of propositional healthcare knowledge has a clear and consistent structure: it is a complex hierarchy, with many levels (see, for example, Blois, 1984, 1988; Patel and Kaufman, 2000). The levels are linked, but each has its own 'emergent' properties and entities, which make sense only at that level. At a lower level, for example, one might note a change in molecular structure; at the next level up a change in a biochemical pathway; at the next, a change in cellular structure; at the next, a disease state in a patient; at the next, the epidemiology of that disease in a population. Each of these levels fits into an appropriate taxonomy: chemical, anatomical, microbiological, disease, and so on.

Blois (1984), in an influential book, suggested that a suitable hierarchy for creating descriptions in the medical area would have ten levels (he did not go beyond an individual patient) as follows (using a slightly clearer numbering scheme than Blois' original):

Level 1 – atoms or ions, e.g. sodium ion

Level 2 – molecules, e.g. glucose

Level 3 – macromolecules, e.g. an enzyme

Level 4 – parts of a cell, e.g. cell nucleus

Level 5 – cell, e.g. epithelial cell

Level 6 – part of an organ, e.g. myocardium

Level 7 – organ, e.g. heart

Level 8 – physiological system, e.g. cardiovascular system

Level 9 – major patient part, e.g. chest

Level 10 – whole patient

Another example of the hierarchical structure of this form of healthcare knowledge is given by the illustration of the basic science courses studied at the medial school of McGill University in Canada during the mid-1990s (Patel and Kaufman, 2000). This is illustrated in Figure 1.2 and shows a breakdown from the concept of 'basic sciences', through the sciences themselves, their sub-components, and then to topics within them, e.g.:

Basic sciences
    Physiology
        Cardiovascular physiology
            Cardiac output

Other forms of hierarchy have been developed, but these are sufficient to provide an idea.

This means that the subject is likely to spawn a variety of detailed hierarchical classifications and nomenclatures, which may be used for coding of the occurrence and treatment of disease, for information retrieval and for

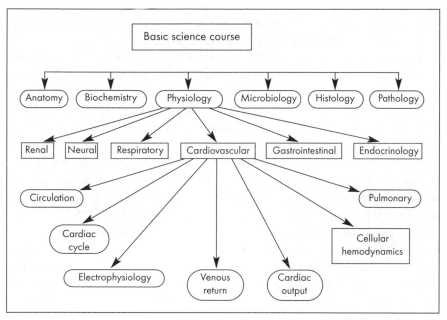

Figure 1.2 A partial model of basic science courses in the medical curriculum at McGill
University
Reproduced with permission from Higgs, J. and Jones, M., *Clinical
Reasoning in the Health Professions*, 2nd edition, Butterworth Heinemann,
2000.

other purposes. As we shall see later, this is indeed the case. While this is
beneficial in allowing the precise communication of information, the existence
of numerous overlapping vocabularies leads to a need for 'translation' between
them, as we shall also see. It also means that the language of formal healthcare
information will be a series of detailed, highly specific terminologies: excellent
for communicating meaning precisely, but tending to form a specialist jargon
which may be inaccessible to lay people.

Non-propositional knowledge

The other forms of healthcare knowledge, the practical craft knowledge based
on experience and the personal 'life knowledge', have been less regarded than
formal scientific knowledge, and hence have been less studied. It is clear, of
course, that these sorts of knowledge, being subjective, context sensitive and
qualitative, will not be amenable to the same kind of detailed, hierarchical
structuring as formal, science-based knowledge. Nor will they be amenable to

being classified and coded, and subjected to statistical analysis, nor so readily retrieved from databases using specialized terminology.

Fleming and Mattingly (2000), for example, cite the case of occupational therapists, who typically have good clinical skills and a great deal of tacit practical knowledge, but lack the rich terminology to describe and explain their practice. 'Therapy stories', qualitative descriptions of what was done and why, are a useful way of expressing this sort of knowledge. Titchen and Higgs (2000, 226) also commend story-telling as a way of creating and communicating knowledge, and suggest that all the health professions have knowledge 'hidden away in reflective accounts in the form of stories, poems, diaries and anecdotes'. The value of such methods, necessarily differing in detail for different professions, has been shown by Urquhart (1998).

This emphasizes the extent to which this kind of knowledge will not be effectively communicated through the kinds of structured formats that are suitable for propositional knowledge. Although the above discussion focuses on the tacit and personal knowledge of healthcare professionals, the same will be true of the experiences of patients, carers and other recipients of healthcare, whose knowledge will certainly take this form.

We can see, from this rather superficial survey, that a range of formats and media will be needed to effectively communicate healthcare information.

Scale and scope

'Today's doctor, physician, surgeon, or medical scientist', wrote Morton and Godbolt just before the impact of the internet was felt (1992, 1), 'requires more information than ever before.' No doubt the same would be said confidently today. But the question of how much healthcare knowledge exists is a difficult one to answer. What is not in question is that it is perceived as having a large and rapidly growing knowledge base, and that this perception has been around for many years. An often-quoted suggestion is that the amount of material published has grown exponentially since 1750 (see, for example, Arndt, 1992), and that the amount of available biomedical knowledge doubles every 20 years (Wyatt and Sullivan, 2005). While such figures are difficult to verify, they give an idea of the scale of the problem.

It has been estimated that experienced doctors call upon two million items of information in their practice (Smith, 1996). It is clear that the volume of information is such that it is now impossible for any person to have a full knowledge of even a small area. A full-time postgraduate student working in their area for five years might stand as good a chance as anyone of doing so, but Prokop (1992) argues that the volume of information in even a single sub-discipline of biomedicine is so great that such a student has no hope of internalizing it all. 'Exogenous memory' in the form of books, databases and other aids is now essential. These aids are themselves now remarkably volum-inous. The series of illustrations and example studies below gives an idea of their scale. This is an example of the 'bibliometrics' aspect of domain analysis, albeit presented here in an informal way. We will look at some specific figures for the size of book and journal collections in libraries in Chapter 5.

Journals

Journals remain a pre-eminent source of professional information. It is estimated that between 15,000 and 17,000 biomedical journals are published worldwide, although only about 6000 of these are judged worthwhile for inclusion by the major bibliographic databases MEDLINE and EMBASE (Gray, 2001, 105). The growth of the journal literature is illustrated by the study of Druss and Marcus (2005), which shows that the MEDLINE bibliographic database included 8.1 million items from about 5,000 source journals between 1978 and 2001. Between 1978 and 1985, the average number of articles in MEDLINE was just short of 250,000; from 1994 to 2001, the average was nearly 450,000, an increase of nearly 50%. Nearly 200,000 randomized clinical trials (the 'gold standard' of evidence-based medicine) were published between 1994 and 2001.

The journal literature of healthcare obeys (as do all such literatures) the Bradford bibliometric law of scattering, which shows that, while the bulk of the literature of any given subject will be concentrated into a small number of sources, for a complete coverage a very large number of sources will be needed. Numerous studies of this kind have been published. For example, it has been shown – in two examples of a numerous series of articles on 'mapping the literature' of various aspects of healthcare, published in the *Bulletin* (and the *Journal*) *of the Medical Library Association* – that the literature of occupational therapy is concentrated in 3 journals, but that nearly 900 are needed for completeness (Reed, 1999), while for cytotechnology the respective figures are 3 and over 1000 journals (Stevens, 2000). Half of all papers providing evi-dence on renal practice were shown in one study to be published in 'non-renal' journals, the authors noting that while scanning top journals in the field is important, 'relevant studies are also scattered across a large range of journals that may not be routinely scanned' by specialists in the area (Garg, Iansavichus, Kastner, Walters, Wilczynski, McKibbon, Yang, Rehman and

Haynes, 2006). The problems are even more acute for a topic which may be of importance to a number of specialities, such a palliative care, where inform-ation may be dispersed over many sources (Tieman, Sladek and Currow, 2008).

This scattering phenomenon presents evident problems for any health librarian seeking to provide a comprehensive collection, whether printed or (increasingly likely) digital. It is partly overcome by the increasing availability of large 'bundles' of electronic journals.

Books

Printed books remain of importance, while e-books are of increasing significance, particularly for reference material. To give an indication of the numbers involved, we may consider the following:

- A study of the personal libraries of family doctors in the USA in the late 1990s showed that each kept an average of 56 books in their office. Nearly 3000 different titles were mentioned, mainly prescribing references and textbooks of general medicine (Ely, Levy and Hartz, 1999).
- CILIP's Health Libraries Group produces a regular listing of a 'core collection of medical books'. Its fifth edition, published in 2006, listed 824 books in clinical medicine, limited to recent in-print material, meeting standards of quality and user demand.
- The Royal Society of Medicine (London) library acquires up to 1000 new books each year.
- A US online bookseller offers 90,000 in-print titles in healthcare and biomedical areas.

Online information

The extent of health information on the internet is difficult to assess, as it is more usual to encounter statements such as 'the net is awash with health information' and there are 'massive amounts of health information on the web'. To get some idea of quantity, we can note that the Health on the Net Foundation (HON), a Swiss non-governmental organization devoted to promoting good-quality health information on the internet, estimates that there are four billion (four thousand million) web pages including some form of health information; this is a significant proportion of the whole web, justifying the dramatic kinds of statement quoted above. Of these, HON's search engine offers access to 140,000 medical websites, and HON promotes 5700 'quality assured' health sites.

Unpublished information

The factors mentioned above relate only to published and generally available information. The information maintained by health services, with a medical record usually available for every person in the population and additional records generated for each episode of healthcare, is also obviously very extensive (see, for example, Taylor, 2006, chapter 2).

Primary care literature

The consequence of this wealth of information is shown in a study of the effort needed to keep up with the literature of primary care, written from the perspective of doctors with particular expertise and interests in epidemiology (Alper, Hand, Elliott, Kinkade, Hauan, Onion, and Sklar, 2004). Their estimate was that over 7000 articles were published monthly in the 341 journals judged to be relevant. They estimated that scanning these for relevance would take over 600 hours per month. To put this into perspective, a study of the reading habits of doctors in the later stages of training (arguably one of the necessarily information-conscious groups) found that they devoted 17 hours per month to the task (Arndt, 1992). Other studies have shown that doctors generate approximately 45 questions about patient care each week (Wyatt and Sullivan, 2005), and that about a third of doctors' time is spent recording and synthesizing information of various kinds (Smith, 1996).

The sheer size of the very large and continually growing body of healthcare information, not to mention its diverse nature, makes its management a challenging task.

Healthcare documents

From the foregoing, it will come as no surprise if we say that, in general, the healthcare domain is characterized by a very large number of documents, of very varied nature, with a wide variety of producers and users, and in a wide variety of languages.

There has been a long-running debate in the information science literature as to exactly what counts as a document; see Frohmann (2009), and references therein, for insight into this. For our purposes, it is enough to note that documents need not be restricted to text-and-image on paper, or a digital equivalent; other kinds of information-bearing objects may be regarded as documents. Such things as anatomical and pathological specimens, histology slides and so on have been very valuable in the creation and communication of medical knowledge, as have dried herbarium specimens for medicinal botany and herbal medicine; many other examples can be given. This is particularly significant now that such items can be represented in digital form and communicated more widely. The most dramatic example of this is the US National Library of Medicine's Visible Human project, which makes available digital representations of images of the whole human anatomy.

Even in more conventional forms of document, healthcare has long been rich in what would now be termed multimedia documents; it was among the first subjects to combine text and images in printed documents. Images of all kinds, video and animation, maps, diagrams and graphics, sound recordings and interactive presentations all form important aspects of healthcare documentation.

An important distinction between document types, clear-cut in the past, but now being somewhat eroded by changes in the technology of communication, is that between formal and informal communication, and associated documents.

Formal communication

Formal communication may be understood to be that involving materials which are 'published' in some way and hence recorded for posterity and, usually, publicly accessible. It includes documents such as books, articles in journals, magazines and newspapers, reports of many kinds, patents, legislation and regulations, guidance notes and procedures, statistical data compilations, handbooks and formularies, and so on. Originally printed, these kind of documents still form the basis of healthcare communication, though they are now often in electronic form. They generally convey the propositional knowledge discussed earlier in this chapter, though published memoirs, lecture notes and suchlike may also include an element of practical experience, and an attempt to convey tacit knowledge. For overviews of this kind of healthcare and bioscience documentation immediately before the main impact of the internet, see Morton and Goldbolt (1992) and Wyatt (1997).

We may notice that this category includes not only documents intended for the use of whoever chooses to read them – books, articles, etc. – but also the kinds of documents, noted above, intended for internal use within health services, and hence confidential. The individual's medical record is the most obvious example, but also included here are the clinical, administrative, managerial and financial records of hospitals and other health service units. The restriction of access to these documents to health service personnel (in Britain until the last years of the 20th century it was taken for granted that a person's medical record belonged to the health service, and the patient was not allowed to see it) does not affect their status as 'formal' documents.

Informal communication

Informal communication comprises the transfer of information which is not 'properly published'. This involves face-to-face communication in discussion, teaching and so on that is never recorded in any way, and also the creation of documents not intended for public dissemination: diaries, notebooks, letters and the like. One of the effects of the digital communication revolution has been to allow this sort of communication to happen in virtual environments, and hence to become accessible in a way not possible before. Personal web pages, blogs, wikis, e-mail lists, podcasts, videos on sites such as YouTube, social networking environments such as Facebook and virtual environments such as Second Life are all means by which personal and tacit knowledge, as well as propositional knowledge, can be communicated and can become accessible (see, for example, Boulos, Maramba and Wheeler, 2006; Gustini, 2006; Cross, 2008; Beard, Wilson, Morra and Keelan, 2009; Hendrix, Chiarella, Hasman, Murphy, and Zafron, 2009). These comprise new types of document and can be seen as moving informal communication towards the formal arena. By comparison with traditional, formal documents, they are typically ephemeral, loosely structured, subjective and personal in presentation.

These newer, Web 2.0 tools may of course be used to convey the more formal style of information, but to date this does not seem to happening to a large extent; the two styles of communication seem to be used for different types of information (see, for example, Robinson, 2007).

With traditional, formal communication, documents were produced by a few distinct groupings of authors, particularly:

* scientific and clinical researchers in academia, government institutes, health services, the scientific industry and international organizations
* health professionals (chiefly doctors, and mainly senior personnel)

- managers, administrators and regulators in government and health services and in international organizations
- providers of medicines, equipment and healthcare products
- medical journalists and commentators.

With the new forms of documents now being produced, a wider range of people contribute to the creation of healthcare knowledge. (We should note that technology is not the only reason for this; it is being increasingly recognized that creating and sharing knowledge is a responsibility of all healthcare professionals.) This includes all the groups listed above, plus some others, particularly:

- a wider range of healthcare professionals
- providers of 'well-being' products and services
- patients, carers and recipients of healthcare, both as individuals and as groups.

This has led, on the one hand, to the benefits of more information being more readily available than ever before and, on the other, to concerns about the validity and usefulness of the information to be found in the greater variety of documents produced by a wider range of creators. To take a specific example (suggested by Christine Urquhart (1998)), a specific item, say a blood sugar reading for diabetic patient, may appear in numerous places, including:

- directly in personal blogs, Twitter messages, etc.
- directly in health social networking sites, such as myHealthSpace
- directly in an individual's medical record
- aggregated in trend analysis for an individual
- aggregated, with data from other patients, in a report or journal article on treatment
- subsumed into data in reports, guidelines, etc.

Structures and institutions

The study of structures and institutions within a discipline is an important aspect for domain analysis, as these not only play a major role in forming the nature of the discipline, but also act as important providers of knowledge and information within it. This is certainly so for healthcare, where very many such institutions and structures exist. Most of these are the kinds of institutions which emerged in the 19th century, with the formation of our modern healthcare system, although, with changing communication patterns, and particularly with the advent of the internet, some have taken new forms.

Many of these will be mentioned later in the book – in Chapter 6 in particular for libraries and information services. Here we will provide a general framework to help understand the area and its information chain, giving a small number of examples for each. Brief information is given for each example, with a web site URL for further information. More details of the services and products offered by these sorts of providers will be given later in the book.

Seven main categories of structures and institutions can be distinguished, though it should be noted that there is overlap between them. Libraries and information centres, for example, may be located within government agencies, professional associations or academic institutions. They are presented here in a rough order of their significance in creating the healthcare knowledge base, with those categories later in the list being largely disseminators and organizers of information.

Academic departments, medical schools, and research institutes

These are the major creators of the scientific and clinical knowledge base of healthcare, through research and scholarship. They are numerous and most countries of the world have such institutions, though basic research is largely still carried out in the West.

Examples of major basic research programmes are the US National Institutes of Health (www.nih.gov) and the British Medical Research Council (www.mrc.ac.uk).

For examples of academic biomedical departments, see the Department of Cell and Development Biology at University College London, UK (www.cdb. ucl.ac.uk), the Department of Physiology at the University of Toronto, Canada (www.physiology.utoronto.ca), and the Department of Pathology at the University of Stanford, USA (http://pathology.stanford. edu).

A listing of medical schools worldwide is provided by World Health Organization (www.who.int/hrh/wdms). As examples, see the College of Medicine and Veterinary medicine at the University of Edinburgh, UK (www.mvm.ed. ac.uk), the School of Medicine at the University of Queensland, Australia (www2.som.uq.edu.au/som), and the Swedish Karolinska Institute (http://ki.se).

National and international institutes and non-profit organizations also provide much health information, usually in quite specific areas. Examples are the Cochrane Collaboration, an international group providing reviews of the effectiveness of treatments (www.cochrane.org), and the King's Fund, a British charity promoting better healthcare policies (www.kingsfund.org.uk).

The healthcare industry

This industry, and the pharmaceutical industry in particular, is an important creator of information, both on its own products specifically and on healthcare issues generally. We will see in the historical overview (Chapter 3) that there has always been controversy about the involvement of industry in healthcare communication, and this continues with debates on the validity of information provided by industry. As well as manufacturers of products, this sector includes insurance companies and providers of private healthcare.

As examples, see the Association of the British Pharmaceutical Industry (www.abpi.org.uk), and BUPA international health insurance provider (www.bupa.co.uk).

Government agencies and national health services

These have been major forces within the healthcare area for over a century and are among the largest creators of information, both for public dissemination and for internal use.

In the United Kingdom, the Department of Health provides policy statements, and guidance and publications on health and social care (www.dh.gov.uk). Healthcare is provided directly by the NHS (www.nhs.uk). The NHS provides numerous information services for professionals and for the public, including a guide to conditions and treatments (www.nhs.uk/conditions) and advice on health for the general public (www.nhsdirect.nhs.uk). Numerous NHS agencies also provide information for various groups; in particular, the National Institute for Health and Clinical Excellence (NICE) provides the official guidance on best practice in promoting health and treating disease (www.nice.org.uk).

Statistical and demographic data relating to health are also largely provided through government agencies: in the UK through the Department of Health and through the UK Statistics Agency (www.statistics.gov.uk).

Government regulatory agents are also important creators of health information: well known examples are the US Food and Drug Administration (www.fda.gov) and the international body, European Medicines Agency (www.emea.europa.eu).

Patient and consumer groups

Such groups play an increasingly important role in the creation and communication of information, usually related to a specific health problem, and increasingly provided through the internet.

As examples of the many patient and consumer groups, see the British charities MacMillan (cancer support) (www.macmillan.org.uk) and Diabetes UK (www.diabetes. org.uk).

Professional associations and institutions

Regional, national and international bodies are important creators and disseminators of information to their professional communities, as well major providers of professional education and training. The UK Royal Society of Medicine maintains an extensive list of British and international organizations of this kind.[1] The best known international example is, of course, the World Health Organization and its many agencies (www.who.int). Other examples are the World Dental Federation (www.fdiworldental.org) and the European Society for Therapeutic Radiology and Oncology (www.estro.org).

As examples of national associations, see the British Royal Society of Medicine (www.rsm.ac.uk), Royal Pharmaceutical Society (www.rpsgb.org.uk) and Royal College of Nursing (www.rcn.org.uk), the American Medical Association (www.ama-assn.org) and the Canadian Physiotherapy Association (www.physiotherapy.ca).

Publishers and database producers

These continue to play a vital role in the dissemination of information, though now just as often through websites or e-books as through traditional tools.

As examples of publishers specializing in medical books, see Oxford Medical, Blackwell/BMJ and Thieme Medical Publishing.[2]

As examples of database producers with several offerings relevant to healthcare, see the National Library of Medicine and Thomson Reuters.[3]

For examples of the increasing range of websites offering copious health information for the public (some from commercial publishers, some from healthcare institutions), see the UK NetDoctor site (www.netdoctor.co.uk), and the American Mayo Clinic's Tools for Healthier Living site (www.mayoclinic.com).

Libraries and information services

Often operated by the kinds of organizations noted above, library and information services play a leading role in the organization and dissemination of healthcare information. Undoubtedly the leading healthcare library in the world is the US National Library of Medicine, which is active in many aspects of research and development into healthcare information, as well as providing a variety of information resources (www.nlm.nih.gov).

A trend is for libraries to adopt a largely digital form, as in the UK NHS Evidence (formerly the National Library for Health) (www.library.nhs.uk); for a rationale for this service, see Leng (2009). For examples of healthcare libraries maintaining both a physical and a virtual presence, see the library of the British Royal Society of Medicine (www.rsm.ac.uk/library), the Hardin Health Science Library at the University of Iowa, USA (www.lib.uiowa.edu/hardin) and the Nursing Library at Yale University, USA (www.med.yale.edu/library/nursing).

Healthcare libraries, of all the sectors of librarianship, have been among the most enthusiastic creators of associations and co-operative groupings. These include local, national, regional and international organizations. Examples of these four types are: CHILL, the Consortium of Independent Health Information Libraries in London (www.chill-london.org.uk); CILIP's Health Libraries Group;[4] EAHIL, the European Association for Health Information and Libraries (www.eahil.net); and the International Federation of Library Associations' (IFLA), Health and Biosciences Libraries Section.[5]

Specialized information services may focus on particular types of information and/or on particular user groups. To show the diversity within this group of services, we can take two British examples. The UK Medicines Information Pharmacists group is an association of pharmacists whose role is to provide information on pharmaceuticals, primarily to other healthcare workers (www.ukmicentral.nhs.uk). The Patient Information Forum is an association for those working with consumer health information, and deals with such topics as the recommendation of relevant information resources and the assessment of the quality of information sources aimed at the general public (www.pifonline.org.uk).

Some providers focus on selecting websites providing 'quality assessed' health information; see, for example, the Health on the Net Foundation, a non-profit organization (www.hon.ch), and the health and life sciences sections of the Intute internet resource directories, supported by the UK higher education community (www.intute.ac.uk).

Drivers for change

A number of factors, very varied in nature, are leading to change in healthcare provision, and thus also in its information communication chain. A brief summary only will be given here, emphasizing the implications for the information chain; for wider surveys see Walton (2000, 2004), Baggott (2004) and Gray (2001). For an example of this issue in, and the difficulties of, analysing current trends in healthcare and predicting the future, see the UK Foresight Health Care 2020 report (DTI, 2000).

Scientific, technical and medical advances have led to improved treatments for many conditions, so that the remit and activities of healthcare services are very different now to how they were in the middle of the 20th century. This, in turn, determines that different kinds of knowledge and information will be needed to support them. These advances have also meant an increase in the size of the knowledge base; quite simply, healthcare practitioners need to know much more than they did in the past. This has led to stronger requirements for practitioners to have good information and IT skills.

These factors are reinforced by an increased emphasis on multidisciplinary teams working in healthcare (Reddy and Spence, 2008), and by an increased internationalization of many health activities, as noted by the British Medical Association (2005) in its recommendations for medical education. This is, of course, accompanied by the need for internationalization of adequate health information (Godlee, Pakenham-Walsh, Ncayiyana, Cohen and Packer, 2004; Madge and Plutchak, 2005).

These advances, among other factors, have led to increased expenditure, and hence to greater emphasis on value for money, this in turn leading to a requirement for better management information. The move towards increasingly evidence-based healthcare also requires improved provision of 'good quality' information. There is also a much greater emphasis on healthcare professionals undertaking continuing professional development, with a consequent need to make use of the evidence base, and to keep up with new knowledge in particular.

Demographic factors, with increasingly ageing populations in Western countries, are also causing changes in the nature of healthcare, with greater emphasis on the treatment of chronic conditions; this further changes the nature of the knowledge base, with more emphasis on long-term care and support for independent living, and also has added implications for costs. Patient expectations are rising, partly as a general 'consumerist' trend, putting further pressure on services. Healthcare has become an intensely political issue, as witness the intense debates in both the USA and Britain during 2009 as to the best form of state-supported healthcare.

Developments in information technology have a direct impact on healthcare, through decision support systems, information accessible directly in clinical settings, telemedicine and so on. They also help to increase the amount of information available, generally by adding new media rather than replacing the old. The move to a generally digital information environment, as will be emphasized throughout this book, influences all aspects of health information provision; for a commentary on its effect on the health information professions, see Groen (2006).

An increased emphasis on individual choice and responsibility for health-care, and an increased interest in 'wellness', together with the impact of web-based information, has led to a much more informed public and to the concept of the 'expert patient'. Perhaps as a result of this has come greater emphasis on 'health information literacy', so that people can find the information that is most appropriate and useful for them. The rise of the so-called 'Google generation', used to accessing information instantly via the web, but arguably lacking the skills to interpret it, may exacerbate this problem.

Conclusion

We have seen that healthcare, and its supporting sciences, forms a broad, complex and 'messy' field of practice. Its systems of information communication, which have developed over a very long period, are necessarily equally complex and broad in scope, supporting a large and ever-growing knowledge base.

Notes

1 www.rsm.ac.uk/welcom/linksocs.php.
2 www.oup.co.uk/academic/medicine; http://blackwellpublishing.com/bmj; www.thieme.com.

3 www.nlm.nih.gov/databases;
   www.thomsonreuters.com/products_services/healthcare.
4 www.cilip.org.uk/specialinterestgroups/bysubject/health.
5 www.ifla.org/en/health-and-biosciences-libraries.

References

AAMC-HHMI (2009) *Scientific Foundations for Future Physicians*, Association
   of American Medical Colleges, available from
   www.hhmi.org/grants/pdf/08–209_AAMC-HHMI_report.pdf.

Alper, B. S., Hand, J. A., Elliott, S. G., Kinkade, S., Hauan, M. J., Onion,
   D. K. and Sklar, B. M. (2004) How Much Effort is Needed to Keep up
   with the Literature Relevant for Primary Care?, *Journal of the Medical
   Library Association*, **92** (4), 429–37.

Arndt, K. A. (1992) Information Excess in Medicine: overview, relevance to
   dermatology, and strategies for coping, *Archives of Dermatology*, **128** (9),
   1249–56.

Baggott, R. (2004) *Health and Health Care in Britain*, 3rd edn, Palgrave
   MacMillan.

Bawden, D. (2002) The Three Worlds of Health Information, *Journal of
   Information Science*, **28** (1), 51–62.

Bawden, D. (2007) Organised Complexity, Meaning and Understanding: an
   approach to a unified view of information for information science, *Aslib
   Proceedings*, **59** (4/5), 307–27.

Beard, L., Wilson, K., Morra, D. and Keelan, J. (2009) A Survey of Health-
   related Activities on Second Life, *Journal of Medical Internet Research*, **11** (2)
   e17, available from www.jmir.org/2009/2/e17/HTML.

Blois, M. (1984) *Information and Meaning: the nature of medical descriptions*,
   University of California Press.

Blois. M. (1988) Medicine and the Nature of Vertical Reasoning, *New
   England Journal of Medicine*, **318** (13), 847–51.

Boulos, M. N. K., Maramba, I. and Wheeler, S. (2006) Wikis, Blogs and
   Podcasts: a new generation of web-based tools for virtual collaborative
   clinical practice and education, *BMC Medical Education*, **6** (41), available
   from www.biomedcentral.com/1472–6920/6/41.

British Medical Association (2005) *Medicine in the 21st Century – Standards for
   the Delivery of Undergraduate Medical Education*, available from
   www.bma.org.uk/careers/medical_education/undergraduate_education/
   M21C.jsp.

Clough, R. W., Shea, S. L., Hamilton, W. R., Estavillo, J. A., Rupp, G., Browning, R. A. and Lal, S. (2004) Weaving Basic and Social Sciences into a Case-based, Clinically Oriented Medical Curriculum: one school's approach, *Academic Medicine*, **79** (11), 1073–83.

Cross, M. (2008) How the Internet is Changing Health Care, *BMJ*, 337:a883.

Dahlgren, M. A., Richardson, B. and Kalman, H. (2004) Redefining the Reflective Practitioner. In Higgs, J., Richardson, B. and Dahlgren, M. A. (eds), *Developing Practice Knowledge for Health Professionals*, Butterworth Heinemann, 15–33.

De Gooijer, W. J. (2002) Health Care Systems in Western Europe: an analytical approach, *World Hospitals and Health Services*, **38** (1), 9–12.

Druss, B. G. and Marcus, S. C. (2005) Growth and Decentralisation of the Medical Literature: implications for evidence-based medicine, *Journal of the Medical Libraries Association*, **93** (4), 499–501.

DTI (2000) *Foresight Heatlh Care 2020*, Department of Trade and Industry, available from www.foresight.gov.uk/Health/Healthcare_2020_Dec_2000.pdf.

Duncan, P. (2007) *Critical Perspectives on Health*, Palgrave MacMillan.

Ely, J. W., Levy, B. T. and Hartz, A. (1999) What Clinical Information Resources are Available in Family Physicians' Offices?, *Journal of Family Practice*, 4892, 135–9.

Engel, G. L. (1977) The Need for a New Medical Model: a challenge for biomedicine, *Science*, **196**, (4286), 129–36.

Fleming, M. H. and Mattingly, C. (2000) Action and Narrative: two dynamics of clinical reasoning. In Higgs, J. and Jones, M. (eds), *Clinical Reasoning in the Health Professions*, 2nd edn, Butterworth Heinemann, 54–61.

Frohmann, B. (2009) Revisiting 'What is a Document?', *Journal of Documentation*, **65** (2), 291–303.

Garbett, R. (2004) The Role of Practitioners in Developing Professional Knowledge and Practice. In Higgs, J., Richardson, B. and Dahlgren, M. A. (eds), *Developing Practice Knowledge for Health Professionals*, Butterworth Heinemann, 15–33.

Garg, A. X., Iansavichus, A. V., Kastner, M., Walters, L. A., Wilczynski, N., McKibbon, K. A., Yang, R. C., Rehman, F. and Haynes, R. B. (2006) Lost in Publication: half of all renal practice evidence is published in non-renal journals, *Kidney International*, **70** (11), 1995–2005.

General Medical Council (2009) *Tomorrow's Doctors*, General Medical Council, available from

www.gmc-uk.org/education/undergraduate/undergraduate_policy/
tomorrows_doctors.asp.

Godlee, F., Pakenham-Walsh, N., Ncayiyana, D., Cohen, B. and Packer, A.
(2004) Can we Achieve Health Information for All by 2015?, *Lancet*, **364**
(9430), 295–300.

Gray, J. A. M. (2001) *Evidence-based Healthcare*, Churchill-Livingstone.

Groen, F. K. (2006) *Access to Medical Knowledge: libraries, digitization and the
public good*, Scarecrow Press.

Gustini, D. (2006) How Web 2.0 is Changing Medicine, *British Medical
Journal*, **333** (7582), (December), 1283–4.

Hendrix, D., Chiarella, D., Hasman, L., Murphy, S. and Zafron, M. L.
(2009) Use of Facebook in Academic Health Sciences Libraries, *Journal of
the Medical Library Association*, **97** (1), 44–7.

Henley, E. and Twible, R. (2000) Teaching Clinical Reasoning Across
Cultures. In Higgs, J. and Jones, M. (eds), *Clinical Reasoning in the Health
Professions*, 2nd edn, Butterworth Heinemann, 255–61.

Higgs, J. and Jones, M. (eds) (2000) *Clinical Reasoning in the Health
Professions*, 2nd edn, Butterworth Heinemann.

Higgs, J. and Titchen, A. (2000) Knowledge and Reasoning. In Higgs, J.
and Jones, M. (eds), *Clinical Reasoning in the Health Professions*, 2nd edn,
Butterworth Heinemann, 23–32.

Higgs, J., Andresen, L. and Fish, D. (2004) Practice knowledge – its nature,
sources and contexts. In Higgs, J., Richardson, B. and Dahlgren, M. A.
(eds), *Developing practice knowledge for health professionals*, Butterworth
Heinemann, 51–69.

Higgs, J., Fish, D. and Rothwell, R. (2004) Practice Knowledge – Critical
Appreciation. In Higgs, J., Richardson, B. and Dahlgren, M. A. (eds),
Developing Practice Knowledge for Health Professionals, Butterworth
Heinemann, 89–105.

Higgs, J., Richardson, B. and Dahlgren, M. A. (eds) (2004) *Developing
Practice Knowledge for Health Professionals*, Butterworth Heinemann.

Higgs, J., Jones, M., Edwards, I. and Beeston, S. (2004) Clinical Reasoning
and Practice Knowledge. In Higgs, J., Richardson, B. and Dahlgren, M.
A. (eds), *Developing Practice Knowledge for Health Professionals*, Butterworth
Heinemann, 181–99.

Hirst, P. (1974) *Knowledge and the Curriculum*, Routledge and Kegan Paul.

Hirst, P. and Peters, R. S. (1970) *The Logic of Education*, Routledge and
Kegan Paul.

Jippes, M. and Majoor, G. D. (2008) Influence of National Culture on the
Adoption of Integrated and Problem-based Curricula in Europe, *Medical*

Education, 42 (3), 279–85.

Lellenberg, J., Stashower, D. and Foley, C. (eds) (2007) *Arthur Conan Doyle: a life in letters*, Harper Collins.

Leng, G. (2009) NHS Evidence: better and faster access to information, *Lancet*, 373 (9674), 1502–4.

Madge, B. and Plutchak, T. S. (2005) The Increasing Globalisation of Health Librarianship: a brief survey of international trends and activities, *Health Information and Libraries Journal*, 22, supplement 1, 20–30.

Mallon, W. T., Biebuyck, J. F. and Jones, R. F. (2003) The Reorganisation of Basic Science Departments in US Medical Schools, 1980–1999, *Academic Medicine*, 78 (3), 302–6.

Morton, L. and Godbolt, S. (eds) (1992) *Information Sources in the Medical Sciences*, Bowker-Saur.

Nutton, V. (1995) Medieval Western Europe, 1000–1500. In Conrad, L. I., Neve, M., Nutton, V., Porter, R. and Wear, A. (eds), *The Western Medical Tradition: 800 BC to 1800 AD*, Cambridge University Press, 139–205.

Nutton, V. (2004) *Ancient Medicine*, Routledge.

Ohio State University (2009) Radiology Program, available from http://amp.osu.edu.

Patel, V. L. and Kaufman, D. R. (2000) Clinical Reasoning and Biomedical Knowledge: implications for teaching. In Higgs, J. and Jones, M. (eds), *Clinical reasoning in the health professions*, 2nd edn, Butterworth Heinemann, 33–44.

Prokop, D. J. (1992) Basic Science and Clinical Practice: how much will a physician need to know? In Marston, R. Q. and Jones, R. M. (eds), *Medical education in transition*, Robert Wood Johnson Foundation, 51–7.

Purdue University (2009) Pharmacy Academic Programs, available from www.pharmacy.purdue.edu.

Quality Assurance Agency (2002) UK Quality Assurance Agency for Higher Education, *Health Studies Subject Benchmark Statement*, available from www.qaa.ac.uk/academicinfrastructure/benchmark/honours/healthstudies.pdf.

Reddy, M. C. and Spence, P. R. (2008) Collaborative Information Seeking: a field study of a multidisciplinary patient care team, *Information Processing and Management*, 4491, 242–55.

Reed, K. L. (1999) Mapping the Literature of Occupational Therapy, *Bulletin of the Medical Library Association*, 87 (3), 298–304.

Richardson, B., Dahlgren, M. A. and Higgs, J. (2004) Practice Epistemology: implications for education, practice and research. In Higgs, J., Richardson, B. and Dahlgren, M. A. (eds), *Developing Practice Knowledge for Health Professionals*, Butterworth Heinemann, 201–20.

Richardson, B., Higgs, J. and Dahlgren, M. A. (2004) Recognising Practice Epistemology in the Health Professions. In Higgs, J., Richardson, B. and Dahlgren, M. A. (eds), *Developing Practice Knowledge for Health Professionals*, Butterworth Heinemann, 1–14.

Robinson, L. (2007) Impact of Digital Information Resources in the Toxicology Literature, *Aslib Proceedings*, **59** (4/5), 342–51.

Robinson, L. (2009) Information Science: information chain and domain analysis, *Journal of Documentation*, **65** (4), 578–91.

Smith, K. A. and Mehenert, R. B. (1986) The National Library of Medicine: from MEDLARS to the sesquisentennial and beyond, *Bulletin of the Medical Libraries Association*, **74** (4), 325–32.

Smith, R. (1996) What Clinical Information Do Doctors Need?, *British Medical Journal*, **313** (7064), 1062–8.

Stevens, S. R. (2000) Mapping the Literature of Cytotechnology, *Bulletin of the Medical Library Association*, **88** (2), 172–7.

Sturgeon D. (2008) Skills for Caring: valuing knowledge of applied science in nursing, *British Journal of Nursing*, **17** (5), 322–5.

Talbot-Smith, A. and Pollock, A. M. (2006) *The New NHS: a guide*, Routledge.

Taylor, P. (2006) *From Patient Data to Medical Knowledge: the principles and practice of health informatics*, Blackwell.

Thompson Rivers University (2009) Nursing courses, available from www.tru.ca/nursing/curriculum.

Tieman, J., Sladek, R. and Currow, D. (2008) Changes in the Quantity and Level of Evidence of Palliative and Hospice Care Literature: the last century, *Journal of Clinical Oncology*, **26** (35), 5679–83.

Titchen, A. and Higgs, J. (2000) Facilitating the Acquisition of Knowledge for Reasoning. In Higgs, J. and Jones, M. (eds), *Clinical Reasoning in the Health Professions*, 2nd edn, Butterworth Heinemann, 222–9.

Titchen, A., McGinley, M. and McCormack, B. (2004) Blending Self-knowledge and Professional Knowledge in Person-centred Care. In Higgs, J., Richardson, B. and Dahlgren, M. A. (eds), *Developing Practice Knowledge for Health Professionals*, Butterworth Heinemann, 110–26.

University of North Carolina Greensboro (2009) Undergraduate Nursing, available from www.uncg.edu/nur.

Urquhart, C. (1998) Personal Knowledge: a clinical perspective from the Value and EVINCE projects in health library and information services, *Journal of Documentation*, **54** (4), 420–42.

Walsh, P. (1993) *Education and Meaning: philosophy in practice*, Cassell Educational.

Walton, G. (2000) Health Services: a contemporary approach. In Booth, A. and Walton, G. (eds), *Managing knowledge in health services*, Library Association Publishing, 3–14.

Walton, G. (2004) New Structures and Principles in Health Services. In Walton, G. and Booth, A. (eds), *Exploiting Knowledge in Health Services*, Facet Publishing, 3–15.

Wear, A. (1995) Early Modern Europe, 1500–1700. In Conrad, L. I., Neve, M., Nutton, V., Porter, R. and Wear, A. (eds), *The Western Medical Tradition: 800 BC to 1800 AD*, Cambridge University Press, 215–361.

World Health Organization (1946) WHO Definition of Health, available from www.who.int/about/definition/en/print.html.

Wyatt, H. V. (ed.) (1997) *Information Sources in the Life Sciences*, 4th edn, Bowker-Saur.

Wyatt, J. C. and Sullivan, F. (2005) Keeping Up: learning in the workplace, *British Medical Journal*, **331 (7525)**, (November), 1129–32.

Further reading

Baggott, R. (2004) *Health and Health Care in Britain*, 3rd edn, Palgrave MacMillan.

Blois, M. (1984) *Information and Meaning: the nature of medical descriptions*, University of California Press.

Groopman, J. (2007) *How Doctors Think*, Houghton Mifflin.

Higgs, J. and Jones, M. (2000) *Clinical Reasoning in the Health Professions*, 2nd edn, Butterworth Heinemann.

Taylor, P. (2006) *From Patient Data to Medical Knowledge: the principles and practice of health informatics*, Blackwell.

2

History of healthcare and its information environment

Introduction

The prevention and treatment of disease is one of the oldest recognizable 'practical disciplines', and among the first to be recorded in documents. Healthcare has always been in the lead in adopting new technologies and media for recording and disseminating information. Considering the history of healthcare and the kinds of recorded information which have been created to support it at various times gives us an essential perspective on the situation today, without which it is not possible to adequately understand how and why healthcare information is as it is. This is the justification for focusing on the historical aspect of domain analysis in this chapter.

The history of the healthcare professions (medicine in particular) and of the scientific research which has contributed to the field is an academic subject in itself, with an extensive literature. Here, we can only attempt an outline view, drawing mainly from a few leading monographs of the subject (Porter 1996, 1997; Bynum, Hardy, Jacyna, Lawrence and Tansey, 2006; Conrad, Neve, Nutton, Porter and Wear, 1995), all of which provide copious further reading for those interested; for a shorter and more popular survey, see Strathern (2005). In view of the main purpose of this book, we will mainly focus on the Western style and tradition of healthcare; for an account of the history of other traditional medical and healthcare approaches, for example those of China and India, see Porter (1997). We will take a chronological approach, focusing only on those aspects which have had a direct influence on the communication of healthcare information. To a large extent, this means focusing on the history of medicine, the other healthcare professions, in an information context, having appeared only relatively recently.

The ancient world

Presumably some attempts were made to treat injury and disease in the earliest human communities, but of this we have no record. The first written records of what we can regard as organized healthcare are found in the earliest known civilization of the Bronze Age, along with the establishment of large settlements, the cultivation of crops, sophisticated metal working and the organization of time and space through calendars and maps. With these, of course, came the development of scripts and writing, and hence administration and bureaucracy. As Porter (1997, 44) puts it, 'All such developments – the ABC of civilization – brought new approaches to healing and, for the first time, the writing down of medical practice. Medicine entered history.' For so long as people have been writing, they have written about healthcare.

The Sumerian civilization of Mesopotamia is generally regarded as the first to have recorded healthcare information, writing in its cuneiform script on clay tablets, in the third millennium BC. Among such tablets, dating from the seventh century BC, found in the library of King Assurbanipal, about one thousand deal with recognizably health issues – descriptions and diagnoses of disease, treatments and recipes for remedies – although much of the nature of the diagnosis and treatment would today be regarded as magic or religious.

A major Sumerian text, translated as *Treatise of Medical Diagnosis and Prognosis*, comprises some 40 clay tables with 3000 individual entries. These are mainly lists of illnesses with their symptoms, some of which seem recognizable today. Porter (1997, 45) suggests, for example, that tuberculosis can be identified from this description:

> The patient coughs continually. What he coughs up is thick and frequently
> bloody. His breathing sounds like a flute. His hand is cold, his feet are warm.
> He sweats easily, and his heart activity is disturbed.

The ancient Egyptian civilization also created healthcare information, in particular 12 'medical papyri' which include rational and reproducible elements of diagnosis and treatment. These provide evidence of healthcare which is supported by limited archaeological evidence, such as the discovery of a sanatorium at the temple of Denderah and study of traces of plant and inorganic pharmacy ingredients (David, 2008).

A tomb inscription from around 2700 BC records that when the tomb's occupant suffered what may have been a stroke, the king 'had brought for him a case of writings', understood to mean advice for those treating him (Lerner, 1998, 18). The earliest surviving writings are to be found in papyri dating from the second millennium BC. As with Sumeria, there is a strong element of magic and ritual, though accompanied by more rational and empirical content. Among the earliest of the medical papyri, the Kahun papyrus (of about 1850 BC) deals with gynaecology and contraception, and the London papyrus (of about 1350 BC) with pregnancy and baby care. The Smith papyrus (about 1600 BC) includes what might now be called case reports of wounds and their treatments, and of surgical procedures. The Ebers papyrus (about 1550 BC, found near Luxor and now held in the University of Leipzig) is regarded as the main Egyptian medical document; Porter (1997) calls it the oldest surviving medical book. Written on a papyrus over 20 metres long (see Figure 2.1), divided into over 100 pages and written in hieratic script, it describes numerous diseases (15 of the abdomen, 18 of the skin, 29 of the eyes, etc.) and treatments, often relying on magical rituals but also listing empirical remedies, largely herbal; for example:

> To drive away inflammation of the eyes, grind the stems of the juniper of Byblos, steep them in water, apply to the eyes of the sick person, and he will be quickly cured.
>
> (Porter, 1997, 48)

Figure 2.1 A page from the Ebers Papyrus, courtesy of the Wellcome Library, London

As we will see in Chapter 5, combined studies of the medical papyri and of archaeological material from Egypt can provide information useful for present-day healthcare.

The origins of healthcare, and its knowledge base, can therefore be traced to the ancient world, as far back as recorded information itself. Activities recognizable as healthcare in any modern sense, however, emerge later, in the classical world (Conrad, Neve, Nutton, Porter and Wear, 1995).

The classical world

Treatment of disease and wounds is mentioned from the earliest stages of writing in the Greek world, from the 5th century BC, another example of the immediate entry of healthcare into the written record at the first opportunity. The most significant of Greek medical writings is the corpus of about 60 works attributed to Hippocrates and dating to around 400 BC, though it is clear that there is a variety of authorship, and by no means all the works deal with healthcare as we would understand it (Nutton, 2004). Their significance is, as Porter (1997) emphasizes, that these are the first significant writings which insist that health can be promoted and disease treated (to use modern idiom) by rational thought and by an emphasis on observation and on the expertise and ethical stance of the physician. The corpus includes advice on diagnosis, on surgical and medical treatment and on diet. Those 'Hippocratic physicians' who practised in this tradition are commonly regarded as the first 'healthcare practitioners' as we would understand the term.

In the Hellenistic world of the Eastern Mediterranean, which succeeded classical Greece, there was a new enthusiasm for the collection of information on natural history, and the beginnings of what would become the sciences of anatomy and physiology (Nutton, 1995a). In this environment, the tradition of Hippocratic medicine was continued, supported by the influential concepts of biology promoted by the philosopher Aristotle and his followers. These were the first to make systematic experimental studies in biology, by observation and dissection, and hence arguably the first to point the way to biomedical science. Their findings, and the medical expertise of the practitioners, were recorded and distributed by the sophisticated manuscript production systems of the time and their associated booksellers and libraries. They were to have a major influence on the theory and practice of healthcare in the Western world for nearly 2000 years, their ideas forming a part of practical medicine up to the 19th century.

The Roman civilization initially embraced Hellenistic medicine, as it adapted Greek ideas for much of its intellectual and cultural life. However, a Roman tradition of healthcare and the creation of healthcare knowledge soon began. The first major work on healthcare in Latin is the set of eight medical books which form part of what we would now term a multi-volume encyclopaedia, compiled by Celsus, and produced in the first century AD. The books survey the whole area of healthcare, presenting diseases and their treatment by body parts, as well as surgical procedures, drug treatments, signs and symptoms, and means of preserving health. Porter (1997) tells us that Celsus was not a physician, but an estate owner, who may be presumed to have treated his family and friends and who wrote for a non-professional readership; he may stand as the first example of the wide, and sometimes unexpected, variety of creators of healthcare information.

The leading healthcare personality of the Roman world was Galen, active in the 2nd century AD, who was to have what Porter (1997, 73) calls 'dominion over medicine for more than a millenium', with some of his anatomical teaching remaining influential until the 19th century. This is undoubtedly due in part to his status as the originator, we may cynically say, of healthcare information overload, being the unquestioned author of over 350 medical books. These include, for example, 16 books on various aspects on the pulse, which he later summarized into a single volume for the benefit of those who might be put off by the original volume of material (Nutton, 1995b). Born into the Greek-speaking empire, and writing in Greek (his books amounting, Porter tells us, to roughly the same as all the other surviving medical writings of classical and Hellenistic Greece put together), Galen saw himself as building on the legacy of Hippocrates, particularly by combining clinical observation and experience with theoretical, primarily anatomical and physiological, considerations. His books present these two aspects in combination for the first time, and may be seen as a forerunner of modern healthcare texts. They cover all aspects of the prevention of disease, and its medical and surgical treatment, as well as providing rational explanations in biological terms. Later generations lamented that no one could any longer 'obtain a mastery of the whole of medical knowledge' as Galen had (Nutton, 1995b).

The Roman world developed a more sophisticated system of healthcare than had been known before, with many forms of healers, in addition to physicians in the sense of Hippocrates and Galen, and also nurses, midwives, herbalists and other 'healthcare professions'. Public and military hospitals were created and the foundations of public health were laid, emphasizing clean water supply, safe food storage and adequate sanitation systems. Books of many kinds were available to support this, and there was a flourishing market for medical books in Rome (Nutton, 2004). From the second century onwards, the scroll or roll, which had been the universal carrier of recorded information, was succeeded by the codex, with parchment pages stitched together to form something with the convenience of use of the modern book. We should, however, be cautious about taking this to mean that there was, in any sense, a Roman 'healthcare information environment' like our own. Books were relatively rare and valuable, and most doctors would probably have owned only a few basic handbooks (Nutton, 2004).

As well as encyclopaedic works of the kind already mentioned and numerous books on specific health topics, there emerged the first form of 'data compilation'. Of these we can mention the two treatises on plants by Theophrastus, *De Historia Plantarum* and *Causis Plantarum* (written about 300 AD), which classify hundreds of species by their characteristics and form the first basis for medicinal botany; and the *De Materia Medica* of Dioscorides, from the first century AD (see Figure 2.2 for later version). The latter, in five separate books, deals with the preparation and use of medicines from a wide variety of sources – animal, vegetable and mineral – in a forerunner of today's pharmacopoeia. Medicinal matters also found their way into handbooks of practical arts, such as farming (Nutton, 1995b).

Nutton (1995b) also points out that medical authors of this time gave some thought to the organization of their information, some being arranged by classifications of body parts, drug actions, etc. and some by the simpler alphabetical order. A perennial concern of health information provision emerges at a very early stage.

Figure 2.2 Dioscorides, *De Medicinali Materia*, courtesy of the Wellcome Library, London

The medieval world

After the end of the Western Roman empire, the development of medicine in Western Europe stultified, with few new developments. Such writings as were produced did little more than attempt to hold on to a simplified and reduced version of classical knowledge. In the monasteries, which are generally regarded as having retained and transmitted knowledge during this time, health held relatively little importance. This may be seen in Britain from the writings of the Venerable Bede, in which medical material is intermingled with metaphysics and mysticism; from our knowledge of the collections of the French Swiss monastery of St Gall, known as a centre of medical knowledge (although only a handful of the many volumes in its library dealt with the subject); and from an existing list of a few, largely practical, medical guides recommended by Cassiodorus (Strathern, 2005; Nutton, 1995c, 2004). In the Eastern Roman empire a tradition of medical knowledge and writing was continued, but, without the input of experiment and observation, it relied largely on the recapitulation and interpretation of classical works: 'medicine was becoming a matter of great texts' (Porter, 1997, 89). A new form of medical text appeared: summaries, handbooks and medical encyclopaedias, passing on classical knowledge without adding to it (Nutton, 1995c, 2004).

Islamic medical scholarship

From the ninth century, Arab-Islamic medical scholarship began to develop, particularly in Baghdad, whereby hundreds of Greek medical texts were translated into Arabic. Medical texts were copied and disseminated on a very wide scale, much more so than texts in other subjects, and formed 'an enormous corpus sufficiently varied so as to be accessible to much of literate society, and it was also well distributed' (Conrad, 1995, 123). Galen's works were particularly favoured. Husayn ibn Ishaq (known in the West as Johannitius) and his pupils alone translated 130 of Galen's works into Arabic (more than survive in the original Greek today), and Galen became regarded as the central figure in Islamic medicine. Subsequently, an Arabic medicine with its own extensive literature arose, well in advance of anything in the West at the time. Its best known product is the *Kitab al-Qanun* (Medical Code or Canon) of Abu Ali al-Husayn ibn Abdullah ibn Sina (known in the west as Avicenna), written around 1000 AD (see Figure 2.3 overleaf). This remains an influential text in Islamic medicine and was equally influential in the Renaissance West. It is an encyclopaedic presentation of all of current knowledge of the medical sciences (particularly anatomy and physiology), the diagnosis and treatment of disease, and the preparation and use of a wide variety of medicines. Its intellectual structure is that of the classical world, augmented by the practical observation and experience of Arab physicians. A similar, though less extensive, encyclopaedic treatment is the *al-Kulliyat* (Book of General Practice) produced around 1160 by Abu-l-Walid Muhammad ibn Ahmad ibn Muhammad ibn Rushd (known in the West as Averroes). A compilation of seven books, its translation into Latin in the 15th century, with that of Avicenna's Canon and other Arabic texts, was of great importance for the Renaissance revival of Western medicine. These books systematized medical knowledge in a way unknown before, so that a doctor in this culture

Figure 2.3 Avicenna, the start of the third book, courtesy of the Wellcome Library, London

could expect to find all the information needed for his practice within a single book (Conrad, 1995).

The Islamic world of this period developed various routes into medical practice, and hospitals in the larger cities, to put into practice the healthcare knowledge set out in the kinds of writings noted above. Hospitals and schools of medicine had small libraries of instructional texts, and medical books were also widely available in the libraries of mosques and schools (Conrad, 1995; Lerner, 1998). This form of healthcare continued until the 19th century, when it was largely abandoned in favour of the Western style of healthcare. However, the Arabic lead in innovation and scholarship in these areas faded after 1300, with the advent of the Ottoman Turks (Porter, 1997, 105).

Western European medicine

The revival of medical knowledge and practice in the medieval West began about 1050, initially with the translation into Latin of classical texts, from the original Greek or from Arabic versions, and also of the later Arabic texts (Nutton, 1995d). The medical school at Salerno in Italy, and particularly the contribution of the translator monk Constantinus Africanus, played a crucial role, 'providing as they did the means whereby Latin Christendom gained access to the tradition of Hippocratic learning rationalized by Galen and digested by the Arabs' (Porter, 1997, 107). Translations into, and original writings in, vernacular languages came rather later; the surgical treatises of John of Arderne in the mid-14th century being the first such in the English language, while German was the other favoured vernacular language (Nutton, 1995d).

The rise of universities in Western Europe in the High Middle Ages – Paris founded in 1110, Oxford in 1167, Cambridge in 1209, Padua in 1222 and so on – provided a further impetus for translations of classical texts into Latin, including much medical material (Nutton, 1995d). They also provided the first academic training in medicine, Padua having a notably large medical school. Such training, by modern standards, was abstract and formulaic, based on study of the classical writing, but 'formulaic teaching was unavoidable in an age when books were few' (Porter, 1997, 115). Hospitals began to be established, almost invariably based in religious foundations, while state authorities began to institute public health measures.

Medical organizations began to form, based originally on the medieval guild structure. In some cases, they concretized the distinctions between healthcare activities: physicians, usually university trained, claiming superiority over surgeons, trained through a guild apprenticeship, for example. In some circumstances, cooperation was favoured: Porter (1997) points out that in small English cities like Bristol and Norwich the physicians, surgeons and barbers (who carried out procedures such as bleeding) joined together, while in Florence the physicians and pharmacists had joined at an early stage.

By the close of the Middle Ages in Western Europe, therefore, many of the components and institutions of the healthcare information chain were beginning to form, although generally not in the form recognized today, while the healthcare literature was still largely restricted to translations of, and glosses on, the classical works, in the form of hand-copied manuscripts. Illustrations were few because of their expense, and fully illustrated manuscripts were rare collectors' items, rather than tools for the practitioner (Nutton, 1995d).

Renaissance and Enlightenment

The Renaissance period, of the 15th and 16th centuries, brought about a renewed spirit of enquiry, focused on rediscovery of the knowledge of the classical world and promoted in particular by the new technology of printing, introduced into Europe with the production of the 'Gutenberg Bibles' in 1454 (Eisenstein, 1983).

The first printed medical literature

Medicine, and health generally, as at other times, were among the subjects which benefited most from the new information technology of printing (Wear, 1995). As well as the reproduction of text, the provision of printed illustrations was particularly valuable for these topics, for anatomical works, herbals and similar material relying on accurate images for communicating information. Printing technology soon developed from reliance on woodcut illustration to techniques using metal plates, which allowed greater exactness of line and varied tone, much improving the quality of illustrations in medical books (Furdell, 2002, chapter 8).

Revival of classical knowledge

Initially, the main enthusiasm among the humanistic scholars of the Renaissance was for better translations of classical works, disseminated through print. Celsus' works were printed in 1478, inspiring the use of Latin terminology in medicine which has lasted to the present day (Strathern, 2005). No less than 590 editions of Galen's works were produced in Europe during the 16th century, together with those of other classical medical authors, leading a commentator of the time to declare that medicine had been raised from the dead (Porter, 1997, 171).

Furdell (2002) gives a detailed account of the production and distribution of printed medical books in England during the 16th and 17th centuries, showing the extent of the take-up of print technology for these purposes. She identifies over 200 printers, publishers and booksellers who handled medical books in London during this period. Some handled a high proportion of health-related material and were clearly specialists in the subjects. The first printed medical bibliography appeared in the first decade of the 16th century, a 57-page text written by the French physician Symphorien Champier (Freeman, 1992). It was succeeded by several more during the following two centuries. There was a gradual trend away from publication in the learned *lingua franca* of Latin and in favour of the vernacular; in England, by the middle of the 17th century, more medical books were being written in English than in Latin (Wear, 1995).

Creation of new knowledge

The printing press, which enabled not merely the wider availability of books of all kinds, but also a new ability to compare editions and translations, initially led learned medicine to focus on the retrieval of past knowledge (Wear, 1995). However, this period also saw an interest in creating new knowledge, particularly in the field of anatomy and not least among artists of the time, of whom Leonardo da Vinci is the best known. A number of medically oriented anatomical texts and atlases were created, taking advantage of the ability to print identical copies of detailed images. The most influential was Andreas Vesalius', *De Humani Corporis Fabrica* (On the Fabric of the Human Body), published in 1543 (see Figure 2.4), which 'marks a watershed in the medical understanding of bodily structures [and] laid the groundwork for observation-based anatomy' (Porter, 1997, 180–1). This impressive work, which Porter (1996, 156) describes as 'one of the jewels of Renaissance printing', had over 700 pages of text and 200 large woodcut illustrations, in seven books, causing problems for the printing technology of the day (Wear, 1995; Furdell, 2002; Strathern, 2005). In terms of information presentation, it was one of the first to link images and text, by means of letters on the anatomical drawings, pointing to text descriptions (Eisenstein, 1983, 25–6). The basis for the first of the supporting 'basic sciences' for healthcare was now in existence.

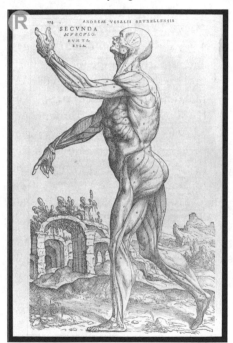

Figure 2.4 Vesalius, *De Humani Corporis Fabrica*, courtesy of the Wellcome Library, London

The beginnings of pharmacy

Printing also supported the development of what would become the profession of pharmacy. The rediscovery of the classical world's stock of *materia medica*, through the translation and printing of the works of authors such as Theophrastus and Dioscorides, 'galvanised the botanical revival' (Porter, 1997, 191). This saw the introduction of the scientifically arranged botanical garden as an adjunct to medicine, and was accompanied by the introduction of many new herbs and other medicinal agents from the voyages of discovery to the Americas and the Far East. New forms of herbals emerged based on naturalistic images, accurately reproduced by printing, in a vegetable analogy to the anatomical atlas (Wear, 1995). Arguably the most famous was the 1565 edition of Andrea Mattioli's illustrated updating of *De Materia Medica* (see Figure 2.5), a massive work for the time, of 1500 pages, and an early example of a regularly updated reference source: 'As Mattioli's commentaries on Dioscorides . . . ran through one edition after another, they were periodically revised and corrected on the basis of specimens and information received from correspondents' (Eisenstein, 1983, 75). All this led to a great increase in status for apothecaries, who began to organize themselves into associations, following the physicians and surgeons.

Figure 2.5 Mattioli, *I Discorsi . . . Nelli Sei Libri*, courtesy of the Wellcome Library, London

The growth of lay medical literature

Printing enabled books on other aspects of healthcare to be created. In particular, texts on obstetrics and the care of the new-born were widely published, in many languages rather than just the professionals' Latin: Porter (1997) gives several examples. The range of material was, from the first, very wide, involving 'a huge range of medical books from elite to popular: textbooks on theory and practice, surgical texts, complicated philosophically based regimens, herbals for apothecaries and wives, plague treatises, suggestions for respite at mineral springs and spas, and modest household recipe books with lists of ingredients and direction for usage. Distinctions between lay and medical readerships blurred: amateurs and professionals both read works which were likely intended for the other. Publishers, both foreign and domestic, benefited from this bonanza and supplied myriad medical titles for increasing customer demand' (Furdell, 2002, 38).

One of the main effects of the printing revolution, as suggested by the quotation above, was the widespread availability, for the first time, of 'popular heath' books aimed at a literate general public (an analogy could be drawn with the advent of the internet, as suggested by Bawden and Robinson, 2000). These books dealt mainly with the 'temperate life', addressing the benefits of a good diet, exercise, avoidance of strong drink, and mental activity.

The 'medical revolution'

The advent of printing provided the means for the wide dissemination of what we would today call healthcare knowledge. The Renaissance, however, saw this mainly used for the rediscovery of classical medical knowledge, and it was not until the so-called Scientific Revolution of the 17th century that healthcare could begin to be set on any sort of scientific basis; the parallel 'medical revolution' is described by the contributors to the survey by French and Wear (2008).

The first leading figure in this movement is Theophrastus Phillipus Bombastus von Hoehenheim, who adopted the name of 'Paracelsus', to show that he was going beyond the status of the Celsus, the classical physician. He is commonly regarded as a kind of founder of modern scientific medicine, and especially of medicinal chemistry, though, as Porter (1997) points out, his views included so many mystical and esoteric aspects that this is hardly a realistic assessment. He was appointed professor of medicine in Basel in 1526, and remained active until his death in 1543, thus pre-dating by many decades the first truly scientific studies. Through his writings and lectures he promoted the idea that observation and experiment, rather than the study of classical texts, was the way to medical understanding: Porter (1997) tells us that he went so far as to publicly burn copies of the works of Avicenna and Galen, regarded as little less then religious texts by most medical authorities of the time. The alchemical, mystical and astrological components of his medicine never gained wide acceptance, but he provided inspiration for those who sought a new form of medical knowledge.

The rise of observational science

This came during the 17th century, with the development of a true observational and experimental science, with its laboratories and equipment – such as the first microscopes and thermometers – and its associated infrastructure of the learned society and the scientific journal (for an overview, see Harvey, 2002 and for a detailed account of the contribution of printing to the emergence of modern science, see Eisenstein, 1983, chapter 7). Based on this, a number of significant developments followed, the most significant being William Harvey's demonstration of the circulation of the blood, in his *Exercitatio Anatomica de Motu Cordis et Sanguinis in Animalibus* (Anatomical Essay concerning the Movement of the Heart and the Blood in Animals) of 1628. The science of physiology was emerging.

Another foundation of modern healthcare appeared during this period, with the first approaches to the compilation and publication of statistics of morbidity and mortality (illness and death), on which healthcare statistics and demographics, and epidemiology, were later to be developed. These statistics followed on the first registers and censuses, developed by government bureaucracies from the 16th century and made widely available through printing (Greenberg, 1997). A well known early example is the analysis of the number of deaths and their causes, maintained on a weekly basis by parish clerks in London, carried out by John Graunt and published as *Natural and Political Observations upon the Bills of Mortality* in 1662. It was not until over a century later that similar tables were produced for an entire nation, this being achieved for Sweden in 1766.

The period of the 18th century, generally known as the Enlightenment, showed a continuation of these trends: a slowly increasing body of relevant knowledge, gained by observation, clinical case study, experiment and rational thought, increasingly widely spread by publications, generally in the form of monographs. Porter refers to a 'stream of books' in obstetrics and gynaecology from the middle of the 17th century and exemplifies many of the influential texts in all aspects of healthcare published throughout the following century (Porter, 1997, chapter 10).

The growth of the medical press

An 'extensive medical press' was operating by 1800, based not merely on monographs but also on the increasing number of medical journals launched by the burgeoning national and regional medical and scientific societies which had come into being during the 18th century (Porter, 1995). The first significant healthcare libraries were by then well established, under the auspices of universities, schools of medicine and professional associations. To give one well known example, the library of the College of Physicians of London, established in 1518, contained over 1300 volumes by 1666, when most were destroyed in the Great Fire (Lerner, 1998). Replenished by wealthy patrons, the library flourishes today as part of the Royal College of Physicians. Its companion library for the London-based Royal College of Surgeons was established in 1800.

The Enlightenment period saw a considerable expansion in hospital provision throughout Europe, as the older pattern of provision was updated by a more modern philanthropy: Porter (1996, 212) gives examples, particularly in England and throughout the Habsburg Empire. Medical practice, however, did not change greatly, and medicine and other healthcare professions certainly did not become true sciences along the model of the developing physics and chemistry. There was, nonetheless, the development of what we might today call a model of professional practice, backed by an extensive printed literature, largely of monographs and textbooks. Surgery, in particular, developed from a rudimentary manual skill to a profession in its own right, backed by scientific understanding and again supported by the dissemination of knowledge through monographs. The outstanding figure in this transformation was the London surgeon John Hunter, who not only wrote numerous treatises in the last three decades of the century but also created a very large collection of specimens of all kinds, 13,000 of which formed the basis for the Hunterian Museum, still maintained by the Royal College of Surgeons in London. The museum is one of the first examples of the important role of organized and documented collections of scientific specimens as a means of transmitting medical knowledge. (Medicine was not, of course, the only subject in which the combination of collections of specimens, painted images and printed books for conveying new knowledge was being developed during this period: see, for example, Attenborough, Owens, Clayton and Alexandratos (2007) for a beautifully illustrated account of these issues in natural history.)

The basic sciences developed further, as a part of a wider discipline which, by the end of the century, was being described as 'biology'. Anatomy flourished, in particular, supported by a range of beautifully illustrated anatomical atlases; Porter (1997, 248) gives examples. These atlases were made possible by an improvement in the process for reproducing illustrations – the use of steel rather than copper plates (Porter, 1995). The books generally illustrated 'gross anatomy', depicting the large and distinct parts of the body, though by the end of the century the study of membranes and tissues was underway, heralded by Bichat's *Traité des Membranes* (Treatise on Membranes) of 1799 (Porter, 1997, 264–5).

Early classification of diseases

Physiology formed the basis for the first attempts at a rational classification of diseases by their underlying cause, rather than simply by body parts and symptoms; Porter (1997, 160–2) gives several examples, including the classification of Cullen, Brown and de Sauvages. William Cullen is an interesting case in point. Originally practising as a surgeon, he was first professor of chemistry at Edinburgh University, and in 1766 became professor in the university's Institute of Medicine, which then encompassed therapeutics, pathology and physiology, his career and his Institute both exemplifying the overlap of the practice of medicine with its scientific base. Cullen, Porter (1997, 263) tells us, 'gathered, sifted and glossed available medical knowledge, his emphasis being on use rather than discovery'. It was only by this stage that sufficient knowledge had been created and disseminated through printed books for such gathering and sifting to be necessary. This was, in general, the age of the encyclopaedia, and medicine and its sciences produced several such: physiology's contribution was Haller's *Elementa Physiologiae*, published in eight volumes from 1759 and generally accepted as including all that was known of the subject (Strathern, 2005, 158). However, such comprehensive coverage could not survive the expansion of knowledge during the following century.

The third of the basic sciences emerged: pathology, the study of the changes in the body brought about by disease. This was first codified by London physician Matthew Bailey in his *Morbid Anatomy of Some of the Most Important Parts of the Human Body* (1793), which went into eight English editions, plus three in America, and was translated – as was increasingly the case with important texts of the time – into the main modern European languages: French, German, Italian and Russian (Porter, 1997, 263–5).

Developments in pharmacy

Pharmacy also developed, with the medical authorities of major centres producing their own pharmacopoeias; the London pharmacopoeia, for example, first appeared in 1618, though German cities had been producing their equivalents many years earlier, with that of Nuremberg the first to appear, in 1546 (Wear, 1995). These were regularly updated and often differed in what substances were included: Porter (1997, 268–71), gives several examples, pointing out, for example, that digitalis as a medicine for heart problems entered the London pharmacopoeia 26 years after it had first been included in Edinburgh's equivalent. (A text often considered the first textbook of chemistry was also produced at this time by a German physician (Wear, 1995) – an indication of early links between subjects that would later become strongly interdependent.)

The greater numbers of books being produced throughout the 18th century included a larger range of relatively cheap popular medical texts, aimed at lay readers and offering practical advice on the treatment of many illnesses. Titles published in Britain inlcuded *Domestic Medicine* of 1769 and *The Poor Man's Medicine Chest* of 1791. Equivalent books were produced throughout Europe (Porter, 1997, 283–5).

Healthcare had built up an extensive and varied system for creating and communicating its knowledge by the end of the 18th century. Bibliographies, now including journal articles and commonly organized by subject rather than by author, reflecting the need for better subject access to the much greater volume of material now available, continued to be produced in several European countries (Freeman, 1992).

It is interesting to note that the phenomenon which we might now term 'information avoidance' had already shown itself, usually in the form of leading authorities decrying 'book learning' in favour of experience and observation. We have seen how Paracelsus made his point by burning copies of classical texts. Less dramatically, the leading English physician of the 17th century, Thomas Sydenham, when asked for his recommendation of the best medical books, advised the questioner to read *Don Quixote*: he also urged that the physician must study 'with his own eyes – and not through the medium of books' (Porter, 1997, 229).

The 19th century to the present day

The 19th century saw the development of modern systems of healthcare, and also of most of the features of the present-day healthcare information environment. These changes resulted from a number of factors. Scientific and technological advances saw healthcare established firmly on a greatly expanded foundation of basic knowledge and led to the introduction of dramatically improved means of prevention and treatment of disease. The healthcare professions were reorganized into the kind of structure familiar today, while national and regional governments took a much more active role in healthcare provision. All of these factors affected the communication of healthcare information. This was itself supported by the communications revolution of the mid-19th century, by the effect of steam power on the production and transmission of printed information, leading to a great increase in the extent and speed of information dissemination. Consequently, this period saw the development and wide adoption of various forms of information resources – particularly scientific and professional journal, mass-produced textbooks, and specialized information sources such as abstracting and indexing services – and the growth of new forms of libraries and information services to deal with the greatly increased extent and diversity of the literature. The healthcare disciplines were at the forefront of these changes. Because these advances and changes were so varied and far-reaching, only a brief account is given here, emphasizing their implications for the communication of information. More detailed accounts are given by Porter (1997, chapters 11, 12 and 13), Bynum (1994), and Bynum, Hardy, Jacyna, Lawrence and Tansey (2006).

Scientific advances

Scientific advances in a variety of disciplines fed through to healthcare practice, so that by the end of the century William Osler, the leading Canadian doctor, could declare that 'the physician without physiology and chemistry flounders along in an aimless fashion, never able to gain any accurate conception of disease, practising a sort of popgun pharmacy' (Porter, 1997, 303). Bynum (2006) notes developments in physiology, pathology, bacteriology and immunology as being particularly significant.

New instruments, particularly modern versions of the stethoscope and clinical thermometer, led to increased sophistication in patient observation (Bynum, 2006), while improved microscopes led to the development of histology (the microscopic study of tissues) and cell biology, and hence to collections of microscopical specimens and images from them (Jacyna, 2006). The first histological textbook, von Kölliker's *Handbuch der Gewebelehre des Menschen* (Handbook of the tissues of man), was published in 1852. The microscope led later to the development of microbiology, ultimately resulting in the control of epidemic diseases through immunization, antibiotic treatment, and insect control for diseases such as malaria and yellow fever – the most dramatic proof of the efficacy of science-based healthcare (Mann, 1999; Porter, 1997, chapter 14).

An improved knowledge of chemistry, and advancement in analytical techniques, led to the development of clinical chemistry, and later biochemistry. These factors also brought the apothecary's practical arts of pharmacy into the scientific spectrum, with the rise of pharmacology. Its sister discipline of toxicology was first established on a scientific basis with Joseph Orfila's *Traité des Poisons* (Treatise on Poisons) of 1814, which first systematized a body of knowledge dating back to the ancient world. Formularies and pocket books, what might now be termed data collections, supplemented the long-standing pharmacopoeias.

Developments in medical publishing

The chief means for the dissemination of knowledge was still the monograph, whose numbers continued to increase dramatically. Leading 19th-century books went through many editions over long lifetimes: the most famous, *Gray's Anatomy*, first published in 1858, is still with us today. Scientific and medical journals, however, expanded greatly in numbers and readership during the period, and became major channels for communication. Several major English-language journals of medicine and science were founded in this period and survive to the present day, some with changes of name: *Lancet* in 1823, *British Medical Journal* in 1857, the *New England Journal of Medicine* in 1812, *Nature* in 1869 and *Science* in 1880. Production of comprehensive bibliographies was abandoned in the face of the volume of material now available; the 'information explosion' had begun (Freeman, 1992).

Both books and papers were frequently translated into several other languages as the market for healthcare literature increased and as the use of Latin as the language of medicine faded away (Bynum, 2006). Such translations became more and more necessary, as significant information was increasingly published in local languages: for example, Semmelweis' work on the reduction of post-natal death by use of antiseptics was published in a Hungarian medical journal and ignored by the outside world (Strathern, 2005).

Reference works such as medical dictionaries, glossaries, disease classifications and biological taxonomies were enthusiastically developed, as well as bibliographic classification and subject heading lists applicable to healthcare topics. The USA was often in the forefront of these developments (see Figures 2.6 and 2.7 on the next page), with tools such as John Shaw Billing's multilingual *National Medical Dictionary* of 1890. Another major development began in 1836, with the foundation of a specialist library for the Surgeon General of the United States Army (Lerner, 1998). In 1840 it had

Figure 2.6 Library at McGill Medical School during Osler's time, courtesy of the Wellcome Library, London

Figure 2.7 National Library of Medicine Reading Room, 1969, courtesy of the [US] National Library of Medicine

134 titles, including 8 journals, and by 1865 it had over 2000. Under the leadership of John Shaw Billings, it embarked on a major expansion and established innovative services, including a detailed subject catalogue and a variety of reference services. In 1879 this library started an abstracting and indexing service for medical literature, Index Medicus, which survives today as Medline, the single most important tool for accessing biomedical literature. It became known as the world's leading centre for healthcare information, a position which – subsumed into the US National Library of Medicine – it still holds (Miles, 1992; Blake, 1986; Smith and Mehenert, 1986).

International conferences and congresses, made feasible by the ease of transport provided by steam-powered ships and trains, were a new feature of academic and professional life in the mid-19th century and medicine was among the first disciplines to take advantage (Bynum, 2006). International conferences on medical and public health topics began to be regularly held from 1851, while rather grand 'general medical congresses' were inaugurated in Paris in 1867 and, by the time of a London congress in 1881, were attracting 3000 participants from 70 countries. Soon conferences were regularly held for the developing medical specializations – the late 1880s saw conferences on topics such as tuberculosis, dermatology and physiology (Porter, 1997, 526). Conference proceedings became an important part of the healthcare literature.

Healthcare organizations

Healthcare structures and organizations changed to match the increased capabilities of scientific medicine (Bynum, 2006). The modern style of hospital was adopted throughout Europe and North America, particularly after the advent of anaesthetics and antiseptics dramatically improved the range of possible treatments. The increasingly common combination of a large hospital, a medical school and university departments of biomedical science formed centres for the creation and dissemination of knowledge, often providing both publishing and library functions. Specialized biomedical research institutes, often government funded and largely devoted to preventive and public health, followed later in the century and also became important information creators and disseminators. Well known examples from the late 19th century are the French Pasteur Institute, the several German Koch Institutes, the American Rockefeller Institute and the British Jenner Institute of Preventive Medicine, later renamed the Lister Institute. These were the forerunners of the large-scale government support for medical research which has been such a feature of the modern healthcare environment, as exemplified by the British Medical Research Council and the American National Institutes of Health (Lawrence, 2006).

The healthcare professions

Healthcare was increasingly professionalized as the century progressed, with the establishment of professional associations: the American Medical Association in 1847, the British Medical Association in 1855 and the Association Générale des Médecins de France in 1858, to give three examples. Other healthcare professions underwent similar changes. Nursing gained a thorough and regulated training as a profession, moving 'from a form of casual labour to a vocation, and a professional one at that' (Bynum, 2006, 161). In Britain the first 'Nightingale school' was established in 1860 and the system spread to Australia, Canada and New Zealand in the next decades and influenced similar initiatives in America; the British Nurses Association was founded in 1887 (Porter, 1996, 226–7). These professional associations were also important participants in the information chain, as both creators and organizers, and they remain so today.

From the middle of the 20th century, changes in the structure of healthcare professions, with nursing, for example, becoming an all-graduate profession in many countries, have raised the level of professional education and, correspondingly, the nature of work done, which is becoming increasingly evidence-based. These healthcare professions have thus become creators and users of professional information in that way that was, at one time, true only for doctors. The result, in the latter part of the 20th century, was a great expansion in the information sources and services specifically catering to nursing and the allied health professions (Kronefeld, Stephenson and Nail-Chiwetalu, 2007).

To return to the 19th century, the expansion and formalization of education and training systems for a variety of healthcare professions was developed, usually based in large hospitals or in universities; early examples in London were the medical schools associated respectively with Saint Bartholomew's and Saint George's hospitals, and with University College and King's College (Porter, 1996, 176–7). This development also ensured that student texts, lecture notes and other learning resources became an important part of information provision. (A early example is Virchow's lecture notes on pathology, which were published in book form, updated through three editions and translated into several languages (Bynum, 2006, 122).)

Medical specialization

Another feature of this time was the development of healthcare specialities. The process 'combined the scientific, the institutional and the therapeutic, and it took myriad forms. Some specialities focused on body parts, some on diseases, some on life events, some on age groups. Specialisms took paths that diverged from country to country and sparked fierce inter- and intra-professional disputes. The proper qualifications, competence and licensing of groups such as obstetricians, dentists, physiotherapists, radiographers and a host of paramedics were endlessly fought over, as were the standing and regulation of the paramedical and ancillary professions and other service groups' (Porter, 1997, 381; see also Jacyna, 2006). The emergence of specialisms, which has continued to the present day, has a strong influence on the creation and communication of information: no specialism is without its textbooks, journals, newsletters, practice guidelines and so on, and from the outset many have also offered library collections and specialized information services. For example, the origination of paediatrics, as a speciality was marked in 1784 by the publication of Underwood's *Treatise on the Diseases of Children*, the first of its kind in English. Institutions for the treatment of childhood diseases soon followed in several countries. In London, the opening in 1816 by John Davis of an out-patient dispensary for children (which later became the Royal Waterloo Hospital for Children and Women and a centre for training in paediatrics) was followed the next year by publication of Davis's *Cursory Survey into some of the Principal Causes of Mortality among Children*. Specialism, institution, education and publication typically went together, around a coherent body of communication and technique relating to a specific medical issue. Other examples of this, for the ear and throat respectively, are Joseph Toynbee, who performed thousands of dissections in research on the ear, oversaw the first specialized unit in a general hospital for treatment of ear disease and was the author of *Pathological and Surgical Observations on the Diseases of the Ear*; and Sir Morrell Mackensie, who 'in 1863 founded the Throat Hospital in Golden Square and wrote a textbook' (Porter, 1997, 385).

Foundation of modern healthcare systems and structures

Medical specialization also emerged as a result of increasing state involvement with healthcare matters (Bynum, 2006). Responding to concerns about health problems in increasingly industrialized and urbanized communities, and to knowledge stemming from more diligent and accurate recording of population data of all kinds, the specialisms of public health, occupational health and epidemiology became established. Here an early landmark was the publication in 1832 of Charles Thakrah's *The Effects of Arts, Trades and Professions on Health and Longevity*, in which for the first time the nature and extent of disease and disability were systematically related to occupation. The demographics of the health of populations as a whole were first studied systematically in Paris by Villermé, whose *Recherches Statistiques sur la Ville de Paris* (Statistical Researches on the City of Paris) of 1821 was the first major analysis of the relation between health, physical surroundings and socio-economic factors for a large population. This approach was followed to some extent in all the countries of Europe and North America, and the resulting data formed the basis for public health planning, with legislation following throughout the century. In Britain, the statistics in the annual reports of the Registrar General from 1836 informed the activities of groups such as the Metropolitan Health of Towns Association and the London Epidemiological Society. These developments strongly influenced regulation and legislation, these in turn producing more information to be communicated.

The rise of the pharmaceutical industry

The pharmaceutical industry also had its origins in this period, developing from the established chemical industry through the insights of scientific pharmacology (Liebenau, 1987, 1990; Lawrence, 2006). Firms such as Squibb, Eli Lily, Parke Davies and Burroughs Wellcome were the progenitors of today's 'big pharma', and from the outset engaged in research and knowledge dissemination, often working closely with academic biomedical scientists. From the earliest days, there was controversy about the role of industry in the communication process, due largely to concerns about the patenting of 'commercial secrets' being contrary to the desirable free communication of scientific information. Scientific associations such as the American Society for Pharmacology and Experimental Therapeutics initially refused membership to employees of pharmaceutical companies. The involvement of commercial interests in healthcare provision and in research has grown steadily to the present day, and controversies over their role in the creation and communication of knowledge have continued.

There has been similar controversy over the newer sciences dealing with genetic information. On the one hand, these developments make possible the creation of very large data collections, with the potential both to develop new treatments for a range of diseases, as well as to profile individuals so as to warn of potential genetically associated health risks and to provide treatments tailored to an individual's genetic make-up. On the other hand, the creation and use of such data lead to ethical concerns, as shown in the linking of genetic data to medical records, performed by a commercial organization that had effective access to data from the whole Icelandic population (Hjorleifsson and Schei, 2006; Merz, McGee and Sankar, 2004).

International health organizations

Healthcare has also become increasingly internationalized, and much of its knowledge is now created and disseminated on an explicitly international basis. The first of the many international health organizations and agencies was the Office International d'Hygiène Publique (International Agency for Public Health), established in 1907 with a membership of 23 European countries. Its purpose was to collect, organize and disseminate data and knowledge about infectious diseases, to act as a forum for discussion and debate on best practice in containing such diseases, and to recommend a framework for international regulations. This information focus is typical of many international health associations formed since, which have been major producers and distributors of information in many formats. Among the best known examples are the World Health Organization, established in 1948, and its many agencies, such as the International Agency for Research on Cancer (IARC).

As we have seen above, governments began to have a closer involvement in healthcare throughout the 19th century: legislating to control public health, licensing practitioners, funding research and overseeing the provision of hospitals and other facilities. This paved the way for a much stronger state control of healthcare in many countries throughout the 20th century, whether through a system of regulated insurance or through provision of state-controlled health services funded through taxation (Porter, 1997, chapter 20). In Britain, a National Insurance scheme commenced in 1911 and the National Health Service was established in 1948 (Baggott, 2004, chapter 4; for a detailed history of the NHS's first 50 years, see Rivett, 1997). National health services and their agencies are now major producers and disseminators of healthcare information.

The twentieth century

The foundations laid in the 19th century have provided the general structure of the healthcare disciplines and underlying sciences and their communication system. This has remained to the present, though greatly altered in detail by scientific, technical and therapeutic advances – including the advent of health informatics, made possible by the digital computer (for introductions, see Taylor, 2006; Bath, 2008) – and by socio-economic factors (Lawrence 2006; Hardy and Tansey, 2006). Although the scientific knowledge base has expanded dramatically, as has the range and nature of available treatments, the basic structure of healthcare systems remains that laid down in the 19th century; the same, broadly speaking, is true of their communication chain. Although the computer was eagerly adopted at an early stage to improve the efficiency of the healthcare information chain, its advent had limited impact on overall communication patterns. Journals moved to electronic form and bibliographic databases are now searched online rather than by hand, but the structure of communication remains the same.

The communications revolution

The internet, and more specifically the world wide web, have had a more fundamental impact since the mid-1990s, along with other forms of digital information provision (see, for example, Welsh, Anagnostelis and Cooke, 2001; Nicholas, Huntington, Jamali and Williams, 2007). Healthcare has been an early adopter, as with all other forms of new information technology. The full impact is difficult to assess (the revolution is still in progress) but one of the main effects has been to blur the boundaries between the formal and informal aspects of communication, with new communication tools such as e-mail lists, blogs, wikis and social networking sites. In particular, these tools have given a new voice to the recipients of healthcare. During most of the history discussed above, knowledge has been created by professionals for communication to other professionals, albeit healthcare has always had a tradition of communicating to the lay person via 'popular' texts – a process recently dignified with the title of 'consumer health information' (Gann, 1991). The web has not merely provided much wider access to all forms of healthcare information to a great diversity of users, but has opened up the information creator's role to an equally great diversity of authors. This has raised concerns about quality of information, even though healthcare already has a long and ignoble tradition of 'quackery' in its publications (Porter, 1997, chapter 10). This dates back at least to 1720, when the Dutch author of a widely read book that promoted tea-drinking as a means to combat diseases caused by thickening of the blood turned out to be in the pay of the tea importers (Strathern, 2005, 151). Nonetheless, the web is certainly the most significant change in healthcare communication since 1800.

Conclusion

We can see, from this brief overview of the history of healthcare and its communication system, that a wide variety of academic disciplines and professional practice areas have evolved, based on an equally wide variety of academic and practice knowledge.

The basic structure of the communication chain that came into being with the development of modern medicine and the concurrent communications revolution of the 19th century is now being changed by the advent of web-based communication, allied with other changes in healthcare itself. The 'traditional' forms of information resource remain in place, supplemented by new forms, and the set of information creators has broadened to match this.

Healthcare is thus one of the largest and most diverse and complex of information domains, as well as being one of the oldest. The consequences of this, for the communication of healthcare information, will be seen throughout the rest of this book. A knowledge of this history and of these consequences is essential for a full understanding of healthcare information, which in turn is essential for effective practice in the area.

References

Attenborough, D., Owens, S., Clayton, M. and Alexandratos, R., (2007) *Amazing Rare Things: the art of natural history in the age of discovery*, Royal Collection Enterprises.

Baggott, R. (2004) *Health and Health Care in Britain*, 3rd edn, Palgrave MacMillan.

Bath, P. A. (2008) Health Informatics: current issues and challenges, *Journal of Information Science*, **34** (4), 501–18.

Bawden, D. and Robinson, L. (2000) A Distant Mirror?; the Internet and the printing press, *Aslib Proceedings*, 2000, **52** (2), 51–7.

Blake, J. B. (1986) From Surgeon General's Bookshelf to National Library of Medicine: a brief history, *Bulletin of the Medical Libraries Association*, 74 (4), 318–24.

Bynum, W. F. (1994) Science and the Practice of Medicine in the Nineteenth Century, Cambridge University Press.

Bynum, W. F. (2006) The Rise of Science in Medicine, 1850 to 1913. In Bynum, W. F., Hardy, A., Jacyna, S., Lawrence, C. and Tansey, E. M. (eds), *The Western Medical Tradition: 1800 to 2000*, Cambridge University Press.

Bynum, W. F., Hardy, A., Jacyna, S., Lawrence, C. and Tansey, E. M. (eds) (2006), *The Western Medical Tradition: 1800 to 2000*, Cambridge University Press.

Conrad, L. I. (1995) The Arab-Islamic Medical Tradition. In Conrad, L. I., Neve, M., Nutton, V., Porter, R. and Wear, A. (eds), *The Western Medical Tradition: 800 BC to 1800 AD*, Cambridge University Press, 93–138.

Conrad, L. I., Neve, M., Nutton, V., Porter, R. and Wear, A. (eds) (1995) *The Western Medical Tradition: 800 BC to 1800 AD*, Cambridge University Press.

David, R. (2008) The Art of Healing in Ancient Egypt: a scientific reappraisal, *Lancet*, **372** (9652), 1802–3.

Eisenstein, E. L., (1983) *The Printing Revolution in Early Modern Europe*, Cambridge University Press.

Freeman, E. (1992) Historical, Biographical and Bibliographical Sources. In Morton, L. and Godbolt, S. (eds), *Information Sources in the Medical Sciences*, 4th edn, Bowker-Saur, 557–491.

French, R. and Wear, A. (eds) (2008) *The Medical Revolution of the Seventeenth Century*, rev. edn, Cambridge University Press.

Furdell, E. L. (2002) *Publishing and Medicine in Early Modern England*, University of Rochester Press.

Gann, R. (1991) Consumer Health Information: the growth of an information specialism, *Journal of Documentation*, 4793), 284–08.

Greenberg, S. J. (1997) The 'Dreadful Visitation': public health and public awareness in seventeenth century London, *Bulletin of the Medical Library Association*, **85** (4), 391–401.

Hardy, A. and Tansey, E. M. (2006) Medical Enterprise and Global Response, chapter 5 of Bynum, W. F., Hardy, A., Jacyna, S., Lawrence, C. and Tansey, E. M. (2006) *The Western Medical Tradition: 1800 to 2000*, Cambridge University Press.

Harvey, J. (2002) *The Scientific Revolution and the Origins of Modern Science*, 2nd edn, Palgrave.

Hjorleifsson, S. and Schei, E. (2006) Scientific Rationality, Uncertainty and Governance of Human Genetics: an interview study with researchers at decode genetics, *European Journal of Human Genetics*, **14** (7), 802–8.

Jacyna, S. (2006), Medicine in Transformation 1800–1849. In Bynum, W. F., Hardy, A., Jacyna, S., Lawrence, C. and Tansey, E. M. (2006) *The Western Medical Tradition: 1800 to 2000*, Cambridge University Press.

Kronefeld, M., Stephenson, P. L. and Nail-Chiwetalu, B. (2007) Review for

Librarians of Evidence-based Practice in Nursing and the Allied Health Professions in the United States, *Journal of the Medical Library Association*, 95 (4), 394–407.

Lawrence, C. (2006) Continuity in Crisis: medicine, 1914–1945, chapter 3 of Bynum, W. F., Hardy, A., Jacyna, S., Lawrence, C. and Tansey, E. M. (2006) *The Western Medical Tradition: 1800 to 2000*, Cambridge University Press.

Lerner, F. (1998) *The Story of Libraries: from the invention of writing to the computer age*, Continuum.

Liebenau, J. (1987) *Medical Science and Medical Industry: the formation of the American pharmaceutical industry*, MacMillan.

Liebenau, J. (1990) The Rise of the British Pharmaceutical Industry, *British Medical Journal*, 301(6754), 724–33.

Mann, J. (1999) *The Elusive Magic Bullet: the search for the perfect drug*, Oxford University Press.

Merz, J. F., McGee, G. E. and Sankar, P. (2004) 'Iceland Inc.'?: On the Ethics of Commercial Population Genomics, *Social Science and Medicine*, 58 (6), 1201–9.

Miles, W. D. (1992) *A History of the National Library of Medicine: the nation's treasury of medical knowledge*, US Government Printing Office.

Nicholas, D., Huntington, P., Jamali, H. and Williams, P. (2007) *Digital Health Information for the Consumer*, Ashgate.

Nutton, V. (1995a), Medicine in the Greek World, 800–50 BC. In Conrad, L. I., Neve, M., Nutton, V., Porter, R. and Wear, A. (eds), *The Western Medical Tradition: 800 BC to 1800 AD*, Cambridge University Press, 11–38.

Nutton, V. (1995b), Roman medicine, 250BC to AD 200. In Conrad, L. I., Neve, M., Nutton, V., Porter, R. and Wear, A. (eds), *The Western Medical Tradition: 800 BC to 1800 AD*, Cambridge University Press, 39–70.

Nutton, V. (1995c), Late Antiquity and the Early Middle Ages. In Conrad, L. I., Neve, M., Nutton, V., Porter, R. and Wear, A. (eds), *The Western Medical Tradition: 800 BC to 1800 AD*, Cambridge University Press, 71–87.

Nutton, V. (1995d), Medieval Western Europe, 1000–1500. In Conrad, L. I., Neve, M., Nutton, V., Porter, R. and Wear, A. (eds), *The Western Medical Tradition: 800 BC to 1800 AD*, Cambridge University Press, 139–205.

Nutton, V. (2004) *Ancient Medicine*, Routledge.

Porter R. (1995) The Eighteenth Century. In Conrad, L. I., Neve, M., Nutton, V., Porter, R. and Wear, A. (eds), *The Western Medical Tradition: 800 BC to 1800 AD*, Cambridge University Press, 371–475.

Porter, R. (ed.) (1996) *Cambridge Illustrated History of Medicine*, Cambridge University Press.

Porter, R. (1997) *The Greatest Benefit to Mankind: a medical history of humanity from antiquity to the present*, Harper Collins.

Rivett, G. (1997) *From Cradle to Grave: fifty years of the NHS*, King's Fund.

Smith, K. A. and Mehenert, R. B. (1986) The National Library of Medicine: from MEDLARS to the sesquisentennial and beyond, *Bulletin of the Medical Libraries Association*, 74 (4), 325–32.

Strathern, P. (2005) *A Brief History of Medicine*, Robinson.

Taylor, P. (2006) *From Patient Data to Medical Knowledge: the principles and practice of health informatics*, Blackwell.

Wear, A. (1995) Early Modern Europe, 1500–1700. In Conrad, L. I., Neve, M., Nutton, V., Porter, R. and Wear, A. (eds), *The Western Medical Tradition: 800 BC to 1800 AD*, Cambridge University Press, 215–361.

Welsh, S., Anagnostelis, B. and Cooke, A. (2001) *Finding and Using Health and Medical Information on the Internet*, Aslib.

Further reading

Healthcare history, introductory

Porter, R. (1997) *The Greatest Benefit to Mankind: a medical history of humanity from antiquity to the present*, Harper Collins.

Strathern, P. (2005) *A Brief History of Medicine*, Robinson.

Healthcare history, in more detail

Bynum, W. F., Hardy, A., Jacyna, S., Lawrence, C. and Tansey, E. M. (2006) *The Western Medical Tradition: 1800 to 2000*, Cambridge University Press.

Conrad, L. I. (1995) The Arab-Islamic Medical Tradition. In Conrad, L. I., Neve, M., Nutton, V., Porter, R. and Wear, A. (eds), *The Western Medical Tradition: 800 BC to 1800 AD*, Cambridge University Press, 93–138.

Conrad, L. I., Neve, M., Nutton, V., Porter, R. and Wear, A. (eds) (1995) *The Western Medical Tradition: 800 BC to 1800 AD*, Cambridge University Press.

Porter, R. (ed.) (1996) *Cambridge Illustrated History of Medicine*, Cambridge University Press.

Library/information history (including healthcare services)

Lerner, F. (1998) *The Story of Libraries: from the invention of writing to the computer age*, Continuum.

Murray, S. A. P. (2009) *The Library: an illustrated history*, Skyhorse Publishing.

3

Producers and users of healthcare information

Introduction

Studies of the production and use of information are important aspects of domain analysis, and they have always had particular significance in the healthcare area; for example, this has always been one of the most popular areas for the study of information use and users. Such studies have a very clear practical importance for information providers in the area: if you do not know who your users are, what their needs are, or how well they are provided for, it will be very difficult to provide an adequate service.

This importance has increased since around 1980 because changes in the information environment, promoted by the drivers for change noted in Chapter 1, have changed the nature of information production and use. In particular, there is now a wider range of both producers and users of healthcare information, and a greater diversity of means for communication between them. This makes it all the more important to have a good understanding of the changing roles of information producers and users in the new environment.

Producers of healthcare information

We noted in Chapter 1 that the 'traditional' producers of healthcare information, namely:

- scientific and clinical researchers, in academia, government institutes, health services, scientific industry, and international organizations

- health professionals (mainly doctors and mainly senior)
- managers, administrators and regulators in government and health services, and in international organizations
- providers of medicines, equipment and healthcare products
- medical journalists and commentators

had been joined by a variety of newer 'voices', particularly:

- a wider range of healthcare professionals
- providers of 'well-being' products and services
- patients, carers and recipients of healthcare, both as individuals and groups.

This reflects a generally more rich and complex environment for information production. In the 'traditional' situation, dominated as noted in Chapter 1 by a relatively small range of types of printed documents, producers and users were closely matched. Researchers wrote primarily for other researchers, and to a limited extent for clinical professionals. Clinicians, mainly doctors and nurses, wrote largely for each other, and to a very limited extent for patients and carers.

In the new healthcare information environment, while these traditional pathways are still of importance, they are subsumed in a more complex pattern of communication, as:

- technology gives a wider range of media and formats
- consumers become a much more important group, both as users and also as producers
- there is greater emphasis on sharing best practice and on building and using an evidence base.

The way in which healthcare information is produced is necessarily becoming more diverse. Much still follows the traditional etiquette for the writing of journal articles, meeting abstracts, case reports, etc. (Hall, 2008). The citing habits of healthcare researchers still tend to the traditional, with little account of new communication formats (Robinson, 2007). Earle and Vickery (1969) showed that medical authors demonstrated their 'information consciousness' by presenting bibliographies up to five times as long as those in articles in other scientific and technical subjects. However, the newer media and formats for communication of health information allow, and perhaps require, different standards, perhaps more usually associated with journalism (Kovic, Lulic and

Brumini, 2008). When, and whether, these will cause a major change in the products of the 'traditional' communication chain is uncertain.

Nevertheless, we should, not imagine that this has led to a situation in which everyone is an author, although the potential for this is certainly much greater than in pre-internet days. In general, there have always been more passive consumers of information than there are active contributors. This remains true even though the internet has made it easier to contribute, and is as true of healthcare information as of any other area. A recent large-scale American survey of internet use by the general public for health information found that 'there are more readers and listeners than writers and creators' (Fox and Jones, 2009). This is confirmed by all other studies of this kind: many more members of the public read health-related web pages, blogs and the like than contribute to them. For example, an analysis of data from 2005 on the general public's use of the internet in the USA related to cancer information found that 58% of users had searched for health information, but less than 4% had contributed to online forums (Atkinson, Saperstein and Pleis, 2009).

The same is true of health professionals. While they all must make use of the healthcare knowledge base, both in training and in practice, only a minority will contribute to it. While Hague wrote in 1992 that 'most members of the medical profession become involved in formal writing at some stage during their careers, whether for a thesis, a book or a journal article', inasmuch as this is still true, it is likely to be restricted to doctors rather than to involve the wider range of healthcare workers, and to involve healthcare professionals in the developed rather than the developing world, and the minority who engage in research and advanced study rather than the majority of practitioners.

Users of healthcare information

For effective healthcare information provision, it is important to understand the use and users of the information. In particular, it is important to know three things:

- who the main users are, actual and potential, of an information service
- what their main characteristics are: what information they need, what they will do with it, whether they have the right tools to find it, etc.
- how their information-related behaviour has changed, and how it may change in the future.

Before we consider these points – using examples of studies from the healthcare area and summarizing what is known – it is necessary to be clear about some of the terminology.

Information behaviour and its modelling

The term 'information behaviour', as it is normally used in information science, covers all aspects of people's dealings with information, including their opinions and judgements.

Tom Wilson, a British information science professor (Wilson, 1999) has devised a simple conceptual model of information behaviour. In this model, information retrieval is a search for information in some information system, such as a catalogue, database or search engine. This is an example of the more general concept of information seeking, which covers any activity performed to find information for some purpose. This, in turn, is just one aspect of information behaviour, which covers all kinds of interaction with information, including using it, communicating it to others, or even ignoring or avoiding it.

In the past, most studies of information users focused on information retrieval, but it is now appreciated that studying the broader context is necessary for full understanding. This context is most associated with the idea of an 'information need'; behaviour and perceived need are closely connected (Bawden, 2006).

There are a great variety of theories and models of information behaviour, mostly developed since the mid-1990s. Fisher, Erdelez and McKechnie (2005) list no fewer than 72 distinct models, theories and philosophical approaches that are relevant to information behaviour. These are mostly conceptual models, rather than mathematical models, and are frequently represented by simple diagrams. Perhaps inevitably, most of them have only ever been applied by their inventors. The few that have had wider usage and have been adopted and extended by others include Wilson's various models for information behaviour, Dervin's 'sense making', Fisher's 'information grounds', and Kuhlthau's 'meaning seeking' (see Fisher, Erdelez, and McKechnie, 2005; Spink and Cole, 2006; and Case, 2006 and 2007, for more details and references).

Although there have been many studies of information users and use in the healthcare area, very few have been designed around any model or theory. Indeed, Peter Bath (2008) argues that 'while these models are very well known within information science, they are relatively unknown among health care professionals and health researchers: increasing awareness of these models may help to develop better information-related interventions'. Similarly, Ina Fourie (2008), in the context of the design of a qualitative study of patient information needs, writes: 'there is, however, little if any acknowledgement of the models and theories from information science and information seeking in the biomedical and healthcare literature'.

As examples of health information user studies that have been based around an established model, we can mention the following:

- Wilson's model compared with another to study the information behaviour of visually impaired people seeking health and social care information (Beverley, Bath and Barber (2007)
- Kuhlthau's model as the basis for studying ways in which women seek information to investigate options for treatment (Procaccino and Warner, 2004)
- Dervin's model used to investigate information needs for parents of babies in a neo-natal intensive care unit (Helliwell, 2003)
- Dervin's model used to study general public use of digital health information sources (Huntington, Nicholas and Williams, 2003).

The lack of a theory or model to support most studies of health information use is unfortunate because the lack of a common basis makes it is difficult to compare these studies in detail or to combine the results with any confidence. Their value in providing solid evidence for improving practice is thus reduced. In particular, it is difficult to obtain a picture of the information-related behaviour of particular groups because the results of each individual study are likely to be affected by its context.

Investigating information behaviour

There are three general ways in which information behaviour can be studied: by inference, indirectly and directly (see Case, 2006 and 2007 for overviews).

Inference

In inferred assessment the information needs and information behaviour of a person or group are determined from what is known about them and the context in which they need information, e.g. work or study. This amounts to an assumption that one can state with confidence; for example, 'A general practitioner needs to know . . . and to find this out this out, they will . . .'. While an experienced health librarian or other information provider may feel confident to infer needs and behaviour in this way, it is risky, especially in times of change. Some studies have shown that information providers were not, in fact, entirely aware of the situation; for example, a study of information provision for midwives and specialist nurses found that their librarians somewhat misunderstood the nature of their information needs (Bawden and Robinson, 1997). Inferring behaviour is therefore not a good idea, if there is an alternative.

Associated with inference is literature analysis, essentially to see what others have said about the target group. This may approach a meta-analysis, although the lack of a common basis for healthcare information behaviour studies, as noted above, causes problems. For examples that analyse studies of information behaviour among doctors, see Coumou and Meijman (2006), Davies (2007), and Masters (2008), and for an example of a meta-analysis of studies on general public use of digital health information see Gunter, Huntingdon, Nicholas and Williams (2003).

Indirect study

Indirect assessment is, essentially, observation. If we can 'see' what people do to access and use information, then we have immediate insight into their behaviour and can draw conclusions about what they need. It is regarded as indirect because we have no first-hand understanding the users' needs, how well they are being satisfied, what they will do with the information and so on.

This kind of study may be, quite literally, visual observation, or it may involve video, recording, web log analysis, examination of documents and records, information audit, etc. There may be an element of participative or action research in which the investigator works alongside users, assisting them at the same time as assessing their needs. With information in digital form, it is much easier to 'see', through use of web logs and so on, what people are doing, than by trying to observe their behaviour in a physical library space. However, interpreting their behaviour and assessing how successful they are may be difficult (Homewood, Huntington and Nicholas, 2003).

Direct study

Direct assessment involves asking people what they need and what they do to get it. This can be done by a variety of methods, including interviews, focus groups, questionnaires, etc. It is the only method that provides insight into motivation, reasons for behaviour, perceived success, etc. The downside is that it is subject to the problem that people do not always do what they say or say what they do in using information – much as in other aspects of life.

Because these methods are frequently complementary, each giving an insight that the others cannot, they are often used together. Each may reveal useful information: analysis of search logs can show what a user did, while an interview can reveal why they did it and with what perceived success. Different methods may also counteract bias: self-reporting usually claims a high use of published literature compared with seeking advice from colleagues, while observation often shows the opposite (McKnight and Peet, 2000).

Studying user information needs and information behaviour is a very appropriate topic for practitioner research, and it is unfortunate that practising librarians and information specialists often leave such studies to academics. Cooperation between the two can be particularly fruitful.

Studying healthcare information behaviour

Information behaviour has been studied more in the healthcare domain than in other academic and professional domains. Studies have focused both on providers (doctors, nurses, midwives, social workers, etc.), on patients and carers, and on the general public.

The methods and results of this large body of work have been reviewed by a number of authors. For a thorough recent review of studies both of healthcare workers and of patients from 1990 onwards, see Case (2007, sections 11.1.4 and 12.2.3). Useful overviews have also been provided by Booth (2000), Urquhart (2000), Dawes and Sampson (2003), Masters (2008) and Bath (2008).

Some of the earliest information 'user studies' were conducted in the 1970s and 1980s (see, for example, Brodman, 1974; Hibberd and Meadows, 1980; Osiobe, 1986), and activity has increased greatly since 1990. There are a number of reasons for the greater attention now being given to health information-seeking behaviour. These include the economic and social importance of healthcare, the increasing public interest in 'wellness' and worry about ill-health, and the sheer amount of information and diversity of resources in the area, as well as the many different professions, activities and roles involved. As well as the producers and users of health information, there are a variety of intermediary roles, including librarians, whose activities have been analysed in Wathen, Wyatt and Harris (2008).

The variety of methods which have been used to study the needs and behaviour of health information users include interviews, questionnaires (paper, telephone and online), focus groups (group interviews), Delphi studies, information audits, observation (including video and audio recordings), critical incident analysis and 'vignettes' (individual case studies of information problems), analysis of search logs and library records, and examination of documents. Qualitative research techniques from adopted anthropology and ethnography have been used in some cases. A literature review may also form part of the study, or may be a study in itself. For an overview of these methods in the information sciences generally, see Gorman and Clayton (2005).

Table 3.1 lists a selection of such studies, showing the variety of approaches to assessment and the diversity of groups studied. Although this variety results in a very rich set of information, the absence of standard models has been noted above. Explicit examination of changes over time is also rare – such studies are particularly valuable in showing how users' needs and behaviour adapt to the changing environment. Although, as the table shows, a wide variety of groups has been studied the focus tends to be on particular groups thought to be of interest, particularly doctors and nurses. Treatment across the full range of health information users is thus uneven. Most of the studies in the selection were carried out in Britain, North America or Australasia, reflecting the predominance of these parts of the world in the literature of the topic. For international comparison, studies from Brazil, France, Iceland, Nigeria and Uganda are included.

As well as these specific studies, the topic has been studied in a number of 'general' social surveys. The most significant of these are the reports of the Pew Internet and American Life Project, which conducts regular surveys of the impact of the internet on all aspects of American society. The results are relevant internationally, given the tendency of worldwide trends to be seen first in the USA, and these reports are generally accepted as among the most reliable indicators of internet trends. They deal with the internet as a source of health information on a regular basis, allowing comparison of trends over time and identifying new issues. The most recent health-related Pew report was based on surveys carried out at the end of 2008 (Fox and Jones, 2009).

Table 3.1 Selection of papers investigating health information behaviour

Paper	Type of user	Study method
P. N. Hider, G. Griffin, M. Walker and E. Coughlan, The information seeking behaviour of clinical staff in a large health care organization, *Journal of the Medical Library Association*, 2009, **97** (1), 47–50.	Healthcare professionals	Postal questionnaires
C. Tenopir, D. W. King, S. Edwards and L. Wu, Electronic journals and changes in scholarly article seeking and reading patterns, *Aslib Proceedings*, 2009, **61** (1), 5–32.	Medical academics	Questionnaires, critical incidents, comparison over time
W. E. Nwagwu and R. Oshiname, Information needs and seeking behaviour of nurses at the University College Hospital, Ibadan, Nigeria, *African Journal of Library Archives and Information Science*, 2009, **19** (1), 25–38.	Nurses	Questionnaires
M. S. Martinez-Silveira and N. Oddone, Information-seeking behavior of medical residents in clinical practice in Bahia, Brazil, *Journal of the Medical Library Association*, 2009, **96** (4), 381–4.	Doctors	Questionnaires, critical incidents
M. I. Trotter and D. W. Morgan, Patients' use of the internet for health related matters: a study of internet usage in 2000 and 2006, *Health Informatics Journal*, 2008, 14 (3), 175–81.	Patients	Questionnaires, comparison over time
M. C. Reddy and P. R. Spence, Collaborative information seeking: a field study of a multidisciplinary patient care team, *Information Processing and Management*, 2008, **44** (1), 242–55.	Emergency care staff	Ethnography
F. M. Dowse and B. Sen, Community outreach library services in the UK: a case study of Wirral Hospital NHS Trust, *Health Information and Libraries Journal*, 2007, **24** (3), 177–87.	Primary care staff	Postal questionnaires, interviews
S. M. Spenceley, K. A. O'Leary, L. L. K. Chizawsky, A. J. Ross and C. A. Estabrooks, Sources of information used by nurses to inform practice: an integrative review, *International Journal of Nursing Studies*, 2008, **45** (6), 954–70.	Nurses	Literature review
K. A. McKibbon, R. B. Haynes, R. J. McKinlay and C. Lokker, Which journals do primary care physicians and specialists access from an online service?, *Journal of the Medical Library Association*, 2007, **95** (3), 246–54.	Doctors	Web log analysis
K. Davies, The information-seeking behaviour of doctors: a review of the evidence, *Health Information and Libraries Journal*, 2007, **24** (2), 78–94.	Doctors	Literature review
R. Jackson et.al., The information requirements and information-seeking behaviours of health and social care professionals providing care to children with health care needs, *Health Information and Libraries Journal*, 2007, **24** (2), 95–102.	Healthcare professionals	Postal questionnaires
K. Ankem, Information-seeking behaviour of women in their path to an innovative alternate treatment for symptomatic uterine fibroids, *Journal of the Medical Library Association*, 2007, **95** (2), 164–72.	Patients	Interviews

Table 3.1 *Continued*

Paper	Type of user	Study method
B. Nail-Chiwetalu and N. B. Ratner, An assessment of the information seeking abilities and needs of practicing speech-language pathologists, *Journal of the Medical Library Association*, 2007, **95** (2), 182–8.	Speech therapists	Postal questionnaires
C. A. Beverley, P. A. Bath and R. Barber, Can two established information models explain the information behaviour of visually impaired people seeking health and social care information?, *Journal of Documentation*, 2007, **63** (1), 9–32.	Patients	Interviews
L. Robinson, Impact of digital information resources in the toxicology literature, *Aslib Proceedings*, 2007, **59** (4/5), 342–52.	Biomedical scientists	Examination of documents
M. McKnight, A grounded theory model of on-duty critical care nurses' information behaviour: the patient-chart cycle of informative interactions, *Journal of Documentation*, 2007, **63** (1), 57–73.	Nurses	Observation, interviews
C. Tenopir et.al., Journal reading patterns and preferences of pediatricians, *Journal of the Medical Library Association*, 2007, **95** (1), 56–63.	Doctors	Postal questionnaires
O. T. Morey, Health information ties: preliminary findings on the health information seeking behaviour of an African-American community, *Information Research*, 2007, **12** (2), paper 297, http://InformationR.net/ir/12-2/paper297.html.	General public	Telephone questionnaires
S. Lewis, Critical care nurses on duty: information-rich but time-poor, *Evidence-based Library and Information Practice*, 2007, **2** (1), 131–3.	Nurses	Observation, interviews, ethnography
E. Sillence et.al., Going online for health advice: changes in usage and trust practices over the last five years, *Interacting with Computers*, 2007, **19** (3), 397–406.	Patients	Online questionnaires
M. G. N. Musoke, Information behaviour of primary health care providers in rural Uganda: an interaction-value model, *Journal of Documentation*, 2007, **63** (3), 299–322.	Healthcare professionals	Interviews
J. A. Burkell et.al., Information needs and information sources of individuals living with spinal cord injury, *Health Information and Libraries Journal*, 2006, **23** (4), 257–65.	Patients	Questionnaires
C. Blake and W. Pratt, Collaborative information synthesis 1: a model of information behaviours of scientists in medicine and public health, *Journal of the American Society for Information Science and Technology*, 2006, **57** (13), 1740–9.	Biomedical scientists	Interviews, document examination, observation
L. C. Wallis, Information-seeking behaviour of faculty in one school of public health, *Journal of the Medical Library Association*, 2006, **94** (4), 442–6.	Biomedical scientists	Postal questionnaires
S. J. Attfield, A. Adams and A. Blandford, Patient information needs: pre- and post-consultation, *Health Informatics Journal*, 2006, **12** (2), 165–77.	Patients	Questionnaires

Table 3.1 *Continued*

Paper	Type of user	Study method
R. M. Harris, C. N. Wathen and J. M. Fear, Searching for health information in rural Canada. Where do residents look for health information and what do they do when they find it?, *Information Research*, 2006, **12** (1), paper 274, http://InformationR.net/ir/12-1/paper274.html.	General public	Telephone questionnaires
M. McKnight, The information seeking of on-duty critical care nurses: evidence from participant observation and in-context interviews, *Journal of the Medical Library Association*, 2006, **94** (2), 145–51.	Nurses	Observation, interviews
H. C. H. Coumou and F. J. Meijman, How do primary care physicians seek answers to clinical questions? A literature review, *Journal of the Medical Library Association*, 2006, **94** (1), 55–60.	Doctors	Literature review
P. Williams and B. Gunter, Triangulating qualitative research and computer transaction logs in health information studies, *Aslib Proceedings*, 2006, **58** (1), 129–39.	General public	Interviews, observation, web log analysis
F. G. Boissin, Information-seeking behaviour and use of the internet by French general practitioners: a qualitative study, *Health Information and Libraries Journal*, 2005, **22** (3), 173–81.	Doctors	Interviews
H. Korjonen-Close, The information needs and behaviour of clinical researchers: a user needs analysis, *Health Information and Libraries Journal*, 2005, **22** (2), 96–106.	Clinical researchers	Online questionnaires, focus groups
D. A. Swinglehurst, Information needs of United Kingdom primary care clinicians, *Health Information and Libraries Journal*, 2005, **22** (3), 196–204.	Doctors	Literature analysis
J. E. Andrews et.al., Information-seeking behaviour of practitioners in a primary care practice-based research network, *Journal of the Medical Library Association*, 2005, **93** (2), 206–12.	Healthcare professionals	Questionnaires
C. Dee and E. E. Stanley, Information-seeking behavior of nursing students and clinical nurses: implications for health sciences librarians, *Journal of the Medical Library Association*, 2005, **93** (2), 213–22.	Nurses	Questionnaires, interviews, observation
P. Longbottom et.al., The information needs of perioperative staff: a preparatory study for a proposed specialist library for theatres [NeLH], *Health Information and Libraries Journal*, 2005, **22** (1), 35–43.	Healthcare professionals	Interviews
P. J. McKenzie, Positioning theory and the negotiation of information needs in a clinical midwifery setting, *Journal of the American Society for Information Science and Technology*, 2004, **55** (8), 685–94.	Nurses, patients	Interviews, observation (recording)
S. L. Bryant, The information needs and information seeking behaviour of family doctors, *Health Information and Libraries Journal*, 2004, **21** (2), 84–93.	Doctors	Interviews, focus groups, library record analysis
P. de Chazal et.al., NHS and social care interface: a study of social workers' library and information needs, *Journal of Librarianship and Information Science*, 2004, **36** (1), 27–36.	Healthcare social workers	Questionnaires, interviews, focus groups

Table 3.1 *Continued*

Paper	Type of user	Study method
J. Harrison and M. Hepworth, A survey of the information needs of people with multiple sclerosis, *Health Informatics Journal*, 2004, **10** (1), 49–69.	Patients	Focus groups, questionnaires
M. Hepworth, A framework for understanding user requirements for an information service: defining the needs of informal carers, *Journal of the American Society for Information Science and Technology*, 2004, **55** (8), 695–708.	Carers	Interviews
A. Palsdottir, Icelandic citizens' everyday life health information behaviour, *Health Informatics Journal*, 2003, **9** (4), 225–40.	General public	Postal questionnaire
P. Huntington, D. Nicholas and P. Williams, Non-use of health information kiosks examined in an information needs context, *Health Information and Libraries Journal*, 2003, **20** (2), 95–103.	General public	Web log analysis, interviews
M. M. Davies and P. A. Bath, Interpersonal sources of health and maternity information for Somali women living in the UK information seeking and evaluation, *Journal of Documentation*, 2002, **58** (3), 302–18.	General public	Interviews, focus groups
O. Sundin, Nurses' information seeking and use as participation in occupational communities, *New Review of Information Behaviour Research*, 2002, **3**, 187–202.	Nurses	Interviews
D. Nicholas, P. Huntington, and P. Williams, Searching intention and information outcome: a case study of digital health information, *Libri*, 2001, **51** (3), 157–66.	General public, patients	Online questionnaires
D. Bawden, T. K. Devon and I. W. Sinclair, Desktop information systems and services: a user survey in a pharmaceutical research organization, *International Journal of Information Management*, 2000, **20** (2), 151–60.	Pharmaceutical research scientists	Interviews, examination of documents and records
S. L. Bryant, The information needs and information seeking behaviour of family doctors: a selective literature review, *Health Libraries Review*, 2000, **17** (2), 83–90.	Doctors	Literature review
M. McKnight and M. Peet, Health care providers' information seeking: recent research, *Medical Reference Services Quarterly*, 2000, **19** (2), 27–50.	Healthcare professionals	Literature review
K. E. Pettigrew, Waiting for chiropody: contextual results from an ethnographic study of the information behaviour among attendees at community clinics, *Information Processing and Management*, **35** (6), 801–17.	Patients	Ethnography
D. Bawden and K. Robinson, Information behaviour in nursing specialities: a case study of midwifery, *Journal of Information Science*, 1997, 23 (6), 407–12.	Nurses	Interviews, examination of documents
C. Urquhart and S. Crane, Nurses' information seeking skills and perceptions of information sources – assessment using vignettes, *Journal of Information Science*, **20** (4), 237–46.	Nurses	Interviews, vignettes

So what do we know?

The numerous studies exemplified above have provided a good deal of understanding about the behaviour of users of health information, and how it is changing. Some of the main points are summarized here.

Commonality and diversity

Some general behaviour patterns can clearly be seen. These are dictated by the nature of the role: for example, there is consistency, in all circumstances, in what a doctor or nurse has to do, and this will determine their information behaviour to a large extent. Similarly, patients or carers will, in general terms, need the same kinds of information and hence go about finding it in the same ways.

However, this commonality is affected to a considerable extent and in various ways by context and circumstances. For one thing, disciplines cannot necessarily be treated as homogeneous: it is known, for example, that different specialities within nursing may have distinctly different attitudes towards and needs for information (Bawden and Robinson, 1997).

It is tempting, and not entirely wrong, to suggest that the likely extent of the use of formal information resources can be predicted by the level of training needed for the role. Doctors and dentists will make greater use of such of sources than, say, healthcare assistants and paramedics; the latter groups will rely mainly on informal sources and 'general' resources such as Google. While studies show that there is a good deal of truth in this, care should be taken, particularly in labelling roles as 'information rich' or 'information poor'. With the increasingly common multidisciplinary working, all roles need good information access. Matters also change over time. Nurses, for example, used to rely on a small number of largely informal sources but now have a wide range of sources of all kinds, and are regarded as a generally information-conscious group.

There are also national differences. Although healthcare has commonality, for both providers and consumers, in all settings, local social, economic and technical contexts may make significant differences. In developing countries there may necessarily be more reliance by health workers on colleagues, personal files and local collections as sources of information, because of lack of access to libraries and networked resources (Nwagwu and Oshiname, 2009; Lundeen, Tenopir and Wermager, 1994). These factors are also time dependent: technical developments and associated information-related behaviours tend to be established first in the USA and Western Europe, and to spread internationally over time.

Even in a particular context, however, differences will be seen between users of the same type, due to factors such as age, gender, education level and personality factors. Age is a particularly strong determinant for use of newer technologies to find health information, among both health professionals and the general public (Case, 2007; Fox and Jones, 2009). Some studies have shown distinct differences in the behaviour and attitudes of information users who appear similar in all respects, such that they can only be attributed to personality (for an example in a pharmaceutical research setting, see Bawden, Devon and Sinclair, 2000). Thus, while a good deal is known about the behaviour of particular groups of health information users, it is unwise to generalize too much: local context may be very significant.

An information-rich environment

The healthcare environment, in all its varied manifestations, has generally been found to be a particularly information-rich environment, with a wide variety of users, sources, systems and services. The following are a few examples for healthcare professionals:

- The multidisciplinary nature of much patient care makes for such an information-rich environment (Reddy and Spence, 2008).
- The pharmaceutical industry has been recognized as the original 'information intensive industry' (Bawden and Robinson, 2010).
- Medical and health academics read the journal literature more intensively than their colleagues in other subject areas (Tenopir, King, Spencer and Wu, 2009; Tenopir, King and Bush, 2004).
- Doctors are also enthusiastic readers of the journal literature (Tenopir, King, Clarke, Na, and Zhou, 2007).
- Pharmaceutical research scientists were found to be particularly information conscious, with one interviewee commenting: 'We are all knowledge workers now' (Bawden, Devon and Sinclair, 2000).

The greater emphasis on evidence-based practice makes it more important for practitioners to be information conscious. As this chapter was being written, the London *Times* carried a story about a British family doctor looking back over his career before retirement and commenting that the biggest change was that 'the quantity of knowledge you need to possess has also increased tremendously' (de Bruxelles, 2009). Similarly, the emphasis on the 'informed' or 'expert' patient and the promotion of 'patient choice' has created a situation where patients and carers feel a necessity to be well informed.

Inertia and change

There seems to be a kind of built-in inertia in the information-related behaviour of healthcare workers. Most users of this kind still rely to a great degree on products of the 'traditional' information chain – textbooks, monographs, encyclopaedias and journal articles still predominate in many cases, although nowadays are often used in digital form, and increasingly on personal digital assistants (PDAs) and similar mobile devices (Tenopir, King, Clarke, Na and Zhou, 2007).

Some forms of change have, however, been recognized enough to be seen as general trends. Although health professionals are still enthusiastic readers, this reading may be less concentrated and in depth than in the past. Less time is devoted to each article and there is increasing reliance on abstracts, while 'power browsing' is increasingly the norm in digital environments (Tenopir, King, Edwards and Wu, 2009).

Similarly, despite the enthusiastic adoption of the internet by patients and carers seeking information, health professionals are still the predominant source of information for this group, supplemented by news sources. Such interactions are, however, increasingly likely to be preceded or followed by an internet search. Reporting the Pew Internet survey, Fox and Jones (2009) summarize their findings as showing that the public 'continue to turn to traditional sources of health information, even as many of them deepen their engagement with the online world'. This study shows that while about 60% will turn to the internet for health information, nearly 70% will ask a friend or family member and nearly 90% will ask a doctor.

With all types of health information user, the picture in relation to the adoption of new technologies – which up to now have largely been used to augment and streamline the traditional communication chain rather than to create radical new alternatives – is rather mixed. However, experience suggests that rapid change could come quite quickly, particularly as both healthcare providers and recipients increasingly come from generations that are accustomed to ubiquitous digital information.

The internet

The importance of the internet as a change factor in the way in which health information is found and used is difficult to overstate (see Cullen, 2006 for an overview). It has been estimated that as long ago as 2003 around 12.5 million health-related searches were conducted worldwide each day (Atkinson, Saperstein and Pleis, 2009). A review of studies into doctors' use of the internet carried out between 1994 and 2004 showed between 60% and 70% of doctors in the developed world having access to internet, rising in later studies to 90% (Masters, 2008). It is likely that, in this environment, the figure is now 100%.

The Pew Internet surveys have shown that in each year since 2002 between 75% and 83% of American internet users looked for health information at some point. The most recent survey suggests that about 60% of American adults used the internet for health information during 2008, compared with 25% in 2002 (Fox and Jones, 2009). The difference in the figures simply reflects the greater penetration of the internet into everyday life. It seems that, once it becomes accessible, it is very often used for health purposes. An Australian survey shows a similar picture, with 16% of patients at a clinic having used the internet for health information in 2000, the figure rising to 55% by 2006 (Trotter and Morgan, 2008).

However, while the web is now a major source of health information, some of the newer forms of internet communication have yet to reach this stage. The Pew Internet survey indicated that less than 40% of users of social networking sites used them for health purposes; for Twitter users, the figure was only 12% (Fox and Jones, 2009). However, these 'new media' users tended to be in younger age groups, and so we may expect this sort of use to grow. A study in late 2009 found 757 Facebook groups for particular disease conditions (Farmer, Bruckner Holt, Cook and Hearing, 2009).

The importance of the personal

Informal and personal sources, typically colleagues, friends and relatives, and popular news sources, have always been among the most widely used means of access to healthcare information, for both providers and patients, and this continues to be the case (Lundeen, Tenopir and Wermager, 1994; Dawes and Sampson, 2003; Spenceley, O'Leary, Chizawsky, Ross, and Estabrooks, 2008). As web 2.0 facilities such as blogs and wikis expand in importance for healthcare areas, we can see an increasing blurring of the hitherto very clear distinction between formal and informal sources. Medical schools and health libraries began to adopt Twitter, perhaps the most informal source of all thus far, in 2009 (Cuddy, 2009).

The 'personal touch' in information provision is important in other ways in the healthcare environment. A variety of roles provide some form of mediation in information provision (Wathen, Wyatt and Harris, 2008; MacIntosh-Murray and Choo, 2005; Lundeen, Tenopir and Wermager, 1994). The long-appreciated role of 'information gatekeeper' – a health professional, in this instance, who finds and communicates information, to the benefit of their colleagues – is still significant (Cullen, 1997; Bawden and Robinson, 1997).

Information problems

The main problems in accessing of health information by users of all kinds seem to have remained remarkably stable over time (see, for example, Ebell, 2009). They are:

- lack of time, first to find, and second to read and assimilate information
- workload too great to allow much information seeking
- lack of easy access to appropriate resources and services
- lack of funds to acquire appropriate resources, or a generally poor information or IT infrastructure; these particularly likely in the developing world (Lundeen, Tenopir and Wermager, 1994)
- lack of appreciation as to what are the best sources for the need
- lack of knowledge as to how best to use resources
- lack of IT skills, or confidence with digital resources
- user attitude, not regarding information as necessary or a priority, 'not knowing what one does not know or needs to know'
- concerns about information overload, 'too much information'.

It is notable how often the issue arises that 'formal' information sources are provided, often at considerable cost, but either they are not provided in the manner most appropriate to the needs of the users, or the potential users are unaware of their value or of how best to use them. This may be despite the fact that information providers have done their best to provide publicity and training, indicating a mismatch in the providers' perceptions of the potential users. There is often also a need (either expressed or which may have to be drawn out by the service planners) for information to be packaged in such a way that users can access it with the all-important factors of convenience and time-saving, while also having confidence in its quality.

Convenience is all

Very often, both for health professionals and for patients and carers, the overriding criterion for whether a service or resource will be used is convenience, which often equates to time-saving (Tenopir, King and Bush, 2004). The meaning of convenience has changed over time, from the convenience of a few familiar, if out-dated, reference books on one's own shelf, to the convenience of an easy-to-use, free search engine. But the principle remains the same; users, all users, tend to rely on the easy and the familiar at the expense of 'quality' sources, even when their advantages are understood. This universal truth is, at bottom, an expression of Zipf's Principle of Least Effort, a very general principle applicable to many social situations, which can be understood in information terms as the idea that information seekers will always try to minimize the effort required to obtain information, even if it means accepting a lower quality or quantity of information (Case, 2005). An excellent example is given by Nwagwu and Oshiname (2009), whose study showed that nearly 90% of nurses cited colleagues as their primary information source, while less than 60% were satisfied with the information received in this way.

Associated with this is another observed factor: that where a large range of potentially useful sources of information is available, users will neither use the whole range nor choose rationally from it. On the contrary, they will typically choose one or a small number of sources, either seemingly randomly or on the basis of familiarity. This is the consequence of the so-called 'paradox of choice', another very general social 'law', which has been noted in information environments as the range of digital resources has dramatically increased (Bawden and Robinson, 2009). This accounts for the continued popularity, attested in many surveys in all kinds of healthcare settings, of the small local collection of reference materials.

This can be seen particularly in the popularity of a few 'big brands', most particularly Google, which often emerges as the single most popular source of health information for both providers and recipients of healthcare. For example, Sim, Khong and Jivva (2008) suggest that Google is the most widely used information tool for Australian family physicians, while Hider, Griffin, Walker and Coughlan (2009) found that it was used more than any other electronic resource by all health professionals in their sample and was rated as 'most valuable' by nurses and allied health professionals.

Impact of information

Several studies of health information use and behaviour have attempted to answer the question of what difference the information provided has made; what impact it has had. This is a fairly fundamental question, not least for information providers seeking to justify their services in economically difficult times. Assessing the 'direct impact' of information provision, ideally in terms of improved patient outcomes or of money saving, is notoriously difficult. A number of methods for 'impact assessment', typically separate from studies of user behaviour, have been devised. These will be discussed in Chapter 6.

Opportunities for providers

Most information behaviour studies do not look explicitly at the provider. Those which do (for example, Bawden and Robinson, 1997) often show missed opportunities and erroneous perceptions on the part of providers. One thing that does emerge clearly from user studies is that many users would appreciate more guidance on the available resources and the best way to use them. Providers should, in particular:

- be aware of possibly important diversity in information-related behaviour within groups of apparently similar uses
- be prepared to accommodate sudden increases in interest in new ways of dealing with information, for example, e-books social networking and delivery to mobile devices
- identify and nurture individuals who may act as gatekeepers
- prioritize simplicity and ease of use over most other criteria.

Conclusion

The many studies of information-related behaviour carried out in the health environment since 1990 have provided much insight into users, their needs and their practices. User behaviour is changing in response to the drivers for change noted in Chapter 1, but as yet quite slowly and unevenly. It is doing so in the context of a richer and more diverse 'producer environment', as a wider range of creators contribute, in a wider range of media.

Knowledge of user needs and user behaviour is an indispensable asset to healthcare librarians and other information providers. It is, of all the possible areas for health information research and evaluation, arguably the one in which it is most important for practitioners to take part, and also the one in which it is most feasible for them to do so.

References

Atkinson, N. L., Saperstein, S. L. and Pleis, J. (2009) Using the Internet for Health-related Activities: findings from a national probability survey, *Journal of Medical Internet Research*, 11 (1), e4, available from www.jmir.org/2009/1/e4/HTML.

Bath, P. A. (2008) Health Informatics: current issues and challenges, *Journal of Information Science*, 34 (4), 501–18.

Bawden, D. (2006) Users, User Studies and Human Information Behaviour: a three decade perspective on Tom Wilson's 'On user studies and information needs', *Journal of Documentation*, 62 (6), 671–9.

Bawden, D. and Robinson, K. (1997) Information Behaviour in Nursing Specialities: a case study of midwifery, *Journal of Information Science*, 23 (6), 407–21.

Bawden, D. and Robinson, L. (2009) The Dark Side of Information: overload, anxiety and other paradoxes and pathologies, *Journal of Information Science*, 35 (2), 180–91.

Bawden, D. and Robinson, L. (2010) Pharmaceutical Information; a 30-year perspective on the literature, *Annual Reviews of Information Science and Technology*, in press.

Bawden, D., Devon, T. K. and Sinclair, I. W. (2000) Desktop Information Systems and Services: a user survey in a pharmaceutical research organisation, *International Journal of Information Management*, 20 (2), 151–60.

Beverley, C. A., Bath, P. A. and Barber, R. (2007) Can Two Established Information Models Explain the Information Behaviour of Visually Impaired People Seeking Health and Social Care Information?, *Journal of Documentation*, 63 (1), 9–32.

Booth, A. (2000) Identifying Users' Needs. In Booth, A. and Walton, G. (eds), *Managing Knowledge in Health Services*, Library Association Publishing, 101–11.

Brodman, E. (1974) Users of Health Sciences Libraries, *Library Trends*, 23 (1), 63–72.

Case, D. O. (2005) Principle of Least Effort. In Fisher, K. E., Erdelez, S. and McKechnie, L. (eds), *Theories of Information Behaviour*, ASIST monograph series, Information Today, 289–92.

Case, D. O. (2006) Information Behaviour, *Annual Review of Information Science and Technology*, 40, 293–327.

Case, D. O. (2007) *Looking for Information: a survey of research on information seeking*, 2nd edn, Academic Press.

Coumou, H. C. H. and Meijman, F. J. (2006) How do Primary Care Physicians Seek Answers to Clinical Questions? A literature review, *Journal of the Medical Library Association*, 94 (1), 55-60.

Cuddy, C. (2009) Twittering in Health Science Libraries, *Journal of Electronic Resources in Medical Libraries*, 6 (2), 169–74.

Cullen, R. (1997) The Medical Specialist: information gateway or gatekeeper for the family practitioner, *Bulletin of the Medical Library Association*, 85 (4), 348–55.

Cullen, R. (2006) *Health Information on the Internet; a study of providers, quality and users*, Praeger.

Davies, K. (2007) The Information-seeking Behaviour of Doctors: a review of the evidence, *Health Information and Libraries Journal*, 24 (2), 78-94.

Dawes, M. and Sampson, U. (2003) Knowledge Management in Clinical Practice: a systematic review of information seeking behavior in physicians, *International Journal of Medical Informatics*, 71 (1), 9–15.

De Bruxelles, S. (2009) After 217 Years David Maurice Ends Marlborough's Dynasty of GPs, *Times Online*, 28 August 2009, available from www.timesonline.co.uk/tol/life_and_style/health/article6812894.ece.

Earle, P. and Vickery, B. (1969) Subject Relations in Science/Technology Literature, *Aslib Proceedings*, 21 (6), 237–43.

Ebell, M. H. (2009) How to Find Answers to Clinical Questions, *American Family Physician*, 79 (4), 293–6.

Farmer, A. D., Bruckner Holt, C. E. M., Cook, M. J. and Hearing, S. D. (2009) Social Networking Sites: a novel portal for communication, *Postgraduate Medical Journal*, 85 (1007), 455–9.

Fisher, K. E., Erdelez, S. and McKechnie, L. (eds) (2005) *Theories of Information Behaviour*, ASIST monograph series, Information Today.

Fourie, I. (2008) Information Needs and Information Behaviour of Patients and their Family Members in a Cancer Palliative Care Setting: an exploratory study of an existential context from different perspectives, *Information Research*, 13 (4), paper 360, available from: http://InformationR.net/ir/13–4/paper360.html.

Fox, S. and Jones, S. (2009) *The Social Life of Health Information*, Pew Internet and American Life Project, available from www.pewinternet.org/~/media//Files/Reports/2009/PIP_Health_2009.pdf.

Gorman, G. E. and Clayton, P. (2005) *Qualitative Research for the Information Professional*, 2nd edn, Facet Publishing.

Gunter, B., Huntingdon, P., Nicholas, D. and Williams, P. (2003) 'Search Disclosure': understanding digital information platform preference and location in a health environment, *Journal of Documentation*, 59 (5), 523–39.

Hague, H. R. (1992) Standard Reference Sources. In Morton, L. and Godbolt, S. (eds) (1992) *Information Sources in the Medical Sciences*, 4th edn, Bowker Saur, 67–86.

Hall, G. M. (2008) *How to Write a Paper*, 4th edn, Blackwell/BMJ.

Helliwell, M. (2003) Building Information Bridges Between Parents and Health Care Providers in the Neonatal Intensive Care Unit, *Canadian Journal of Information and Library Science*, 27 (3), 134.

Hibberd, P. L. and Meadows, A. J. (1980) Use of Drug Information Sources by Hospital Doctors, *Journal of Information Science*, 2 (3/4), 169–72.

Hider, P. N., Griffin, G., Walker, M. and Coughlan, E. (2009) The Information-seeking Behavior of Clinical Staff in a Large Health Care Organization, *Journal of the Medical Library Association*, 97 (1), 47–50.

Homewood, J., Huntington, P. and Nicholas, D. (2003) Assessing Used Content Across Five Digital Health Information Services Using Transaction Log Files, *Journal of Information Science*, 2996), 499–516.

Huntington, P., Nicholas, D. and Williams, P. (2003) Non-use of Health Information Kiosks Examined in an Information Needs Context, *Health Information and Libraries Journal*, 20 (2), 95–103.

Kovic, I., Lulic, I. and Brumini, G. (2008) Examining the Medical Blogosphere: an online survey of medical bloggers, *Journal of Medical Internet Research*, 10 (3), e28, available from www.jmir.org/2008/3/e28/HTML.

Lundeen, G. W., Tenopir, C. and Wermager, P. (1994) Information Needs of Rural Healthcare Practitioners in Hawaii, *Bulletin of the Medical Library Association*, 82 (2), 197–205.

MacIntosh-Murray, A. and Choo, C. W. (2005) Information Behavior in the Context of Improving Patient Safety, *Journal of the American Society for Information Science and Technology*, 56 (12), 1332–45.

McKnight, M. and Peet, M. (2000) Health Care Providers' Information Seeking: recent research, *Medical Reference Services Quarterly*, 19 (2), 27–50.

Masters, K. (2008) For what Purpose and Reasons do Doctors use the Internet: a systematic review, *International Journal of Medical Informatics*, 77 (1), 4–16.

Nwagwu, W. E. and Oshiname, R. (2009) Information Needs and Seeking

Behaviour of Nurses at the University College Hospital, Ibadan, Nigeria, *African Journal of Library Archives and Information Science*, 19 (1), 25–38.

Osiobe, S. A. (1986) A Study of the Use of Information Sources by Medical Faculty Staff in Nigerian Universities, *Journal of Information Science*, 12 (4), 177–83.

Procaccino, J. D. and Warner, D. (2004) Towards Wellness: women seeking health information, *Journal of the American Society for Information Science and Technology*, 55 (8), 709–30.

Reddy, M. C. and Spence, P. R. (2008) Collaborative Information Seeking: a field study of a multidisciplinary patient care team, *Information Processing and Management*, 44 (1), 242–55.

Robinson, L. (2007) Impact of Digital Information Resources in the Toxicology Literature, *Aslib Proceedings*, 59 (4/5), 342–52.

Sim, M. G., Khong, E. and Jivva, M. (2008) Does General Practice Google?, *Australian Family Physician*, 37 (6), 471–4.

Spenceley, S. M., O'Leary, K. A., Chizawsky, L. L. K., Ross, A. J. and Estabrooks, C. A. (2008) Sources of Information Used by Nurses to Inform Practice: an integrative review, *International Journal of Nursing Studies*, 45 (6), 954–70.

Spink, A. and Cole, C. (2006) Human Information Behaviour: integrating diverse approaches and information use, *Journal of the American Society for Information Science and Technology*, 57 (1), 25–35.

Tenopir, C., King, D. W. and Bush, A. (2004) Medical Faculty's Use of Print and Electronic Journals: changes over time and in comparison with scientists, *Journal of the Medical Library Association*, 92 (2), 233–41.

Tenopir, C., King, D. W., Clarke, M. T., Na, K. and Zhou, X. (2007) Journal Reading Patterns and Preferences of Pediatricians, *Journal of the Medical Library Association*, 95 (1), 56–63.

Tenopir, C., King, D. W., Spencer, J. and Wu, L. (2009) Variations in Article Seeking and Reading Patterns of Academics: what makes a difference?, *Library and Information Science Research*, 31 (3), 139–48.

Trotter, M. I. and Morgan, D. W. (2008) Patients' Use of the Internet for Health Related Matters: a study of internet usage in 2000 and 2006, *Health Informatics Journal*, 14 (3), 175–81.

Urquhart, C. (2000) Health service users of information. In Booth, A. and Walton, G. (eds), *Managing Knowledge in Health Services*, Library Association Publishing, 15–30.

Wathen, N., Wyatt, S. and Harris, R. (eds) (2008) *Mediating Health Information: the go-betweens in a changing socio-technical landscape*, Palgrave MacMillan.

Wilson, T. D. (1999) Models in Information Behaviour Research, *Journal of Documentation*, 55 (3), 249–70.

Further reading

Case, D. O. (2007) *Looking for Information: a survey of research on information seeking*, 2nd edn, Academic Press.

Fox, S. and Jones, S. (2009) *The Social Life of Health Information*, Pew Internet and American Life Project, available from www.pewinternet.org/~/media//Files/Reports/2009/PIP_Health_ 2009.pdf.

Wathen, N., Wyatt, S. and Harris, R. (eds) (2008) *Mediating Health Information: the go-betweens in a changing socio-technical landscape*, Palgrave MacMillan.

4

Healthcare information organization

Introduction

The characteristics of information and knowledge in the healthcare domain, and the variety of users and uses involved, mean that the subject area, by its very nature, requires a series of detailed and specific technical terminologies, and a variety of classifications and nomenclatures. All are based on the underlying hierarchical structure of healthcare knowledge, at least in its predominant scientific aspects. The result is that healthcare information is organized by a variety of alternative, and generally overlapping, controlled vocabularies. 'Controlled' implies, in a sense, artificial vocabularies, designed to avoid the redundancy and inconsistency of natural spoken and written language. These information organization tools are the subject of this chapter. They are too many to deal with each in detail, and instead we will consider a number of examples, each illustrating some general principles. They are divided into two main categories: first classifications and taxonomies, then subject headings and thesauri. The first group are arranged hierarchically, showing the semantic structure of the area and bringing together concepts that are similar in meaning. The second are arranged alphabetically.

There are many good treatments of the principles of knowledge organization, and we will not repeat this material here. For overviews of these topics, see Chowdhury and Chowdhury (2007), Taylor (2004), Hjørland (2003) and Svenonious (2000).

The chapter looks first at some general issues in the organization of healthcare information specifically. It then examines in more detail four forms of controlled vocabularies of importance for healthcare information: dictionaries and glossaries; classifications and taxonomies; subject headings and thesauri; and meta-vocabularies. Finally, it looks at abstracting and indexing in the context of healthcare.

Organizing healthcare information: overview

The healthcare information domain has generated a rich variety of classifications and vocabularies (for overviews, and some of the issues involved, see Cimino, 1998 and Taylor, 2006. It is also one of the oldest fields of recorded knowledge, and one with a consistent sense of innovation. Tools for organizing its knowledge base have a long history, with the earliest classifications dating back to classical times, as was noted in Chapter 2. Statistical classifications, in a modern sense, began in the 18th century and medical abstracting and indexing services, with their associated vocabularies, in the mid-19th century. As a result, there are many controlled vocabularies for information organization in the healthcare domain, more so than for any other subject area. These are often categorized as:

- nomenclatures: comprehensive lists of names with definitions and synonym cross-references
- classifications: logical hierarchies of concepts, with their interrelations indicated
- clinical terminologies: for creation of clinical records
- coding schemes: for statistical data collection.

However, in practice, distinction between these is blurred and other terms, such as taxonomies, thesauri, and subject headings are used.

The diversity is explained by the varied purposes and user groups which these vocabularies have to serve, including:

- statistical recording of illness and death
- coding of diagnosis, treatment and outcome, for management purposes in health services
- indexing for retrieval of information in books, articles, websites, etc.
- structuring of printed and electronic collections of data and information for browsing and navigation.

The British NHS has also broken down the second of the above points further, by distinguishing the processes of:

- terming: detailed coding for patient care
- classifying: providing less detailed statistics for management
- grouping: providing broad groups for costing and similar analyses.[1]

These uses of structured vocabularies are not, perhaps, so familiar to library/information workers as are information retrieval applications; but they are fundamental to effective operation of health services (Gardner, 2003).

All of these vocabularies, however defined, have some form of hierarchical arrangement, necessarily reflecting the hierarchical structure of healthcare knowledge. They differ in their

- scope: some are very broad, others much more subject specific
- depth: some have great detail, others stay at a more general level
- intended users: most are intended to be used by healthcare experts and professionals, but some are at least partly aimed at the general public.

Because the large number of these vocabularies tends to cause confusion, there is a trend towards providing *mappings* or *cross-walks* between vocabularies, so that concepts or queries expressed in one may be translated into another. The most elaborate example of this is the US National Library of Medicine's Unified Medical Language System (UMLS), which will be discussed later in this chapter.

We will now discuss and exemplify the four tools or forms of controlled vocabulary used in the organization of healthcare information:

- dictionaries and glossaries
- classifications and taxonomies
- subject headings and thesauri
- meta-vocabularies.

In the examples given below a web reference to the original will be provided, but the examples are shown in 'plain text', rather than as screen shots. The plain text presentation makes comparison between tools easier. 'Administrative' information, such as the date of introduction of a concept into the vocabulary, has been omitted from the examples of terms.

Metadata

Metadata are the standards, schemas and formats which allow the consistent recording of information about information resources. Most of the vocabularies discussed below can be used to provide the content of metadata records, in library catalogues, for example, or bibliographic databases. However, these records will use standard metadata schemas: Dublin Core, IEEE-LOM, AACR/MARC, and so on. None of the metadata schemas is healthcare specific, so they will not be described here (see Zeng and Qin, 2008) for a full discussion of metadata).

Dictionaries and glossaries

The language of healthcare is detailed, complex and technical. The most basic tools used to handle it are dictionaries and glossaries, which simply provide alphabetic listings of terms, with a definition and perhaps an explanation of varying length, possibly with diagrams or photographs, depending on the purpose of the tool. The distinction between a dictionary and glossary is not sharply defined, but dictionaries tend to cover a wider subject area, and hence to be larger vocabularies.

Most of these tools are now available in digital form, many still with a print equivalent. Their usual method of use is simply for alphabetic look-up, with a degree of cross-referencing, but the digital formats allow more complex searching. They are typically not used for indexing and retrieval because of the limited structure within the vocabulary; they usually point to synonyms and related terms, but, being purely alphabetical, cannot represent hierarchical knowledge structures. Most only offer terms in one language, but a few are multilingual.

A well known example of a dictionary is the *Oxford Concise Medical Dictionary*, with 11,000 terms, available in both printed and digital formats. Typical entries in this vocabulary are:

abarticulation n. 1. The dislocation of a joint. 2. Synovial joint (*see* DIARTHROSIS).
abasia n. an inability to walk for which no physical cause can be identified. *See also* ASTASIA.
abbreviated injury scale a quick method for determining the severity of a case of serious trauma. It can be used for purposes of *triage and *clinical audit.

Note the use of *see*, *see also* and the * symbol to make cross-references and build up a structure within the vocabulary.

Another well known example, primarily intended for the general public, is the online medical dictionary in the US National Library of Medicine's Medline Plus service,[2] which uses the Merriam-Webster Medical Dictionary with about 6,000 terms. An example of a leading dictionary aimed at a specific professional audience is *Stedman's Medical Dictionary for the Health Professions and Nursing*, now in its sixth edition of 2007.[3] With 54,000 entries, it includes numerous graphs, colour images and photographs, so that it verges on being more of an encyclopaedic reference work than a simple terminology listing. Its digital versions include audio pronunciations of terms, animations and other interactive elements, moving further away from the simple terminology concept.

Some of these tools are primarily concerned not so much with defining and explaining concepts, as with 'translating' terms between natural languages and between professional and lay terminology. An example is the European Union's *Multilingual Glossary of Technical and Popular Medical Terms in Nine European Languages*, which, as its name implies, offers brief definitions of about 2000 medical terms, in professional and lay terminology, in nine European languages.[4] It offers, for example, the English terms *rubella* (technical) and *German measles* (popular), equating it to the Italian *rosolia* (both technical and popular usage), the Dutch *rubella* (technical) and *rodehond* (popular), and so on.

These tools are certainly the most familiar form of healthcare information organization for healthcare workers, and are important for terminology control and for aiding information access by clarifying terminology and concepts. However, they are not suitable in themselves for direct use in information systems, because of their limited semantic structure, lacking consistent hierarchical relationships.

Classifications and taxonomies

Classifications and taxonomies are forms of knowledge organization which aim to show the relationships between concepts – generally hierarchical relationships – by bringing together terms representing similar meanings. They are sometimes referred to as 'systematic' vocabularies (according to a 'system') by contrast with alphabetical vocabularies. For a description of such tools from a library/information viewpoint see Broughton (2005) and for a more scientific perspective see Bowker and Star (2000a).

The difference between classification and taxonomy is not clearly defined and the terms are, to a large extent, used interchangeably. These types of tools are also sometimes referred to as 'categorizations', 'coding schemes', or 'ontologies' (two useful articles which help to clarify the issue are Gilchrist, 2003 and Jacob, 2003). They are widely used with healthcare information, for a variety of purposes, including:

- arrangement of physical materials in libraries and record centres
- allowing browsing and navigating in digital collections
- organizing material in printed handbooks and reference works
- tagging items for retrieval
- coding individual episodes of patient care
- organizing statistical and epidemiological data.

A considerable number of such tools are therefore needed, differing greatly in their size and complexity, according to their purpose. Even within one purpose there may still be a variety of solutions. A survey of 660 UK health libraries and information centres (Ryder, 2002) asked about the classification schemes used for shelf arrangement. The results were:

National Library of Medicine classification	38%
Wessex (a UK variant of NLM)	12%
Dewey Decimal	21%
Own scheme	19%
Library of Congress	4%
Bliss, Barnard, UDC	2% each

It is noticeable that a fifth of services use a 'home grown' system. In most cases these are individual schemes for small collections, but small numbers used classification schemes produced by and for major libraries, such as the Royal College of Nursing.

We will look at six major tools, mentioning others in passing, as examples of different types of classification and taxonomy relevant to healthcare. Four of the six are specifically designed for healthcare and two are general purpose tools which include healthcare concepts:

- Dewey Decimal Classification – a large, general-purpose library classification scheme
- National Library of Medicine classification – a healthcare-specific library classification scheme
- International Classification of Diseases – a healthcare-specific special classification scheme
- Systematized Nomenclature of Medicine (SNOMED) – a healthcare-

specific hierarchical coding system
- Integrated Public Sector Vocabulary – a general-purpose web taxonomy
- British National Formulary classification – a small classification for a specific aspect of healthcare.

Dewey Decimal Classification

The Dewey Decimal Classification (DDC) is a large general purpose classification scheme, originally designed for the physical arrangement of materials on library shelves, though subsequently adopted for many other purposes, such as the organization of internet subject directories. The other widely used examples of this type of classification are the Universal Decimal Classification (UDC) and the Library of Congress Classification (LCC). A full description of the DDC is given by Bowman (2005) and by Satija (2007), and by its maintainers, OCLC (Online Computer Library Center) at www.oclc.org/dewey.

The Dewey classification is certainly the best known vocabulary for information organization, being used for shelf arrangement in a quarter of a million libraries worldwide, as well as in digital environments, such as internet subject directories. Dating from the late 19th century, it is now in its 22nd edition, being revised regularly by an international editorial board. DDC is available in complete and abridged editions, and in print and digital formats.

Its ten main classes are divided into ten, and then again, to give 1000 concepts, each of which is divided further as appropriate. Complex subjects can be denoted by combining class numbers, in the so-called 'number building' process. Healthcare topics are to be found mainly in the section 610:

000	Computer science, information and general works
100	Philosophy and psychology
200	Religion
300	Social sciences
400	Language
500	Science
600	Technology
610	Medicine and health
611	anatomy, cytology, histology
612	physiology
613	promotion of health
614	incidence and prevention of disease
615	pharmacology and therapeutics

616		diseases
617		surgery and related specialities
618		gynaecology and related specialities
619		experimental medicine
620	Engineering
630	Agriculture
	. . .
700	Arts and recreation
800	Literature
900	History and geography

The hierarchical notation is an aid to finding one's way around the structure to a quite detailed level, for example:

600	Technology
610		Medicine and health
615			Pharmacology and therapeutics
615.9				Toxicology
615.905					Prevention of poisoning

Dewey is, like other classifications of its kind, fundamentally organized by discipline, and healthcare is a multi-faceted subject. Consequently, that healthcare material is not all in the 610 section but is scattered throughout the classification (Connaway and Sievert, 1996). Public health issues and material on healthcare systems, for example, are typically classified at 362.1, in the social services and planning sections.

Even within the 610s, scattering occurs. For example, material dealing, with particular organs or systems is dispersed according to its disciplinary treatment. Material on the heart is dispersed in this way (only a selection of class numbers are shown here, and the headings are paraphrased for clarity):

611	Human Anatomy
611.12		Heart (anatomy)
612	Human physiology
612.17		Heart (physiology)
614	Incidence of diseases
614.591		Cardiovascular diseases – human – incidence
615	Pharmacology and therapeutics
615.71		Drugs affecting cardiovascular system
616	Diseases

616.12	Diseases of the heart
617	Surgery
617.4112	Heart surgery
618	Other branches of medicine
618.921	Cardiovascular diseases – human – paediatrics

To counter this scatter, and to find all relevant material, the alphabetical index to DDC's headings must be used. Other classifications (though not now used widely) have organized material by subject rather than by discipline. The Brown classification is an example (Beghtol, 2004). This sort of classification will bring material on, say, the heart together in one place, but at the cost of splitting material on, say, human physiology or surgery. There is no single perfect classification for a multi-faceted subject such as healthcare and its sciences.

The advantages of DDC, as with other general-purpose classifications of its kind, are:

- its scope, covering all human knowledge and therefore necessarily having a place for all healthcare topics and issues
- its familiarity to many users, particularly in the English-speaking world, where it is very widely used in public and educational libraries
- the intuitive simplicity of its decimal notation, which makes it easy to navigate.

Its disadvantages are:

- its rather dated main structure, which dates from the 1870s
- its lack of detail for any particular subject, no general classification being able to compete for specificity with subject specific tools.

Despite these limitations, Dewey is used to classify healthcare materials, both printed and electronic, particularly as part of more general collections, e.g. in an academic or public library, or in an internet directory with broad subject coverage. The Bulletin Board for Libraries (BUBL) directory is an example of the latter (www.bubl.ac.uk). Ryder's 2002 survey found that DDC was used in over 20% of UK health libraries. It has also been used to classify web resources for healthcare students (Bremner, 2001).

The UDC and LCC are used in much the same ways, though the UDC, by virtual of its facilities for creating new classification numbers by synthesis, is better adapted for specification of detailed subjects, including medicine

(McIlwaine, 1995; Slavic, Cordeiro and Riesthuis, 2008). Ryder found that LCC had 4% of use in UK health libraries, and UDC 2%, as did the Bliss classification scheme, a relatively little-used scheme with a strongly faceted structure.

National Library of Medicine classification

Developed and maintained by the US National Library of Medicine (NLM), this classification scheme is designed for the arrangement of library materials – initially printed, but now encompassing digital sources – in the healthcare area. It is widely used internationally in medical and nursing libraries and for special healthcare collections within larger libraries. The only scheme of its kind, it dates from 1950. It is provided only in digital format, may be downloaded free of charge, and is updated annually. The closest possible integration with the MeSH vocabulary (see below) is one of the aims. Full details are available on the classification's web pages (www.nlm.nih.gov/class), and the scheme is discussed by Chan (2007).

Its overall structure is very similar to that of the Library of Congress Classification, which it follows in its general 'style' and with which it shares an alphanumeric (rather than decimal) notation. NLM uses parts of the alphabetic notation (QS–QZ and W–WZ) which are not used by LCC, so that the two may be combined in a single collection: in a general collection, NLM can be used for the medical sections as an alternative to LCC's less detailed treatment of these subjects; or a healthcare collection mainly using NLM can use LCC schedules for any 'non-health' material. Because of this relationship with LCC, the NLM scheme does not need any provision for 'ancillary' subjects, apart from a listing of geographic descriptors.

The NLM Classification is divided into two main sections: for pre-clinical sciences and for medicine and related subjects. These, in turn, are divided into 8 and 27 sub-sections respectively, giving the following main structure of the classification:

PRE-CLINICAL SCIENCES

QS   Human Anatomy
QT   Physiology
QU   Biochemistry
QV   Pharmacology
QW   Microbiology and Immunology
QX   Parasitology

QY   Clinical Pathology
QZ   Pathology

MEDICINE AND RELATED SUBJECTS
W   Health Professions
WA   Public Health
WB   Practice of Medicine
WC   Communicable Diseases
WD   Disorders of Systemic, Metabolic or Environmental Origin, etc
WE   Musculoskeletal System
WF   Respiratory System
WG   Cardiovascular System
WH   Hemic and Lymphatic Systems
WI   Digestive System
WJ   Urogenital System
WK   Endocrine System
WL   Nervous System
WM   Psychiatry
WN   Radiology, Diagnostic Imaging
WO   Surgery
WP   Gynecology
WQ   Obstetrics
WR   Dermatology
WS   Pediatrics
WT   Geriatrics. Chronic Disease
WU   Dentistry. Oral Surgery
WV   Otolaryngology
WW   Opthalmology
WX   Hospitals and Other Health Facilities
WY   Nursing
WZ   History of Medicine
19th   19th Century Schedule

As with all hierarchical classifications, the NLM scheme allows specification of detailed concepts in each of the sub-sections, for example:

QV   Pharmacology
QV 600   Toxicology
QV 601   Antidotes and other therapeutic measures

Again, as with all schemes of this kind, there is an element of scatter. Although toxicology appears in the QV (Pharmacology) section, industrial poisons appear in WA (Public Health), food poisoning in WC (Communicable Diseases), and so on. Lopez-Mertz (1997) shows that almost half of a sample of books dealing with pharmacy and pharmaceutics were scattered throughout the scheme, outside the QV (pharmacology) section. Connaway and Sievert (1996) also give an example of scatter in the NLM scheme. An alphabetical index using MeSH headings allows users to overcome this scattering effect.

The 19th Century Schedule, a simplified version of the whole classification, is intended for organization of historical materials.

The NLM Classification is a popular way of organizing healthcare libraries: Womack (2006), for example, found it was used in 75% of a sample of academic health science libraries in the USA. It is also used to a limited extent with digital collections of healthcare material, and was used, for example, as a browsing tool in the OMNI (Organizing Medical Networked Information) listing of web resources, now succeeded by InTute (www.intute.ac.uk/medicine). However, the MeSH subject headings are usually regarded as the primary means of organizing such collections because of their greater specificity. The NLM Classification seems likely to be used in future mainly with printed collections.

A very similar scheme, the Wessex Classification, derived from NLM, is used in some British healthcare libraries.[5] NLM, or its Wessex derivative, were used in 50% of the UK health libraries in Ryder's 2002 survey. Accounting for 2% of use was the Bernard classification, the only other generally available classification designed specifically for medical and veterinary subjects (Glanville, 1981).

International Classification of Diseases

The International Classification of Diseases is the most widely used of a number of classifications of diseases, causes of ill-health and treatments, used mainly for organizing compilations of statistical, epidemiological and health management information. This classification began as the International List of Causes of Death in the 1850s was adopted by the World Health Organization in 1948, and has been maintained by it ever since. It is now in its 10th edition (2003), commonly referred to as ICD-10. It is the main classification used for statistical compilations of data on diseases and health problems worldwide. It is both broad and detailed, with about 20,000 concepts.

Full details of the classification are available from the International Classification of Diseases (ICD) web pages.[6] Bowker and Star (2000b) also give a detailed analysis of the structure of the ICD, albeit dated in detail.

The website states that it has become 'the international standard diagnostic classification for all general epidemiological and many health management problems [including] the analysis of the general health situation of population groups and the monitoring of the incidence and prevalence of diseases and other health problems . . . It is used to classify diseases and other health problems recorded on many types of health and vital records including death certificates and hospital records. In addition to enabling the storage and retrieval of diagnostic information for clinical and epidemiological purposes, these records also provide the basis for the compilation of national mortality and morbidity statistics by WHO member states.'

ICD-10 is a hierarchical classification with 22 main sections, referred to as 'chapters': e.g. 'mental and behavioural disorders', 'diseases of the respiratory system', 'injury, poisoning and certain other consequences of external causes'. The hierarchical structure covers several levels, as shown in the following example:

Diseases of the digestive system
      Diseases of oesophagus, stomach and duodenum
           Gastric ulcer
               Gastric ulcer acute with haemorrhage
External causes of morbidity and mortality
     Transport accidents
          Pedal cyclist injured in transport accident
             Pedal cyclist injured in collision with railway train

There is an alphanumeric code for each specific term, e.g.:

K25.0   Gastric ulcer acute with haemorrhage
V15   Pedal cyclist injured in collision with railway train

ICD-10 has also been adapted for special purposes, including: the International Classification of Diseases for Oncology, now in its third edition (ICD-O-3); the International Classification of External Causes of Injury (ICRCI); and the International Classification of Primary Care, now in its second edition (ICPC-2). WHO maintains related classifications in the WHO Family of International Classifications, including the International Classification of Functioning, Disability and Health (ICF), and the

International Classification of Health Interventions (ICHI). Full details of all of these are available from the WHO classifications website.[7] ICF, in particular, complements ICD-10. The latter describes a 'diagnosis' of disease or health problems, while the former describes disability, functioning, activities and participation.[8]

ICD-10 is not the only statistical classification of its kind. In the UK, the 4th revision of the Classification of Surgical Operations and Procedures,[9] maintained by the Office of Population, Censuses and Surveys, is used for coding in the UK health services, alongside ICD-10. The classification is based on anatomy and systems of the body, e.g.:

Z50.7 – skin of ankle

and allows detailed specification of procedures, e.g.

S54.6 – cleansing and sterilization of burnt skin of neck or head.

Similar coding schemes are used in many countries, Germany, for example, using the OPS (Operationen und Przeduernschlüssel) classification.[10]

ICD-10 and Office of Population, Censuses and Surveys (OPCS) codes are used as the basis for deriving Healthcare Resource Groups (HRG), a broad categorization used for management and accounting purposes within the British National Health Service.[11] There are about 1400 terms in the vocabulary, encoding treatments and types of patients, e.g.:

urgent dental care
dressing a major wound or burn

As health services move to more devolved operation and payment by results, so the applications of these codes, which are used to justify activity, and hence resources, become more important. See Reid and Sutch (2008) for a comparison of several such coding systems used in different countries, and Doyle and Dimitropoulos (2009) for an Australian perspective on keeping such systems current. At present, the available tools seem far from perfect: one UK study of the use of OPCS and HRG for coding of head and neck operations reported that 'the current coding system was found to be complicated, ambiguous and inaccurate' (Mitra, Malik, Homer and Loughran, 2009).

This is likely to be a significant area for future development (Tatham, 2008). It seems probable that comprehensive vocabularies such as ICD-10 and SNOMED will replace specific-purpose tools such as OPCS and HRG for detailed recording of healthcare activities.

Systematized Nomenclature of Medicine (SNOMED)

SNOMED/CT (Systematized Nomenclature of Medicine/Clinical Terms), like other clinical terminologies, is a structured list of terms for use in clinical practice to describe the care and treatment of patients, for either a single incident or a full care record. It is a particularly comprehensive and carefully structured vocabulary. It was developed jointly by the British health services and the American College of Pathologists, the latter having devised the original SNOMED. It is now maintained by the International Health Terminology Standards Development Organization (IHTSDO) and is regularly updated and extended, with recent developments including the extension of the vocabulary to nursing and radiology. Full details of the vocabulary, its development and current status can be found on the IHTSDO website.[12]

SNOMED has been adopted as the standard clinical coding system within the English health service, replacing the Read Codes used previously. Details of its UK implementation may be found on the Connecting for Health website.[13] An introductory guide for healthcare practitioners has been provided within the UK health service (Connecting for Health, 2007).

This is a very large vocabulary, with nearly one million concepts, and a very detailed hierarchical organization. An example is:

Substance
      Drug or medicament
            Anti-infective agent
                  Local anti-infective
                        Carbol-fuschin topical solution

A complex alphanumeric notation parallels the text terms.

The UK SNOMED/CT browser requires registration, but a freely available browser for the vocabulary may be found at the Virginia/Maryland Regional College of Veterinary Medicine.[14]

Among the current applications for SNOMED are electronic medical records, intensive care monitoring, knowledge summaries, clinical decision support, clinical trials, disease surveillance and consumer health information systems. Richesson, Fung and Krischer (2008) report the application of

SNOMED for the monitoring of the potential side-effects of drugs. They compare it with two specialist vocabularies, the Medical Dictionary for Regulatory Affairs (MedDRA) and the Common Terminology Criteria for Adverse Events (CTCAE), noting the different structures and features of the three. Some problems have been identified with the consistency of coding among different coders using SNOMED/CT (see, for example, Andrews, Richesson and Krischer, 2007).

It is likely that this comprehensive vocabulary will be further developed and even more widely used in the future. A comparably widely used coding system, though for more narrowly defined purposes, is WHOART, the World Health Organisation's Adverse Reaction Terminology for coding the adverse reactions of drugs.[15] The need for detailed recording of adverse events and side-effects of drugs has led to the development of several alternative coding schemes (Bawden and Robinson, 2010), including those noted above and others such as the US Food and Drug Administration's (FDA), Coding Symbols for a Thesaurus of Adverse Reaction Terms (COSTART).

Integrated Public Sector Vocabulary

The Integrated Public Sector Vocabulary (IPSV)[16] is the standard terminology for subject description in the metadata of UK government websites. It is aimed at use by the general public and it is the successor to the Government Category List.

IPSV is a hierarchical taxonomy – although its maintainers do not like this term, and prefer 'encoding scheme'. There are 16 main sections covering all aspects of public information, e.g. 'education and skills', 'housing' and 'life in the community'. There are many 'non-preferred terms', synonyms which point a user to the appropriate taxonomy term. The vocabulary is updated regularly. It has over 3000 preferred terms and nearly 5000 synonyms.

Healthcare concepts appear in the 'Health, well-being and care' section, which itself has 13 sub-sections, e.g. 'animal health', 'cosmetic treatments', 'disability' and 'food and drink'. The concept of healthcare itself appears in the sections 'health', 'health care', 'health and social care professions' and 'National Health Service'. (It is a feature of this kind of taxonomy that a concept may appear in several places, which is not allowed in other kinds of vocabulary.)

There are several levels of hierarchy, e.g.:

Health, well-being and care
    Health care
        Complementary medicine
           Aromatherapy
Health, well-being and care
    Health
        Illnesses
           Digestive system disorders
                Liver diseases
                    Hepatitis

Coverage of diseases and treatments is neither complete nor systematic. This is because the vocabulary is mainly intended to cover those health issues on which central and local government are likely to provide information to the public. In this way, it is typical of many vocabularies in use worldwide for public information, including health.

British National Formulary classification

The British National Formulary (BNF)[17] is a reference work intended 'to provide UK healthcare professionals with authoritative and practical information on the selection and use of medicines in a clear, concise and accessible manner' by 'providing key information on the selection, prescribing, dispensing and administration of medicines'. It is produced jointly by the Royal Pharmaceutical Society and the British Medical Association. Intended for rapid reference, it is available in paper and digital versions. The paper versions are updated twice a year, the digital versions more frequently.

It is organized by a hierarchical classification, covering prescription drugs available in the UK. The classification, used in all versions for the formulary, printed and digital, is primarily intended to guide the user quickly to the choice of drugs for particular purposes. It has 15 top terms, corresponding to chapters of the formulary, each covering a system of the body or a type of medical care, e.g. 'respiratory system', 'infections' and 'anaesthesia'. There is a hierarchical structure, with a numeric notation, for classes of drugs, after which specific examples are listed by generic name and brand names, e.g.

13   skin
13.11   skin cleaners and antiseptics
13.11.2   chlorhexidine salts

chlorhexidine
Chlorhexidine 0.05%
Cepton
Hibiscrub
. . .

The listing of specific examples outside the hierarchical structure and notation 'breaks the rules' of formal classification, so this is best regarded as a specialist taxonomy.

The classification is well suited for a quick look-up of particular topics, or for navigating to the kind of information required. It is complemented by an index, enabling look-up of specific topics or products without going via the classification. It typifies the pragmatic, and relatively simple, taxonomies used to organized reference works with specialist content.

Subject headings and thesauri

These vocabularies consist of lists of terms in alphabetical order. At their simplest, usually in the form of so-called 'keyword lists', that is all they are: a bare list of terms that are used for indexing and retrieval. This is the simplest form of controlled vocabulary, but also the least useful.

All the widely used healthcare vocabularies are more sophisticated than this. At a minimum, they will allow for:

• synonyms, so that someone seeking information can be guided to the 'preferred' or 'approved' term
• broader and narrower terms, reflecting the hierarchy almost always present in healthcare information, and allowing an indexer or searcher to be guided to the appropriate level of specificity
• related terms, providing the 'see also' function which guides the user to other possible useful concepts
• notes for some or all terms, providing definition, explanation or instruction.

A vocabulary with these facilities will match the British and international standards for retrieval thesauri (the current relevant British Standard is BS8723); and indeed, most such vocabularies in the healthcare area are termed thesauri. An evident exception is the most widely used health vocabulary of all, MeSH (Medical Subject Headings), applied to many kinds of health-related information, which is described as a set of subject headings –

although it allows for all the thesaural features, though not quite in the way recommended by the standards. (More details of these issues are provided by Broughton, 2006 and Aitchison, Gilchrist and Bawden, 2000.)

There are many such vocabularies used with healthcare information. They are more numerous than the classification/taxonomy type of vocabulary, though less diverse in nature. Their main function is the indexing of information, whether in printed sources, bibliographic databases, library catalogues or directories of web resources. The one which will be examined first, is MeSH. We will then consider three vocabularies as examples of those designed, according to the thesaurus standards, to deal with particular aspects of health information:

- the Pharmline thesaurus (for medicines information)
- the Public Health Language
- the Maternal and Child Health Thesaurus.

These examples will also show how vocabularies, though all including the features required by the thesaurus standards, can differ in content and in the facilities provided to the user, according to the requirements of the context for which they are designed.

Medical Subject Headings (MeSH)

MeSH is the vocabulary most widely used for the indexing of collections of bibliographic records, library materials and internet resources in healthcare. Originating in the 1860s, it is administered by the US National Library of Medicine (NLM), with international advisers, and revised frequently – in principle, on a weekly basis, since the MeSH files are updated every Sunday. Full details, and access to the vocabulary itself, are available from NLM; MeSH is now available only in digital form.[18]

The vocabulary is both broad and detailed, with 23,000 terms. MeSH headings have synonyms and related terms shown, with extensive information about each term and its use. Hierarchical relations are shown by a complementary tree structure. Related term ('see also') links are included. Although termed 'subject headings', this vocabulary has all the sophistication of a thesaurus. There are 16 main headings, or sections, in the hierarchy:

ANATOMY
ORGANISMS

DISEASES
CHEMICALS AND DRUGS
ANALYTICAL, DIAGNOSTIC AND THERAPEUTIC TECHNIQUES AND EQUIPMENT
PSYCHIATRY AND PSYCHOLOGY
PHENOMENA AND PROCESSES
DISCIPLINES AND OCCUPATIONS
ANTHROPOLOGY, EDUCATION, SOCIOLOGY AND SOCIAL PHENOMENA
TECHNOLOGY, INDUSTRY, AGRICULTURE
HUMANITIES
INFORMATION SCIENCE
NAMED GROUPS
HEALTH CARE
PUBLICATION CHARACTERISTICS
GEOGRAPHICALS

Note the very broad scope of subjects included here, reflecting the breadth of what may be relevant to healthcare.

The hierarchy extends down several levels of detail. Terms may be allotted 'qualifiers' to improve precision of indexing: for drug terms, as an example, qualifiers include 'therapeutic use of' and 'adverse effects of'. An example of a MeSH heading (with some detail omitted, and slightly altered for clarity) is:

MeSH heading	Chlorhexidine
Tree number	D02.078.370.141.100
Scope note	A disinfectant and topical anti-infective agent used also as a mouthwash to prevent oral plaque
History note	Introduced in 1980: previously was biguanides
Entry term (i.e. synonym)	Chlorhexidine acetate
	Chlorhexidine hydrochloride
	Novalsan
	. . .
Qualifiers	Therapeutic use
	Adverse effects
	Analysis
	. . .
Pharmacological action	Mouthwashes
	Anti-infective agents, local
	. . .

The equivalent tree structure, with alphanumeric notation, is:

Chemicals and drugs [D]
  Organic chemicals [D02]
    Amidines [D02.078]
      Guanidines [D02.078.370]
        Biguanidines [D02.078.370.141]
          Chlorhexidine [D02.078.370.141.100]
            . . .

The MeSH browser software allows both direct look-up or terms, and also convenient browsing up and down the hierarchies, so that the user can get maximum value from the vocabulary structure in selecting terms.

MeSH terms are linked to NLM classification codes, and also to Chemical Abstracts registry numbers for chemical substances, thus providing integration with a large extent of the scientific and healthcare literature. Many initiatives have mapped MeSH terms onto other parts of healthcare terminology (see Schultz, 2006, mapping onto acronyms as an example).

The best known application of MeSH is its use in indexing the NLM's bibliographic databases, most notably Medline/PubMed. It is also used to index resources in several collections of healthcare internet resources, such as the medical/dental and nursing/allied health sections of the InTute directory (www.intute.ac.uk), and for some of the indexing of individual periodicals (Jones, 1994 gives the example of the *British Medical Journal*). MeSH headings are also used as subject headings in many health libraries; Womack (2006) found that 95% of academic health libraries in the sample studied used MeSH in this way. MeSH has a great influence on the indexing of healthcare materials generally and is the one vocabulary of its kind likely to be familiar outside the library/information community, being known to students, teachers, practitioners and even the general public (McGregor, 2002).

Aside from their main function of information retrieval, MeSH headings have also been used in the development of knowledge-based systems and in systems for the discovery of unappreciated ideas implicit in the literature (see, for example, Swanson, Smalheiser and Torvik, 2006). MeSH is usually regarded as the epitome of the healthcare vocabulary, as well as the oldest example. Its importance and the extent of its use show no signs of decreasing.

Pharmline thesaurus

The Pharmline thesaurus[19] is maintained by the UK Medicines Information Pharmacists Group and used for indexing that group's medicines information resources, particularly the Pharmline bibliographic database on pharmacy practice and clinical use of drugs. The vocabulary is therefore strongly centred on concepts directly related to pharmacy and associated areas, with a particularly rich set of terms for drug types and drug actions. The great majority of its terms are brand names or generic names for medicines. It is closely equivalent in purpose to the BNF classification.

It is a full thesaurus, with synonyms (preferred and non-preferred), broader and narrower terms, related terms, and scope notes (explanatory notes for individual terms). There is, unusually, a very 'flat' structure, with limited hierarchy and with numerous 'top terms' and, in effect, no sections within the thesaurus, so that 'top-down' browsing is not well supported. This means that this thesaurus will be most effective when used for fairly specific searches, rather than for general browsing. This seems appropriate, considering the tightly focused database that it is designed to search, and it is a good example of a thesaurus designed for the searching of a particular database, in a particular area of healthcare.

An example of a Pharmline term is:

ANTIFUNGALS

SN	used in therapeutics – do not confuse with FUNGICIDES
USE FOR	Antibiotics, antifungal
	Antimycotics
BT	Anti-infective agents
	Drugs-anti-infective
NT	Amorolfine
	Ampotericin
	Antifungals – imidazole
	Antifungals – triazole
	Butenafine
	[21 additional specific examples are listed] . . .
RT	Fungicides

Public Health Language

The Public Health Language (PHL)[20] (formerly known as the National Public Health Language) was designed to meet the needs of the then UK Health Development Agency (now part of NICE), the Association of Public Health Observatories and the Public Health electronic Library. It is used to index websites, online libraries and databases from these three organizations, and others in the UK and internationally.

PHL is a full thesaurus, with synonyms, broader and narrower terms, related terms and explanatory scope notes. Unusually, it was created not from scratch, but from the combination and restructuring of two existing vocabularies. It was also designed to be compatible with terms used in other vocabularies relevant to the UK public health setting: MeSH, IPSV and a taxonomy maintained by the UK Department of Health. It has ten sections, or 'top terms' in thesaurus parlance:

COMMUNICATION AND KNOWLEDGE
DEATH, DISEASE AND DISABILITY
DETERMINANTS OF HEALTH
EQUIPMENT
HEALTH SERVICES AND THEIR MANAGEMENT
HEALTH, PUBLIC HEALTH AND HEALTH PROMOTION
PEOPLE AND POPULATIONS
PUBLIC HEALTH METHODS, THEORY AND RESEARCH
SETTING AND PLACE
TIME FACTOR

These reflect the breadth of subject coverage necessary for the broad field of public health, with its overlaps with health policy.

An example of a PHL term is:

PUBLIC HEALTH
The science and art of promoting health, preventing disease and prolonging life, through the organised efforts of society (Health Promotion Glossary, 1998)
Use for: PUBLIC HEALTH MEDICINE
BT: HEALTH, PUBLIC HEALTH AND HEALTH PROMOTION
NT: ENVIRONMENTAL HEALTH
RT: PREVENTION
            PUBLIC HEALTH WORKER

Note the full set of thesaurus relations (synonym, broader and narrower terms, related terms), and the use of the note to give a definition of the term from an 'approved' source, in effect justifying, as well as explaining, the terminology.

This thesaurus is a good example of those that have been created for broad areas of healthcare, on the basis of existing vocabularies, with the need to satisfy more than one user group and with a need to link to other vocabularies in the area. This situation requires more compromises on the choice of structure and terminology than when the vocabulary can be created from scratch to fulfil one clear need.

Maternal and Child Health (MCH) thesaurus

This, again, is a full thesaurus, developed according to the standards by the US National Center for Education in Maternal and Child Health, based in the Maternal and Child Health Library at Georgetown University, Washington DC. An example of vocabulary tools which are revised as formal 'new editions' rather than updated 'as and when', it is now in its third edition.[21]

It was developed to provide a standard vocabulary for health professionals working in this subject area. Its focus is on public health in the specific context of MCH. Its core topics are women's health, child health, oral health, nutrition, injury and violence prevention, chronic illnesses and disabilities related to MCH, children with special healthcare needs, genetics and public health programmes and services. The thesaurus largely excludes clinical medicine, and includes terms for diseases and treatments only when they are directly relevant to MCH; it is therefore complementary to 'general' medical vocabularies such as MeSH.

The vocabulary is designed for indexing and retrieval of information from MCH resources in a variety of forms, including government documents, learning resources, audiovisual materials, technical reports and information on funding, grants and health programmes. Its primary use is with a variety of databases, containing bibliographic, educational and administrative information relevant to MCH, hosted at the sponsoring library.[22]

The thesaurus includes 4000 terms, divided into 21 sections which are referred to as 'subject categories':

Agencies and Organizations
Chemicals and Drugs
Diseases and Disorders
Diagnosis and Intervention
Economics and Politics
Education and Training
Facilities and Buildings
Field, Discipline, and Occupational Groups
Geography
Health Promotion and Disease Prevention
Health Services Management

Law and Legal Issues
Nutrition and Food
Psychology and Development
Population Groups
Program Types
Research and Data
Reproduction and Genetics
Social and Demographic Issues
Service Types
Technology, Information and Publications

Note the emphasis on public health and 'social' issues, and the consequent similarity with the structure of the PHL.

An example of a term from this vocabulary is:

DENTAL HYGIENE
Use for personal dental care and for the profession of dental hygiene
Use for ORAL HYGIENE
BT   HYGIENE
          ALLIED HEALTH OCCUPATIONS
NT   FLOSSING
RT   DENTAL CARIES
          DENTAL HYGIENISTS
          DENTAL PROPHYLAXIS
          ORAL HEALTH

The two broader terms show that this thesaurus has a multi-hierarchy. Each concept may be in two or more sections, in this case one for the concept of hygiene and one for the concept of the related healthcare profession. Although multi-hierarchies make construction and use of vocabularies more complicated, they are quite common in healthcare vocabularies (more so than in any other subject area) because of the complex and hierarchical nature of healthcare knowledge. All the other alphabetic vocabularies shown in this chapter, MeSH, PHL and the Pharmline thesaurus, also have multi-hierarchy.

The online presentation of this vocabulary emphasizes selection of specific terms rather than browsing the hierarchies. Unusually, a 'rotated' term access is provided, giving access to each word within a term. So, for example, the term ALLIED HEALTH OCCUPATIONS could be accessed by scanning the alphabetical list under A, H or O.

This is a good example of a vocabulary created to be complementary to the major tools (and the introduction makes clear that many existing vocabularies were compared in its design) for a specific healthcare sector, and designed for indexing of particular collections of information, not all of them bibliographic.

Meta-vocabularies

Because of the proliferation of classifications, taxonomies, thesauri and other forms of controlled vocabulary in the healthcare domain, there is a natural desire for some way of linking or integrating them. This approach offers a number of advantages, most particularly that those who are looking for information need not be familiar with several vocabularies in order to search a variety of information sources.

One way of achieving this is for individual vocabularies to provide links to terminology from other vocabularies; we have seen some examples of this earlier in the chapter. Another way is to provide explicit mapping or 'cross-walks' between vocabularies; again, some examples of this have already been mentioned. However, the most comprehensive way of dealing with this issue is to provide an integrating framework or meta-vocabulary, sometimes termed an ontology. This includes, in one consistent structure, several vocabularies or sections of vocabularies, showing how the terms in each are equivalenced or otherwise related.

There have been a number of attempts to create such meta-vocabularies for healthcare information, but the only one which has been developed fully, and is still in active use is the Unified Medical Language System (UMLS), developed by the US National Library of Medicine. This provides a mapping structure between vocabularies in the form of a so-called metathesaurus, supported by a semantic network which clarifies and makes explicit the meaning of terms.[23]

Over 170 individual vocabularies or sections of vocabularies are integrated into the UMLS Metathesaurus, although many of these are different editions of sources or national modifications of major vocabularies such as ICD-10 and MeSH, or their translations into a variety of languages. They include older editions of vocabularies and those which have been replaced, allowing older sources to be searched without re-indexing, or allowing for automatic updating. A full listing of the vocabularies covered is available on the NLM website.[24] Among the well known vocabularies included are:

- the WHO family of classifications, including ICD-10 and ICF
- MeSH
- SNOMED
- Read Codes (formerly used in clinical coding in the USA)
- relevant Library of Congress Subject Headings
- the MedDRA regulatory vocabulary
- medicines classifications, including RxNorm and the US pharmacopoeia
- vocabularies for adverse effects of drugs, including WHOART and COSTART
- a variety of thesauri in diverse subject areas, including alcohol abuse, osteopathy and psychology.

This is certainly the most sophisticated and extensive healthcare meta-vocabulary so far devised. It is unlikely that any others will be created to duplicate or compete with it, given the effort involved, so that it is likely to gain wider use in future. At present it is freely available to system developers and is used mainly in support of the NLM's database systems.

For an analysis of current and future use of UMLS, see Chen, Perl, Geller and Cimino (2007). For accounts of various aspects of the creation of UMLS, and issues of structure and meaning involved, see Mougin, Bodenreider and Burgun (2009); Fung, Hole, Nelson, Srinvasan, Powell and Roth (2005); and Perl and Geller (2003).

Abstracting and indexing of healthcare information

Access to healthcare information depends to a great extent on the processes of abstracting or summarizing and of indexing or coding. Even in an age when full-text searching has become readily available, particularly through search engines like Google, these more traditional approaches retain their place.

Much effort has been put into devising approaches for automatic, or at least computer-assisted, abstracting and indexing, but these have not yet gained sufficient quality and reliability to displace the expert human for these purposes (see Neveol, Rogozan and Darmoni, 2006 for a typical example of semi-automatic indexing of healthcare information, and Roberts and Souter, 2000 for an account of the possibility of fully automatic healthcare indexing, and the problems encountered).

Abstracting

The writing of abstracts or summaries of documents, typically books, articles and reports, to make it easier for users to become aware of them, to assess their possible value and to save time in appreciating their contents, has a very long history, going back to antiquity (Borko and Lerner, 1975). For healthcare, the 19th century saw the start of specific abstracting services. The Index Medicus abstracting service commenced in 1879, and this is often taken as the starting point. Borko and Lerner (1975) and Sutherland and Jenkins (1992) remind us that this was preceded by the abstracts in the *American Medical Intelligencer* from 1837, and in *Braithwaite's Retrospective of Practical Medicine and Surgery* from 1840. Abstracts are now ubiquitous – in articles and reports, in specifically designed abstracting and indexing services such as Medline, and in many other forms of information service. They still appear, though not as commonly as they once did, as sections in medical journals; the *British Medical Journal*, for example, published an abstract section as the 'Epitome of Current Medical Literature' from 1892 until 1939. The best source of information on all aspects of abstracting is Lancaster (2003).

Various types of abstracts have been recognized. For the healthcare setting, the significant types are:

- indicative: succinct, and aiming simply to alert the reader to the content of the item
- informative: longer, and aiming to inform the reader in some detail of the content, and perhaps acting as a surrogate for the original
- critical: again longer, and adding the abstracter's evaluation and opinions of the original, and thereby going beyond it.

Sometimes another type is recognized – the mini-abstract or telegraphic abstract, created by taking extracts from the original. This type of abstract is the easiest to create automatically. It is related to the idea of an 'extract', a short piece of text which incorporates the essence of the original. A variant of this, specific to the healthcare setting, is a synopsis of an original 'professional' article or report for the benefit of a lay audience. An example is the use of 'plain language summaries' in the Cochrane database of systematic reviews. These are short summaries of the review's main findings, using the minimum of technical or specialist terminology.

Abstracts usually aim to report the original as accurately as possible, reporting the content without comment and retaining the balance of importance of the matters discussed in the original. Critical abstracts are the exception; here the abstracter may introduce new ideas not in the original.

The 'balance' aspect may also be avoided in abstracts targeted for a particular readership. A writer of abstracts for a pharmaceutical company's information service, for example, will certainly give emphasis to that company's products, even if they were only mentioned in passing in the original.

Lancaster (2003) gives examples of all these kinds of abstracts. All have been used at some time in the healthcare domain, reflecting the perceived importance of abstracts as a way of handling the great numbers of documents produced.

Abstracts may be written by an abstracter (who is typically also an indexer) who is contributing to the creation of an information service, either publicly available or for use within an organization. More commonly, however, they are written by the author of the original document and used with little, if any, modification in an abstract database. Authors, lacking the training and perhaps a professional abstracter's appreciation of the qualities of a good abstract, may be less likely to produce consistently useful abstracts. Buschlauer (1995), in a comparative genre analysis of abstracts in medical journals, identified particular problems when author abstracts had been translated between languages.

To overcome the problems of inconsistency of abstracts, there is an increasing tendency for them to be structured, that is to say, written to a consistent format, with certain elements (e.g. purpose of study, methods and their limitations, results, implications for practice) required. The general consensus from studies is that this increases readability and comprehension, and encourages abstracters to include all relevant material. (For comments on structured abstracts for healthcare material, see Booth and O'Rourke, 1997; O'Rourke, 1997; Nakayama, Hirai, Yamazaki and Naito, 2005; Hartley, 2004.)

The convenience of abstracts, and their value in saving time, cannot be doubted. There is an increasing tendency for professional and academic users of health information users to rely on abstracts, at the expense of studying the original documents. This may be unwise if decisions are to be taken on the basis of the information in the abstracts. Numerous studies have shown that abstract contents do not always faithfully reflect the original. They may omit relevant information, and may give an impression of the content of the original which is misleading or downright contradictory. In particular, negative or inconclusive findings are often downplayed in abstracts. For examples relating specifically to healthcare, see Harris, Standard, Brunning, Casey, Goldberg, Oliver, Ito and Marshall (2002) and Smith, Dunstone, and Elliott-Rudder (2009), both of which found significantly misleading material in about one-third of items, and Ward, Kendrach and Price (2004), who found 60% of a sample of abstracts in seven pharmacy journals to have omissions or inaccuracies.

Indexing

Like abstracting, systematic indexing of healthcare information has a history going back to the 19th century and retains its importance to the present day. The NLM and its forerunners set the standard, with Index Medicus and the Index-Catalogue of the Library of the Surgeon-General's Office (Greenberg and Gallagher, 2009).

Lancaster (2003) is the best source for an authoritative discussion of the issues involved.

The title of the British Standard on indexing (BS6529), *Recommendations for Examining Documents, Determining their Subjects and Selecting Indexing Terms*, neatly summarizes the indexing process. First the document must be examined and its contents understood (requiring some subject expertise). Then the 'aboutness' of the document must be determined so as to decide which concepts are to be indexed (again requiring subject expertise, as well as an understanding of the purpose of the index and the needs of its users). Finally, the terms to describe these concepts must be chosen; in the case of healthcare, probably from the sorts of vocabularies discussed above. The influence of widely known vocabularies, particularly Medline, affects much health information indexing practice (McGregor, 2002; Jones, 1994). The process of clinical coding, discussed above, is essentially the same, except that here the documents are records of episodes of patient care.

Indexing is clearly an intellectual process, demanding human expertise. Much ink has been spilt in pursuing the sterile argument as to whether human indexing, using a controlled vocabulary, or full-text searching is 'better'. The answer, that the two are complementary, seems rather self-evident. Hence, human indexing, at least for what is regarded as crucial information resources, has survived into the 21st century despite many predictions to the contrary. In the healthcare area the most obvious examples are the abstracting and indexing services, the indexes to individual journals (see, for example, Jones, 1994), and the many internet resource directories, as well as the coding functions within health services.

Indexing principles are the same in all these cases. The principles and practice of the indexing of healthcare material in particular are set out from an American perspective by Whyman (1999), and from a British perspective by Blake, Clarke, McCarthy and Morrison (2002). Specific issues are noted in the indexing of pharmaceutical information by Bawden and Robinson (2010), of systematic review articles by Wilczynski and Haynes (2009), and of the pharmacology literature by Barber, Moffat, Wood and Bawden (1988). Lancaster's (2003) overview also includes numerous examples of medical literature indexing.

The indexing process in healthcare is not without its problems, of course. We noted earlier the concerns about demonstrated inconsistencies in clinical coding. Many studies, most particularly Lancaster's series of studies of Medline indexing, have shown that consistency in the indexing of bibliographic material is equally difficult to obtain (Lancaster, 2003, chapter 5). Of course, the counter-argument is often made that human indexers are consistent in their treatment of the most significant aspects of a document, and that it is at the margins of importance where inconsistency can appear.

Conclusion

Healthcare has a diverse range of controlled vocabularies for organizing its information resources. This diversity will not disappear, but it is likely that there will be some consolidation, due to the clear advantages of consistency and the resource implications of providing many alternative, or local, vocabularies.

The vocabularies which seem certain to retain and perhaps increase in their importance are: MeSH, SNOMED, ICD-10 and possibly the NLM classification scheme. Relatively small thesauri and taxonomies for specific purposes are also likely to thrive.

Health information professionals need, for obvious reasons, to be familiar with those vocabularies that are relevant to their activities. They may also be involved in indexing and abstracting, traditional activities which show no signs of disappearing.

But more than this, there is an opportunity for them to contribute to the development of the discipline, by taking part in the construction and modification of vocabularies and evaluating their adequacy. These are tasks in which the information practitioner can make a valuable contribution, as has been shown particularly in the healthcare area. The major vocabularies are maintained by large groups of people, often with international advisory boards to guide them, and it is unlikely that anyone would seek to create an alternative to these, But the construction of taxonomies and thesauri for specific contexts, to complement the well-established vocabularies for particular purposes, is a task well within the capabilities of individuals or small groups. An example is the concise medical taxonomy developed by the American Medical Association to improve access to material on its websites (McGregor, 2005).

Notes

1 NHS Connecting for Health, Frequently asked questions on classifications and coding, www.connectingforhealth.nhs.uk/systemsandservices/data/clinicalcoding/codingadvice/faqs.
2 www.nlm.nih.gov/medlineplus/mplusdictionary.html.
3 www.stedmans.com/product.cfm/570.
4 http://users.ugent.be/~rvdstich/eugloss/welcome.html.
5 www.swimsnetwork.nhs.uk/modules/cataloguing/wessex/classification.htm.
6 www.who.int/classifications/icd/en.
7 www.who.int/classifications/en.
8 www.who.int/classifications/icf/en.
9 www.connectingforhealth.nhs.uk/systemsandservices/data/clinicalcoding/codingstandards/opcs4.
10 www.dimdi.de/static/en/klassi/prozeduren/ops301.
11 www.ic.nhs.uk/services/the-casemix-service/new-to-this-service/what-are-healthcare-resource-groups-hrgs.
12 www.ithsdo.org.snomed-ct.
13 www.connectingforhealth.nhs.uk/systemsandservices/data/snomed.
14 http://terminology.vetmed.vt.edu/SCT/menu.cfm.
15 www.umc-products.com.
16 www.esd.org.uk/standards/ipsv.
17 http://bnf.org (registration required).
18 www.nlm.nih.gov/mesh.
19 www.pharm-line.nhs.uk/htmlthesaurus.
20 www.nphl.nhs.uk
21 www.mchthesaurus.info.
22 www.mchlibrary.info/databases/about_databases.html.
23 www.nlm.nih.gov/research/umls. For introductory information, www.nlm.nih.gov/pubs/factsheets/umls.html; for an online tutorial, www.nlm.nih.gov/research/umls/online_learning/index.htm.
24 www.nlm.nih.gov/research/umls/metaa1.html.

References

Aitchison, J., Gilchrist, A. and Bawden, D. (2000) *Thesaurus Construction and Use: a practical manual*, 4th edn, Aslib.
Andrews, J. E., Richesson, R. L. and Krischer, J. (2007) Variation of

SNOMED CT Coding of Clinical Research Concepts Among Coding Experts, *Journal of the American Medical Informatics Association*, 14 (4), 497–506.

Barber, J., Moffat, S., Wood, F. and Bawden, D. (1988) Case Studies of the Indexing and Retrieval of Pharmacology Papers, *Information Processing and Management*, **24** (2), 141–50.

Bawden, D. and Robinson, L. (2010) Pharmaceutical Information: a 30-year perspective on the literature, *Annual Reviews of Information Science and Technology*, in press.

Beghtol, C. (2004) Exploring New Approaches to the Organization of Knowledge: the subject classification of James Duff Brown, *Library Trends*, **52** (4), 702–18.

Blake, D., Clarke, M., McCarthy, A. and Morrison, J. (2002) *Indexing the Medical Sciences*, 2nd edn, Society of Indexers.

Booth, A. and O'Rourke, A. J. (1997) The Value of Structured Abstracts in Information Retrieval from MEDLINE, *Health Libraries Review*, 14 (3), 157–66.

Borko, H. and Lerner, C. L. (1975) *Abstracting Concepts and Methods*, Academic Press.

Bowker, G. C. and Star, S. L. (2000a), *Sorting Things Out: classification and its consequences*, MIT Press.

Bowker, G. C. and Star, S. L. (2000b), The ICD as an Information Infrastructure. In Bowker, G. C. and Star, S. L., *Sorting Things Out: classification and its consequences*, MIT Press, 107–34.

Bowman, J. (2005) *Essential Dewey*, Facet Publishing.

Bremner, A. (2001) Introducing Open University Health Studies Students to Internet Resources, *Health Information and Libraries Journal*, **18** (1), 57–9.

Broughton, V. (2005) *Essential Classification*, Facet Publishing.

Broughton, V. (2006) *Essential Thesaurus Construction*, Facet Publishing.

Buschlauer, I. A. (1995) Abstracts in German Medical Journals – a linguistic analysis, *Information Processing and Management*, **31** (5), 769–76.

Chan, L. M. (2007) National Library of Medicine Classification and Other Modern Classification schemes. In Chan, L. M., *Cataloguing and Classification: an introduction*, 3rd edn, Scarecrow Press.

Chen, Y., Perl, Y., Geller, J. and Cimino, J. J. (2007) Analysis of a Study of the Users, Uses, and Future Agenda of the UMLS, *Journal of the American Medical Informatics Association*, 14 (2), 221–31.

Chowdhury, G. G. and Chowdhury, S. (2007) *Organizing Information: from the shelf to the web*, Facet Publishing.

Cimino, J. J. (1998) Desiderata for Controlled Medical Vocabularies in the Twenty-First Century, *Methods of Information in Medicine*, **37**, 394–403.

Connaway, L. S. and Sievert, M. C. (1996) Comparison of Three Classification Systems for Information on Health Insurance, *Cataloguing and Classification Quarterly*, **23** (2), 89–104.

Connecting for Health (2007) SNOMED CT – the language of the NHS Care Records Service, available from www.connectingforhealth.nhs.uk/systemsandservices/data/snomed/snomed-ct.pdf.

Doyle, K. and Dimitropoulos, V. (2009) Keeping our Classifications Up to Date, *Health Information Management Journal*, **38** (1), 50–2.

Fung, K. W., Hole, W. T., Nelson, S. J., Srinivasan, S., Powell, T. and Roth, L. (2005) Integrating SNOMED into the UMLS: an exploration of different views of synonomy and quality of editing, *Journal of the American Medical Informatics Association*, **12** (4), 486–94.

Gardner, M. (2003) Why Clinical Information Standards Matter, *British Medical Journal*, **326** (7399), 1101–12.

Gilchrist, A. (2003) Thesauri, Taxonomies and Ontologies – an etymological note, *Journal of Documentation*, **59** (1), 7–18.

Glanville, V. J. (1981) A Classification for Medical and Veterinary Libraries by C. C. Barnard, *Aslib Proceedings*, **33** (4), 177–81.

Greenberg, S. J. and Gallagher, P. E. (2009) The Great Contribution: Index Medicus, Index-Catalogue and IndexCat, *Journal of the Medical Library Association*, **97** (2), 108–13.

Harris, A. H. S., Standard, S., Brunning, J. L., Casey, S. L., Goldberg, J. H., Oliver, L., Ito, K. and Marshall, J. M. (2002) The Accuracy of Abstracts in Psychology Journals, *Journal of Psychology*, **136** (2), 141–48.

Hartley, J. (2004) Current Findings from Research on Structured Abstracts, *Journal of the Medical Library Association*, **92** (3), 368–71.

Hjørland, B. (2003) Fundamentals of Knowledge Organization, *Knowledge Organization*, **30** (2), 87–111.

Jacob, E. K. (2003) Ontologies and the Semantic Web, *Bulletin of the American Society for Information Science and Technology*, **29** (4), 19–22, available from www.asis.org/Bulletin/Apr-03/jacob.html.

Jones, R. (1994) Indexing the British Medical Journal, *The Indexer*, **19** (1), 13–18.

Lancaster, F. W. (2003) *Indexing and Abstracting in Theory and Practice*, 3rd edn, Facet Publishing.

Lopez-Mertz, E. M. (1997) The Adequacy of the Structure of the National Library of Medicine Classification Scheme for Organizing Pharmacy

Literature, *Library Resources and Technical Services*, 41 (2), 123–35.

McGregor, B. (2002) Medical Indexing Outside the National Library of Medicine, *Journal of the Medical Library Association*, 90 (3), 339–41.

McGregor, B. (2005) Constructing a Concise Medical Taxonomy, *Journal of the Medical Library Association*, 93 (1), 121–3.

McIlwaine, I. C. (1995) UDC Centenary: the present state and future prospects, *Knowledge Organization*, 22 (2), 64–9.

Mougin, F., Bodenreider, O. and Burgun, A. (2009) Analyzing Polysemous Concepts from a Clinical Perspective: application to auditing concept categorization in the UMLS, *Journal of Biomedical Informatics*, 42 (2), 440–51.

Mitra, I., Malik, T., Homer, J. J. and Loughran, S. (2009) Audit of Clinical Coding of Major Head and Neck Operations, *Annals of the Royal College of Surgeons of England*, 91 (3), 245–8.

Nakayama, T., Hirai, N., Yamazaki, S. and Naito, M (2005) Adoption of Structured Abstracts by General Medical Journals and Format for a Structured Abstract, *Journal of the Medical Library Association*, 93 (2), 237–42.

Neveol, A., Rogozan, A. and Darmoni, S. (2006) Automatic Indexing of Online Health Resources for a French Quality Controlled Gateway, *Information Processing and Management*, 42 (3), 695–709.

O'Rourke, A. J. (1997) Structured Abstracts in Information Retrieval from Biomedical Databases: a literature survey, *Health Informatics Journal*, 3 (1), 17–20.

Perl, Y. and Geller, J. (2003) Research on Structural Issues of the UMLS – past, present and future, *Journal of Biomedical Informatics*, 36 (6), 409–13.

Reid, B. and Sutch, S. (2008) Comparing Diagnosis-related Group Systems to Identify Design Improvements, *Health Policy*, 87 (1), 82–91.

Richesson, R. L., Fung, K.W. and Krischer, J.P. (2008), Heterogeneous but 'Standard' Coding Systems for Adverse Events: issues in achieving interoperability between apples and oranges, *Contemporary Clinical Trials*, 29 (5), 635-45.

Roberts, D. and Souter, C. (2000) The Automation of Controlled Vocabulary Subject Indexing of Medical Journal Articles, *Aslib Proceedings*, 52 (10), 384–401.

Ryder, J. (2002) *Directory of Health Library and Information Services in the UK and the Republic of Ireland 2002–03*, 11th edn, Library Association Publishing.

Satija, M. P. (2007) *The Theory and Practice of the Dewey Decimal Classification*

System, Chandos.

Schultz, M. (2006) Mapping of Medical Acronyms and Initialisms to Medical Subject Headings (MeSH) Across Selected Systems, *Journal of the Medical Library Association*, **94** (4), 410–14.

Slavic, A., Cordeiro, M. I. and Riesthuis, G. (2008) Maintenance of the Universal Decimal Classification: overview of the past and preparation for the future, *International Cataloguing and Bibliographical Control*, **37** (2), 23–9.

Smith, J., Dunstone, M. and Elliott-Rudder, M. (2009) Health Professional Knowledge of Breastfeeding: are the health risks of infant formula feeding accurately conveyed by the titles and abstracts of journal articles?, *Journal of Human Lactation*, **25** (3), 350–8.

Sutherland, F. M. and Jenkins, S. R. (1992) Indexes, Abstracts, Bibliographies and Reviews. In Morton, L and Godbolt, S. (eds), *Information sources in the medical sciences*, Bowker Saur, 43–66.

Svenonious, E. (2000) *The Intellectual Foundation of Information Organization*, MIT Press.

Swanson, D. R., Smalheiser, N. R. and Torvik, V. I. (2006) Ranking Indirect Connections in Literature-based Discovery: the role of medical subject headings, *Journal of the American Society for Information Science and Technology*, **57** (11), 1427–39.

Tatham, A. (2008) The Increasing Importance of Clinical Coding, *British Journal of Hospital Medicine*, **69** (7), 372–3.

Taylor, A. G. (2004) *The Organization of Information*, 2nd edn, Libraries Unlimited.

Taylor, P. (2006) Clinical terms. In Taylor, P. *From Patient Data to Medical Knowledge: the principles and practice of health informatics*, Blackwell/BMJ, 98–121.

Ward, L. G., Kendrach, M. G. and Price, S. O. (2004) Accuracy of Abstracts for Original Research Articles in Pharmacy Journals, *Annals of Pharmacotherapy*, **38** (7/8), 1173–7.

Whyman, L. P. (ed.) (1999) *Indexing Specialities: medicine*, Information Today.

Wilczynski, N. L. and Haynes, R. B. (2009) Consistency an Accuracy of Indexing Systematic Review Articles and Meta-analyses in MEDLINE, *Health Libraries and Information Journal*, **26** (3), 203–10.

Womack, K. R. (2006) Conformity for Conformity's Sake? – the choice of a classification system and a subject heading system in academic health sciences libraries, *Cataloguing and Classification Quarterly*, **42** (1), 93–115.

Zeng, M. L. and Qin, J. (2008) *Metadata*, Facet Publishing.

Further reading

Bowker, G. C. (2005) *Memory Practices in the Sciences*, MIT Press.

Bowker, G. C. and Star, S. L. (2000) *Sorting Things Out: classification and its consequences*, MIT Press.

Taylor, P. (2006) *From Patient Data to Medical Knowledge: the principles and practice of health informatics*, Blackwell/BMJ, part 2.

Detailed information about coding and vocabularies in the UK health services from:

NHS Classifications Service, www.connectingforhealth.nhs.uk/systemsandservices/data/clinicalcoding.

NHS Terminology Service, www.connectingforhealth.nhs.uk/systemsandservices/data/terminology.

5

Healthcare information sources, services and retrieval

Introduction

Healthcare information resources are diverse and very numerous. It is therefore not possible to give anything approaching a complete list here, nor to produce a list of the 'best' resources, since healthcare is a dynamic domain and its resources change over time.

The nature of guides to healthcare resources has also changed as the extent and diversity of these resources has increased, as is clearly shown by the multi-edition series of guides edited by Leslie Morton. In the first edition (Morton, 1974), the editor's statement was that:

> The book attempts to provide a comprehensive guide to the general and
> specialized literature covering the medical sciences . . . limitations of space have
> not permitted a separate chapter for every branch of medicine, but readers will
> find that several of the contributors have covered their subjects very broadly.

By the fourth edition (Morton and Godbolt, 1992), the attempt at comprehensive coverage had been abandoned:

> This book is intended to serve as an evaluative guide to the most important
> sources of information that each contributor has recommended from experience
> of the subject, rather than as a directory of sources.

Morton and Godbolt's 1992 guide was the last of its kind. Since then, guides either have been restricted to specific subjects within healthcare, for example Snow's (2008) guide to pharmacy resources, or have been devoted to finding knowledge for evidence-based practice, for example De Brún and Pearce-Smith's (2009) 'toolkit'. These latter may emphasize analysis and evaluation of information as much as, or more than, resources (see, for example, Guyatt, Rennie, Meade and Cook, 2008).

Morton and Goldbolt's book stands as an excellent and thorough account of the information sources in healthcare and the health sciences just before the advent of the internet, which has been one of the major drivers for change. It is still worth consulting, to get an understanding of the nature of the 'traditional' sources in the domain.

Since it is not possible to enumerate all resources, or the 'best' resources, we will focus here on an explanation of the types of resources available and their purpose, value and significance, giving examples for each. The examples will sometimes be the best known or most widely used, of their kind, but often will just be 'typical' examples.

A framework is needed to structure the explanation of this complex set of resources. Four typologies of materials have commonly been used, either alone or in combination, to describe scientific and medical resources:

- by subject, e.g. 'communicable diseases'
- by format, e.g. 'podcasts'
- by location, e.g. 'North America'
- by type of material, e.g. 'systematic reviews'.

While all are useful in some respects, the last, organizing by type of material, is the best overall way of arranging a guide to healthcare resources, and will be used here. A fourfold framework is used for categorizing resources according to type and purpose of material, loosely based on Robinson (2000), and denoting resources as:

- primary: the 'original information'
- secondary: value-added information, from some organization of primary material
- tertiary: materials pointing to, and aiding the use of, primary and secondary materials
- quaternary: giving access to resource listings at a higher level, essentially, 'lists of lists'.

It is possible also to consider 'zeroth' order information, raw information before it enters the communication chain, for example, the output from laboratory instruments. While such information is certainly vital in scientific and clinical investigations, it is not discussed here because it does not constitute a generally available resource. The internet even offers quintenary resources: 'lists of lists of lists'. These higher-level resources are not usually subject specific in any way, so are not included here.

Primary sources

These are the original sources of information, in whatever form of documents (understood very loosely) they occur. We will consider them under the following 12 headings:

* journal articles
* meetings proceedings and abstracts
* theses and dissertations
* reports
* patents
* healthcare news sources
* legislation, regulations and standards
* information on individuals, organizations and products
* personal messages and sharing of experience
* training materials
* local documents
* unconventional documents.

Journal articles

An academic or professional journal is usually understood as a publication which appears in individual issues at regular intervals, each issue containing a number of independent articles, and the whole intended to be preserved indefinitely as a record of knowledge in the subject area. Healthcare journals can be found on a spectrum from the scientific and research-based journals, through journals for the practitioner, to less formal and more news-oriented publications which might be better referred to as newsletters. Those at the 'academic' end are usually international in scope. Those aimed at the practitioner may also be international, particularly if they deal with a specialist area of practice, or may be national, while the 'newsletter' style of publication is typically national, regional or local.

It has usually been assumed that journals of medicine and of the basic biomedical sciences publish research studies, while other healthcare journals publish largely practical advice and experience. There has been a trend since around the year 2000 for the journals of other healthcare professions, particularly nursing, also to focus on research (see, for example, Oermann, Nordstrom, Wilmes, Denison, Webb, Featherstone, Bednarz, Striz, Blair and Kowalewski, 2008; Mantzoukas, 2009).

Although it is presumed that the most recent journal literature is always the most heavily used, studies have demonstrated the 'long tail' effect, by which older journal material contributes a good deal to total use, particularly when this is made easier through digital access (see, for example, Starr and Williams, 2008).

The professional journal still retains a very important place in the healthcare communication chain. Medicine, and health generally, were among the first subjects to adopt the scientific journal format. They remain among the subjects with the largest number of journal titles and healthcare professionals are still very active readers of journals. There has been remarkably little change in the overall purpose and structure of journals over the years. The steadily increasing number of journal titles has been a constant factor since the 19th century, as the increased specialization within healthcare leads each section of a sub-discipline to want 'its own' journal.

E-journals

Other changes in healthcare journal access have resulted from technical advances. The great majority of the academic and scientific styles of journal now have an electronic format alongside print, and an increasing number are electronic only. Most large healthcare libraries, at least in Europe and the USA, have moved to predominantly, if not wholly, to electronic journal provision. Local practitioner journals and newsletters have tended to retain their printed format, especially in parts of the world where computer access is not widespread; we may see a migration of such journals to web formats in the near future. It is also increasingly common for journal access to be arranged through subscription to an e-journal 'bundle', rather than by subscription to individual titles. E-journal contents can also be provided via mobile devices (for early examples using personal digital assistant (PDA) devices, see Cuddy, 2006). Producing a journal in digital format also means that it is possible to publish 'supplementary material' – typically voluminous data tables – which in a print environment would have to be labelled as 'available from the author', leaving the reader having to make contact to obtain them.

With the move to e-journal formats has come the possibility of offering journals in so-called 'open access' form: free to use with subscription, the costs being borne by authors or sponsors. The best known of these are the 200 open access biomedical journals published by the BioMed Central online publisher (www.biomedcentral.com). Articles published in 'paid for' journals may also be 'self-archived' by their authors in a repository, usually maintained by a university or research institution, and will then be freely available.

E-publication also means that articles can be made available immediately they have been accepted by the journal, rather than having to wait for compilation into one of the journal's regular issues. An example is the *British Medical Journal*'s 'Online First', which also allows more detail to appear than in the final, printed version (www.bmj.com/onlinefirst). These developments mean that, following some early experiments, there is no well-established 'preprint exchange' system, as there has been in subjects such as physics (for an overview of these issues, see Pinfield, 2009).

Quantity of titles published

The number of healthcare periodicals is impossible to measure accurately, but some attempt can be made. Ulrich's *Periodicals Directory* is the single most comprehensive listing of journals, conference proceedings series and similar publications. It categorizes periodicals into overlapping subjects, so that any title may come under one or several subjects. Using data from September 2009, we find 24,097 titles listed for 'Medical Sciences'. Within this can be identified a large number of sub-categories. 'Nurses and Nursing' is the largest, with 1212 titles, while 'Oncology' has 1031. The others can be counted in the hundreds, as illustrated by these examples:

Obstetrics and gynaecology	819
Pediatrics	799
Radiology and nuclear medicine	677
Opthalmology	602
Endocrinology	569
Allergology and Immunology	521
Experimental medicine, laboratory techniques	515
Gastroenterology	417
Physical medicine and rehabilitation	398
Respiratory diseases	355
Anaesthesiology	236

Rheumatology	231
Forensic sciences	172

There are other relevant subject categories which may overlap with 'Medical Sciences', but which have 'extra' journals not included in that category, for example:

Psychology	3258
Pharmacy and pharmacology	2729
Gerontology and geriatrics	1956
Nutrition and dietetics	973
Occupational health and safety	834
Alternative medicine	478
Physiology	455

The number of healthcare-related journals in Ulrich can be estimated at between 20,000 and 30,000. We can compare this with Duckitt's (1991) estimate that a reasonable figure for the number of journals needed to encompass the medical and biological interests of the pharmaceutical industry was about 10,000. The pharmaceutical industry is not interested in all aspects of healthcare, and the journal literature has grown considerably in the intervening 20 years, so these estimates seem in accord. We can also compare this estimate with the collections of the largest medical library in the world. The NLM in Washington, DC, had a collection of 20,901 active journals as of September 2009. It is therefore reasonable to conclude that the current number of active healthcare journals is somewhere around 25,000.

Healthcare library collections

Of course, no healthcare library, other than NLM, will approach having anything like this number. Based on data from their websites in September 2009, these are the approximate healthcare journal collection figures for some major healthcare libraries:

German National Library of Medicine	7800
Johns Hopkins University, USA	5000
Duke University Medical Library, USA	4400
Mayo Clinical Medical School, USA	4300
Harvard Medical Schools, USA	3500

Royal Society of Medicine, UK	1300
Cambridge University, UK	1000
University of Queensland, Australia	1000

It seems that somewhere between 1000 and 5000 journals form the basis of the collection of most major healthcare libraries. Similarly, about 5000 journals are indexed for the Medline/PubMed database.

This seeming limitation in size of journal collections reflects the well known concept that, out of a large number of active journals in any subject area, a 'core' or important or significant titles can be identified. For example, although Ulrich lists nearly 3000 titles in the pharmacy and pharmacology area, it has been suggested that there is a core of about 300 significant journals (Bawden and Robinson, 2010). And while Ulrich lists 1200 nursing titles, the ISI journal collection, which focuses on 'high impact' journals, lists 58 in this area.

Many smaller healthcare libraries have to manage with considerably smaller journal collections, with typically between 100 and 300 journals. The so-called Brandon-Hill list was a list of recommended books and journals for the small (American) medical library, updated biannually for 38 years; the final listing, in 2003, recommended a set of 141 journals, categorized into 46 specialities, with 59 selected as particularly important and for 'initial purchase'. An equivalent list for nursing, last produced in 2002, listed 86 journals, with 35 for initial purchase. A listing for allied health professions, again last published in 2002, contained 79 journals, with 32 for initial purchase. Details of this significant innovation in healthcare collection management, with details of the lists, are provided by Brandon-Hill[1]; although the details are dated, the concept is still of relevance. An international equivalent, a 'core collection of medical books and journals', known as the Hague list and last produced in 2001, listed 249 journals. Lists of this kind are used to create bundles of high-impact journals, such as Ovid's 'Premier International', which is explicitly based on the Brandon-Hill and Hague listings.

Identifying 'cores within cores', we can note that there are a few journals in all aspects of healthcare which are recognized internationally as the 'top' journals. For medicine, for example, these are usually regarded as *Lancet*, the *New England Journal of Medicine* and the *Journal of the American Medical Association*. This gives an interesting 'scale' of numbers of journals:

'Top' journals	2–5
Small library collection	100–300
Large library collections	1000–5000
Total published	about 25,000

This is not to suggest that journals outside the 'cores', however defined, are of no importance; they may be very significant locally, or to a particular group of practitioners or researchers. A study of Croatian doctors, for example, showed that they considered national journals more important for supporting medical practice than international journals (Sambunjak, Huic, Hren Katic, Marusic and Marusic, 2009).

Categorized lists of healthcare journals can be found on the websites of libraries such as those noted above, from healthcare information providers such as Ovid,[2] and from commercial sites such as medical-journals.com.

As a contrast to the statistics, and for a personal and controversial view of medical journals and their role in the communication of health information, see Richard Smith's 'The trouble with medical journals' (2006).

Meetings proceedings and abstracts

Scientific and clinical meetings are an important source of information, since it is often at such meetings and congresses that new information is announced for the first time, particularly for topics such as results of clinical trials of new medicines. As a source of information, however, although valuable, the information is somewhat difficult to handle (Illig, 2008; Kelly, 1998). The content may be offered in the form of abstracts or of full papers. It may or may not be circulated previously, in the form of meeting preprints; may or may not appear on the website of the relevant meeting or of the sponsoring organization; and may or may not be published subsequently in the journal literature (Scherer, Langenberg and von Elm, 2007). Material for major meetings will be included in the major disciplinary databases such as EMBASE, Cumulative Index to Nursing and Allied Health Literature (CINAHL), Chemical Abstracts and Biological Abstracts. BMC Proceedings, one of the BioMed Central (BMC) open access databases, specializes in publishing biomedical conference papers and abstracts. Some commercial information providers specialize in providing meetings abstracts; examples are Medscape[3] and various pharmaceutical 'drug pipeline' databases, such as Investigational Drugs database (IDdb) Meeting Reports (Snow, 2008). Identifying and accessing such material is likely to be a challenge for the healthcare information specialist.

Theses and dissertations

Rather like conference materials, these are a type of document that has long been recognized as valuable because it may be the form in which information first appears and may include useful detail which is not subsequently published in the journal literature. Like the meetings literature, it is a challenging form of information, since it may only be available from the awarding institution, which may or may not make it readily available. Increasingly, theses and dissertations are included in online catalogues and digital versions are appearing in institutional repositories (see Piorun and Palmer, 2008 for a medical school example). However these can only be useful if the existence of the thesis and the institution are known. This kind of material is included in some disciplinary databases, such as CINAHL and Chemical Abstracts, and in the format-specific Dissertation Abstracts International, which includes theses and dissertations from all academic subject areas.

Reports

The healthcare report literature is extensive and diverse, mirroring the domain as a whole. Publicly accessible reports, together with the meetings materials and theses just discussed, make up what was traditionally termed 'grey literature': publicly available, but not published through formal channels. Like the other forms of grey literature, reports often contain information which cannot be found elsewhere. Institutional reports may be useful sources for analysing trends and issues in the domain; an example is the analysis of 25 years of reports from the Indian National Institute of Occupational Health (Bhatia, Rao and Saiyed, 2006).

Regarded in the past as difficult to find and manage, this sort of literature has been greatly affected by the advent of the web, which provides ready access to much of this material. An example of a healthcare service whose remit includes particular concern for this kind of source is FADE, the library service of the Liverpool healthcare authority, which acts as the grey literature service for health services in the north-west of England.[4]

Reports in the healthcare area may contain scientific, clinical, regulatory, managerial or financial information and may be produced occasionally, regularly, or as parts of report series. They originate from all the information-producing agencies: universities and research institutes, industry, hospitals and other healthcare settings, libraries and information services, consultancies, regulators and government agencies, and healthcare providers.

Some reports, typically but not solely those from industry, will be confidential and will not be publicly available. Others, though not confidential, are produced for in-house purposes and not regarded as of any public interest. While they will not be externally available as information sources, they may be important sources of internal information. The management of such internal sources is an important task for information professionals, including records management, in many healthcare organizations.

Access to reports which are made publicly available is most often achieved through the web, via search engines, since they are usually made available on the websites of the producing organizations. They are not well covered by the disciplinary databases, apart from Chemical Abstracts, although reports sponsored by the US government may be found in the National Technical Information Service (NTIS) database.

Some institutions act as publishers or 'clearing houses' for reports of a particular nature. For example:

- The UK King's Fund has a collection of many thousands of reports relating to health management and planning, and also produces many reports itself.[5]
- The World Health Organization produces numerous reports on public health and epidemiology.[6]
- Bioportfolio is an example of healthcare consultancies providing commercial reports on healthcare research and markets.[7]

The following examples give a flavour of the variety of the healthcare report literature:.

- a series of reports from the Institute of Medicine of the US National Academies on health issues stemming from the 1991 Gulf War[8]
- perceptions of patients and professionals on rheumatoid arthritis care, a consultancy report by the King's Fund for the Rheumatology Futures Group, 2009[9]
- an international comparison of early childhood initiatives: from services to systems, report by the Commonwealth Fund, USA, 2009[10]
- a series of reports on cancer incidence and care in Scotland, from the Scottish health service[11]
- the annual World Health Report from the World Health Organization[12]
- annual reports of the Medical Library at Yale University, USA.[13]

Patents

The patent literature often contains the first announcements of new discoveries or innovations. It may contain detailed information difficult to find elsewhere and is an underutilized resource in the health and life sciences (MacMillan, 2005). In the healthcare domain, patent information is particularly relevant to pharmaceuticals and to medical devices and instruments. This kind of information is of particular importance to researchers, especially in industry, but may also be useful more generally in healthcare libraries to answer a variety of queries, as pointed out by Hogan and Scarborough as long ago as 1996.

Patents information can be found in disciplinary databases such as Chemical Abstracts and Biological Abstracts, and in specific patents databases such as those of Derwent Publications.

Healthcare news sources

Among the drivers for change identified in Chapter 1, several have combined to increase the 'newsworthiness' of the healthcare domain. These include the greater economic and political impact of healthcare systems and the healthcare industry, the increased concern for wellness among the public, and the emphasis on patients and consumers being knowledgeable about their conditions. All these have led to an increased extent of healthcare news coverage, both in sources aimed at the public and in those aimed at health professionals, with a particular increase since the mid-1990s, when the internet joined the factors promoting it.

As an illustration, we might consider local television as the major source of news for most Americans. Studies have shown that 65% of bulletins on these stations include some health items (Pribble, Goldstein Fowler and Greenberg, 2006) and that 10% of all stories are health related (Wang and Ganz, 2007).

Healthcare news for the general public is provided, in addition to television, by radio, newspapers, magazines and, increasingly, the internet. Magazines have been seen for a long time as a particularly influential source of health information, for both men and women (Turner, Vader and Walters, 2008; Graham, Bawden and Nicholas, 1997), while British newspapers have been shown to publish health and medical items in preference any other science-related news (Weitkamp, 2003). One influence of the internet has been to promote the provision of health news through 'mixed media', of which the most obvious example is websites associated with broadcasters, news being integrated with advice and other features. An example is the British

Broadcasting Corporation's (BBC) popular Health service.[14] Examples of the diverse forms of health and medical news resources on the internet are compared by Cunningham (2005).

News items have been shown to have immediate effects on the public's behaviour (see Li, Chapman, Agho and Eastman, 2008 for a study on the effects of an Australian news story about lack of iodine in the diet, and consequent increase in sales of iodized salt). They can have equally immediate effects on the finances of companies in the healthcare industry (see Ewing, Kruse and Thompson, 2005 for a study of the effects on healthcare providers, producers of drugs and supplies and insurance companies in the USA).

There has, of course, been much concern about the accuracy of health material in the news media, the way in which topics are chosen for coverage and the context into which they are put. An editorial in the *New England Journal of Medicine* in 2009 put it bluntly: 'all too frequently, what is conveyed about health by [some] journalists is wrong and misleading' (Dentzer, 2009). Even when not incorrect, the content and format of health news can vary greatly between sources, as illustrated by Guillaume and Bath (2008) for news stories about the MMR vaccine. (For more examples, see Harrabin, Coote and Allen, 2003; Pribble, Goldstein Fowler and Greenberg, 2006; Sankofa and Johnson-Taylor, 2007; and Turner, Vader, and Walters, 2008; and for a thoughtful analysis of why news media often get medical stories wrong, see Barbour, Clark, Peiperl, Veitch, Wong and Yamey, 2008).

Several initiatives have tried to overcome these problems. The UK National Health Service provides a 'Behind the Headlines' service, which aims to offer an unbiased analysis of health news stories, intended for both the general public and health professionals.[15] A similar American initiative, based at the University of Minnesota is HealthNewsReview,[16] while the US National Library of Medicine offers a digest of health-related news, organized by date and by topic.[17]

Professional newsletters

Health professionals are likely to use all of these public news services, but also to have services for professional news. The most familiar of these are the wide variety of professional newsletters and magazines, some edited by professional associations and some provided free by commercial suppliers and funded by advertising. Still largely in paper form, many are now adding a web presence. A typical example is *Pulse*, aimed mainly at British family doctors, and offering a paper newsletter and a variety of e-mail alerts, as well as web-based information.[18]

News alerting services and databases

Given the influence of news items noted above, it is obviously important to be able to identify items quickly. The internet, through search engines, is now the predominant means of identifying news items and for keeping up to date through use of alerting tools such as RSS feeds. There are also many health news sources and databases, often with 'added value' commentary and typically aimed at the healthcare industry, and the pharmaceutical industry in particular (Snow, 2008). Examples are:

- Reuters Health, with sections for health professionals, the healthcare industry and the consumer[19]
- Scrip, primarily aimed at the pharmaceutical industry.[20]

Legislation, regulations and standards

All aspects of healthcare provision, without exception, have formal constraints. From the treatment of experimental animals to the obtaining of consent from patients in clinical trials, from the licensing of medicines to the conduct of medical practitioners, and from the operation of diagnostic equipment to the maintenance of public health, all are controlled by a plethora of laws, regulations, good practice guidelines, protocols and standard operating procedures. These may be specified and operated at international, national, regional or local level.

It is helpful for a healthcare information specialist to have some insight into the nature and complexity of these constraints on healthcare. It is unlikely that any individual could have an understanding of all of them, nor that any information specialist would have an immediate knowledge of where to locate information on all of them. The most that can be expected is an understanding of those constraints affecting their speciality and local situation. (For an introduction to the laws affecting healthcare in Britain, see Brazier and Cave, 2007, and for an insight into the regulation of medicines see Feldschreiber, 2008. For an overview of the kind of clinical guidelines mandated by the UK National Health Service, see the introduction to NHS Evidence's guidelines library.)[21]

The documentation setting out all these constraints and how they are to be applied is voluminous. The advent of the internet has meant that the supporting documentation has mainly moved from print to the web, at least in Europe and North America, so that access to the relevant documents is easier once they have been identified. For examples of the kinds of resources needed to provide access to this voluminous documentation, see:

- NHS Evidence – National Library of Guidelines (clinical guidelines for the UK health services)[22]
- European Medicines Agency regulatory guidance (medicines licensing regulations)[23]
- Food and Drug Administration (USA) Good Clinical Practice (standards for clinical trials)[24]
- UK Nursing and Midwifery council legislation summary (laws governing the practice of nursing and midwifery in the UK)[25]

These sorts of constraint are relevant in another way – standards and guidelines are available for the operation of healthcare libraries and information services, as will be seen in Chapter 6.

Information on individuals, organizations and products

This is another category of information where access has been greatly changed by the internet. Now that most health professionals, and all departments and organizations, at least in the developed world, have a web presence, this is the natural way to find information about them. Information about organizations, including company reports and financial data, and about individuals is now widely available through corporate and personal websites, replacing the files of paper brochures and contact lists kept in the past by many healthcare information services. Access to such information is generally via a search engine, or one of the numerous directory sources which will be discussed later in this chapter. Product, and 'trade', information is similarly now almost exclusively web-based, with technical manuals and instrumentation operating protocol also in this format.

One kind of healthcare product information is an exception. Patient information leaflets, which must by law be included with medicines, are still provided in paper form. The most appropriate content and format for such leaflets has been much discussed, in one of the longest-running debates in the consumer health area (Bawden and Robinson, 2010).

Personal messages and sharing of experience

In this category come such resources as:

- letters and memoranda

- entries in diaries and blogs
- postings to mailing lists, newsgroups and web forums (largely replaced by blogs)
- e-mail messages and text messages
- entries on social networking sites such as MySpace and Facebook
- instant messages and Twitter messages ('tweets')
- voicemail messages.

With the exception of some, largely historical, paper documents, all these materials are now digital. Some are the digital equivalents of earlier formats, others are quite new. Although most come from individuals, a small proportion – arguably the most useful as information resources – come from institutions and organizations.

Accessing the digital versions is far easier than trying to find such documents on paper. Indeed, apart from records management and archiving activities within an organization, these were rarely available, or indeed thought of, as accessible information resources. In large measure, they have replaced the printed notices of events, library news posters and similar informal paper communications of earlier days.

The digital transition has led to a great volume of such material becoming available, though not necessarily being permanently stored. Much of the information in, for instance, the blogs and Facebook pages being set up by many healthcare library services is likely to be of ephemeral value, and media such as Twitter are even more personal and ephemeral. Twitter messages, for example, typically disappear after about 10 days unless actively archived by the reader, although authors can see their whole timeline.

Users of the 'social internet' do not typically write much substantive health-related material. Nonetheless, there may be very valuable information in such formats, for example, in the 'self-help' forums for particular diseases. In late 2009, 757 Facebook groups were identified, with over 290,000 members, including healthcare professionals as well as patients and carers, devoted to particular diseases and including information on scientific research, as well as educational material and exchange of experiences (Farmer, Bruckner Holt, Cook and Hearing, 2009). Useful detailed information may also be found in professional internet newsgroups, mailing lists and other forums, although these are being slowly replaced by newer media.

Many of these communication media are so new that health information users and information specialists are still assessing the best way to use them. There is also a considerable turn-over in the popularity of media. Web-rings, one of the earliest forms of social networking on the web, have largely fallen out of favour, although a few health-related rings survive (www.webring.com). Conversely, the Second Life virtual environment, created in 2003, was only beginning by 2009 to make a significant impact in health-related areas such as patient education, health promotion, training and so on (Beard, Wilson, Morra and Keelan, 2009). Similarly, Twitter began to be used by medical schools and health libraries in 2009 (Cuddy, 2009).

A few of the many health-related examples of such media are given below, to show the diversity within each format. They are chosen from institutional, rather than personal, sites. Not all institutions, however, are hospitable to such media; in late 2009 many parts of the British health services banned their staff from using Facebook and Twitter, in particular, regarding them as unprofessional communications channels.

Blogs

- Wellcome Library, London (history of medicine collection)[26]
- Medical education blog, University of Saskatchewan[27]
- British Medical Association (Wales)[28]
- Community and District Nursing Association (UK)[29]Journal of the Medical Library Association (JMLA) case studies in health sciences librarianship (Medical Library Association, USA)[30]
- Trust the Evidence blog (Centre for Evidence Based Medicine, UK[31]
- FADE (provision of 'grey literature' for healthcare information, UK).[32]

Facebook pages

- Weill Cornell Medical College Library, USA
- Medical Library Association, USA
- National Institute for Occupational Safety and Health (NIOSH), USA
- Friends of Harefield Hospital, UK
- University of Maryland Medical Center, USA
- Reckefeller Medical Library, Institute of Neurology and National Hospital for Neurology and Neurosurgery, UK.

Twitter

- Shared Twitter feed for medical librarians[33].

Mailing lists

- LIS-MEDICAL (discussion list for UK medical and health library community)[34]
- MIUA (Medical Image Understanding and Analysis, UK-based forum)[35]
- Nurse-philosophy (aims to foster a sense of community among philosophically minded academic nurses).[36]

The value of sharing experiences, for those affected by illness, is well recognized, particularly in helping them to make informed decisions. Some initiatives have aimed to present personal experiences in a structured and reliable way, rather than relying on the partial, anecdotal and possibly inaccurate material obtained from social networking sources. An example is the healthtalkonline site, which presents the experiences of patients and carers, including their involvement in clinical trials, in multimedia formats. The information is based on interviews carried out by health professionals.[37]

Training materials

Support for formal education and training, and then for in-service updating, is an important role for many healthcare libraries and information services. Therefore training materials, to support journals, textbooks and similar training resources, are a significant type of health information source. These come in a variety of formats, including lecture notes, case studies, syllabi, examination papers and other forms of assessment. Video and audio materials and a wide variety of interactive materials are as important as text-based formats. Increasingly, such materials are available in digital form, either stand-alone or within e-learning systems, and hence more readily accessed and shared via the web.

This kind of material will obviously be a major resource in academic healthcare libraries, but is relevant elsewhere because of in-service training needs and because health libraries must increasingly serve both practitioners and students (Dorrington, 2006). There is also an increasing role for information providers in 'patient education', by maintaining collections of information resources for hospital patients or providing patient education tutorials (Siess, 2008), while organizations such as the NLM in the USA have developed interactive tutorials to explain aspects of healthcare information to the public.

Examples of these resources are:

- Harvard-MIT (USA) Division of Health Sciences and Technology Open Courseware, teaching materials from a large number of health and biomedical courses[38]
- Microbiology and Immunology Online, an online multilingual textbook, including audio and video materials, from the University of South Carolina School of Medicine, USA[39]
- Human Physiology, lecture notes from Eastern Kentucky University, USA[40]
- Blue Histology, course notes, including numerous microscope images and multi-choice quizzes, from the University of Western Australia[41]
- Interactive Health Tutorials for patient education, from the NLM, USA[42]
- Medical school instructional videos on a YouTube channel, from St George's Medical School, UK[43]
- Interactive Medical Animations for healthcare education[44]
- examdoctor, revision aids and mock exams, from Royal Society of Medicine, UK[45]
- ToxTown, an interactive tutorial for school students on environmental health issues, from the NLM, USA[46]

Local documents

We have largely focused in this section on healthcare information resources which are publicly accessible, although we noted that many reports were intended only for use within an organization and might indeed be restricted to that setting because of confidentiality or sensitivity of the content. There are various other forms of primary documents which are intended to be created and used solely within the organization.

Research records

In health research settings these will include the primary documentation coming from the research process, both scientific and clinical. Examples are laboratory notebooks and the 'raw' data from clinical trials. These have to be stored carefully for future access, partly because of the detailed information in them, which may never appear in any other form, and partly because they are part of the documentation which regulations such as Good Laboratory Practice and Good Clinical Practice require, and, as such, they have a legal status. Maintaining such documentation is an important information and records management function in all health research organizations.

Notebook-type records that are not 'born digital' are commonly digitized (Bawden and Robinson, 2010; Caporizzo, 2008). The management of clinical trials data is a major undertaking (as an example, see Pon, Nahm, Wakim, Cushing, Poole, Tai and Pieper, 2009), and although library/information professionals are typically not involved, they need to be aware of the nature of such data sources. The raw data from such trials has traditionally been regarded as confidential, and even the results of such trials have often not been available; this situation has been criticized for many years (see, for example, Manheimer and Anderson, 2002), and several initiatives now aim to make this information accessible, for example the clinical trials registry of the US National Institutes of Health (http://clinicaltrials.gov/).

Patient records

Within healthcare settings, the equivalent internal documentation is the case notes and associated clinical data generated in patient care. In some circumstances, typically where the case and its treatment have general lessons, this will appear in anonymised form in the literature. Case reports, individual or in series, usually appearing as journal articles, are a significant part of the healthcare evidence base (Carey, 2006).

Most such documentation, however, is used purely in-house, where it is linked to the patient's medical record and is, of course, a vital resource for ongoing care (Taylor, 2006, chapter 2). The transition of such data from paper to digital form is a major task, generally regarded as beneficial, although the value and the success or otherwise of such initiatives has been a source of controversy in several national health services (see, for example, Ayatollahi, Bath and Goodacre, 2009; Randell, 2007; Uslu and Stausberg, 2008; Williams and Boren, 2008; O'Neill, 2009). The British health services' proposed Care Records Service, initially proposed to be implemented in 2008, has had a particularly troubled history (see, for example, Jones, 2004 and Fisher, 2006).

This type of data is organized according to the clinical coding schemes discussed in Chapter 4. The management of such data is an aspect of healthcare information in which library/information services have not traditionally been involved, though such involvement can be worthwhile (Ewing, 2007; Ellero, 2009). The management of these records will be mentioned again in Chapter 6.

Unconventional documents

Without revisiting the academic debates about what a document is (Frohmann, 2009; Buckland, 1997), we can note that the healthcare domain has collections of items which might not normally be thought of as documents. Nonetheless, they play an important role is supporting education, practice and research, as well as historical study (Suarez and Tsutsui, 2004). They include collections of anatomical specimens, microscope slide specimens, instruments and equipment, photographs and other images, sound and video recordings and so on. All have some documentation associated with them, if only simple labelling. Many such collections are now being digitized to promote their wider use, and increasingly they are being 'born digital' – the most obvious example being the Visible Human projects. They are integrated to varying extents with other healthcare information collections at the sponsoring institutions.

Examples include:

- NLM, USA Visible Human Project, a complete digital representation of human anatomy[47]
- Warren Anatomical Museum (Boston Medical Library and Harvard Medical School) – includes anatomical and pathological specimens, images of different kinds, images, etc.[48]
- Wellcome Images Biomedical Collection, 40,000 images of all kinds from the clinical and biomedical sciences[49]
- MacKinney collection of medieval medical illustrations, University of North Carolina Library, USA, historical resource with all images digitized[50]
- Royal College of Surgeons London, Wellcome Museum, a modern anatomical and pathological teaching collection of physical specimens, slides and X-rays[51]
- Podcasts and videocasts on healthcare topics, compiled in wiki format from the Health Library, University of British Columbia, Canada[52]
- Portraits of historical medical personalities as prints, photographs, engravings, drawing, and cartoons, paper only, with a card catalogue, Royal Society of Medicine, UK[53]
- Digitized collection of photographs of the life of Sir William Osler, 19th-century physician.[54]

There are also collections of materials which may not at first sight seem relevant to healthcare, but which are in fact significant. One such is the plant materials stored in herbaria, which act as the fundamental reference for scientific study and identification of plants which may be of value as sources of medicines. The herbarium at Kew Gardens in London, whose resources are being digitized for worldwide access, is an example.[55]

Another unusual example is the International Ancient Egyptian Mummy Tissue Bank at Manchester Museum (UK), with over 2000 samples, which may be examined pathologically. In conjunction with study of the medical papyri (mentioned in Chapter 2), these samples can yield information about the epidemiology of disease in ancient times. This has proved to be of very practical use, for example in a study of the prevention of schistosomiasis (Lambert-Zazulak, Rutherford and David, 2003; David, 2008).

Secondary sources

These are sources which provide value-added information from some collection, organization and analysis or processing of primary sources. They may point to primary sources – indeed, for some secondary sources, such as abstracting and indexing services, that may be a main purpose – but they will always provide information directly themselves.

This category includes some of the oldest forms of healthcare information provision, such as monographs and encyclopaedias. But it also encompasses some of the newer formats. Frequently asked questions (FAQ) files, ubiquitous in web information services, are a modern format for a classic form of secondary information provision (see, as examples, a report of the effectiveness of an FAQ facility on a website for cancer patients, Coleman, Olsen, Sauter, Baker, Hodgin, Stanfield, Emerling, Hruban and Nolan, 2005; and a study of the use of FAQs for providing information about e-journals in medical school libraries (Lingle, 2004). Wikis, collaboratively written information sources, are similarly a novel technological solution to an old problem: how to enable experts to collaborate in providing validated information (see, as examples, the use of wikis in health science libraries, Lombardo, Mower, and Mcfarland, 2008; in nurse education, Ciesielka, 2008; in public health training, Cobus, 2009).

Most of these sources, with the exception of some which are very clearly and explicitly aimed at consumers and the public in general, are used only by professionals. Their content is certainly relevant to a wider audience, but their style and structuring, as well as the specialist terminology of anatomy, physiology, diseases, medicines, etc. render these sources largely incomprehensible to the general public, as was shown in a study of medical textbooks (Baker and Gollop, 2004).

We will examine secondary sources under the following eight headings:

- textbooks and monographs
- encyclopaedias and comprehensive reference sources
- quick-reference sources and handbooks
- reviews and summaries
- consumer advice services
- abstracting and indexing services
- databanks and statistical compilations
- terminologies and classifications.

The section will end by considering an issue usually associated with secondary resources: searching features and strategies.

Textbooks and monographs

These are among the best established secondary healthcare resources. There is no sharp dividing line between them, as witnessed by common use for reference by healthcare practitioners of the textbooks which served them well during their education. Monographs are typically written for an advanced audience and are generally specialized in topic. Textbooks are typically written for students, but, with a nod to the practitioner audience, often cover wider subject areas and are more likely to include pedagogic devices such as exercises and key learning points.

The printed textbook and monograph is still very much alive and well in the healthcare domain, although e-books have had a significant impact, since their introduction (MacCall, 2006). Like electronic journals, e-books may be ordered separately or acquired in 'bundles' from publishers such as Ovid, Springer and Karger. Some studies suggest that books in electronic format have much greater use than in their printed form, particularly in educational and research settings (see for example, Ugaz and Resnick, 2008).

The 'core collections' recommendations, noted above for journals, also listed books. The 2003 Brandon-Hill list for small medical libraries recommended 672 books in 59 subject categories, with 104 noted as a 'minimal core'. The equivalent figures for the other two lists, both from 2002, were: nursing, 370 books, with 143 for initial purchase; allied health, 434 books, with 169 in the 'core of the core'.[56] The Brandon-Hill and equivalent international Hague listings are no longer current, although their approach is still influential (Ugaz and Resnick, 2008). They have been succeeded by the commercial US-based *Doody's Core Titles*, which similarly recommends core lists, with 'core of the core' essential purchase recommendations.[57]

Although such lists were designed for small libraries, they have value in larger collections: one study showed that items on core lists were used much more than average, suggesting that priority should be given to these core items (Schmidt and Eckerman, 2001). In general, usage of these resources has been shown to follow a Zipfian or 'Vital Few' pattern, with a few sources accounting for a large proportion of use of the collection (see, for example, Eldredge, 1998).

We can contrast these figures for typical small library book collections with those of larger libraries. Apart from truly major collections – the NLM, for example, has 12 million books – most large medical libraries hold around half a million monographs. Typical figures from library websites in late 2009 were:

Yale Medical School, USA	462,000
Harvard Medical School, USA	630,000
Royal Society of Medicine, UK	500,000

Encyclopaedias and comprehensive reference sources

'It must be admitted', wrote Hague in 1992, 'that encyclopaedias are now of little value in the medical field. Even when updated by means of annual supplements, they are unsatisfactory for finding information on particular topics, when compared with other sources, such as textbooks, monographs and reviews.'

The situation has not changed in the intervening years, and the medical or healthcare encyclopaedia, covering the whole of the subject and intended for the professional, is now effectively extinct. This type of comprehensive reference volume is now available only for the consumer audience, where it still enjoys some popularity, in both printed and online formats (now even for mobile devices). Examples include:

- The British health services' interactive 'Health A-Z'[58]
- the A.D.A.M. online Medical Encyclopaedia, included in the NLM's MedlinePlus consumer health system[59]
- the University of Maryland Medical centre online Medical Encyclopaedia, which has a mobile version for the iPhone[60]
- The Royal Society of Medicine's printed *Health Encyclopaedia* (compiled by R. Youngson, published by Bloomsbury, 2nd edn, 2002)

Online reference

The best known and most used encyclopaedia, so far as most of the computer-using public is concerned, is, of course, Wikipedia (for an overview, see O'Sullivan, 2009). There have been many concerns about the quality of information in such an open access source. One study, comparing Wikipedia with a conventional database of drug information, showed that it was largely free of factual errors (these tend to be corrected by other users) but was seriously incomplete (Clauson, Polen, Boulos and Dzenowagis, 2008). Such sources do, however, have a capacity for rapid improvement, and it is clear that Wikipedia has to be counted as a significant source of health information for the consumer (Laurent and Vickers, 2009).

Several professional equivalents of Wikipedia have been created in healthcare areas. The best established is RadiologyWiki (Streeter, Lu and Rybicki, 2007); under development (in late 2009) are WikiSurgery and, covering all of healthcare, Medpedia.[61]

The status of the wiki as an adequate stand-alone resource still seems to be questionable. A suggestion in the *British Medical Journal* that professional wikis could constitute the 'libraries of the future' (Jhetam, 2009) was met by a series of responses in the vein 'libraries are the libraries of the future'.

Printed reference works

For the professional, the encyclopaedia still exists as a multi-volume printed reference work, but on a specialized aspect of healthcare and its science base. A good example is the series published by Academic Press, dealing with medicine and the medical science, and including, among many others:

- *Encyclopaedia of Microbiology*, 6 volumes, 2009
- *Encyclopaedia of Human Nutrition*, 4 volumes, 2008
- *Encyclopaedia of Public Health*, 6 volumes, 2008
- *Encyclopaedia of Endocrine Diseases*, 4 volumes, 2004
- *Encyclopaedia of Forensic and Legal Medicine*, 4 volumes, 2004
- *Desk Encyclopaedia of Human and Medical Virology*, 2009

The 'Desk Encyclopaedias' in this series are one-volume abridgements of multi-volume works.

Similar comprehensive reference sources are the 'medical atlases', effectively visual encyclopaedias in subjects where images are crucial to understanding. Examples are:

- *Atlas of Clinical Gastroenterology*, Mosby, 2004
- *Atlas of Clinical Dermatology*, Churchill Livingstone, 2002

Because of the need for interactive examination of such images, this type of book is typically accompanied by a CD-ROM or a website. It is likely that this sort of resource will move into a fully digital environment; an example is images.MD, an online encyclopaedia of 70,000 medical images consolidated from a variety of published atlases (King, 2009).

Finally, we might note some comprehensive sources which do not seek to provide detailed information so much as a readable overview of a very wide area. The best known of this style of book is the *Oxford Companion to Medicine*, whose latest (2001), edition includes comprehensive ('from abortion to zombification') coverage of the history of medicine, cultural links with music and the arts, international comparisons, and so on.

Quick-reference sources and handbooks

This type of source invariably emerges as among the most used and useful, according to surveys of health information users. Virtually every field of healthcare practice and medical science has its sources of this kind, providing validated and structured facts and figures. They are variously referred to as handbooks, databooks, encyclopaedias (though they are really nothing of the sort, lacking substantial articles), formularies, pharmacopoeias and so on.

Still provided in printed form, often in handy, 'pocket-sized' editions and with a specially robust binding to stand heavy use, they generally now also have a digital version. This latter is usually web-based, but many of the sources are now also provided in forms for mobile devices: PDAs and, increasingly, smart mobile phones. The digital formats have the advantage of rapid updating, although the printed versions are typically updated at least annually, and often more frequently. The few examples given here illustrate the diversity of this kind of resource:

- *Monthly index of Medical Specialities* (MIMS). UK-based commercial source of medicines information. Monthly printed reference book for doctors and pharmacists, with special versions for nurses and other practitioners, plus web resource.[62]
- *Merck Index*. Reference source on chemicals, drugs and biological agents. Printed book, plus CD-ROM and web versions.[63]
- Oxford Handbooks.[64] A series of over 50 pocket handbooks for doctors,

nurses, medical students and specialist trainees, and other health professionals. Some are available for PDAs, and some as subscription e-books, via the Oxford Medical Handbooks Online website. Examples of titles are:

- *Oxford Handbook of Dialysis*
- *Oxford Handbook of Clinical Dentistry*
- *Oxford Handbook of General Practice*
- *Oxford Handbook of Cardiac Nursing*
- *Oxford Specialist Handbook of Hand Surgery*

Reviews and summaries

The knowledge base of healthcare and its supporting sciences is so great, and expanding so rapidly, that it has been recognized for many years that some means is needed to summarizing new findings, to set them into the context of existing knowledge, to explain their significance and to make connections between different parts of the knowledge base.

This is done to some extent by monographs and specialized encyclopaedias. The classic tool for achieving this end has been the review. There are many different types of review: Grant and Booth (2009) identify 14 kinds, just in the context of evidence-based healthcare. But they all share the general characteristics of requiring an initial collection of relevant information from the literature or other sources, which is then analysed by some appropriate method.

Reviews appear in many journals and in some major conference proceedings, but a main forum has been specialized review journals, which publish only this kind of article, in defined subject areas. Typically, these have titles such as *'Reviews of . . .', 'Advances in . . .'*, and *'Progress in . . .'*. Usually published annually, they fall somewhat awkwardly into the gap between books and journals. Many are still published, and have now largely migrated to electronic form. Most retain a print equivalent, since there is a general perception that relatively lengthy and densely written articles, as reviews typically are, can be better appreciated in paper form. The trend towards more evidence-based healthcare practice has led to the emergence of new forms of reviews and summaries, intended to encapsulate knowledge in ways more immediately accessible to the practitioner than the traditional, rather academic, review article.

A good example of the traditional review journal format are the numerous *'Advances in . . .'* journals, published by Elsevier in clinical medicine and health sciences (http://Elsevier.com). Typical titles, current in 2009, are:

- *Advances in Cancer Research*
- *Advances in Clinical Chemistry*
- *Advances in Genetics*
- *Advances in Immunology*
- *Advances in Parasitology*
- *Advances in Pediatrics.*

Similar in nature are the '*Recent Advances in . . .*' series, published by the Royal Society of Medicine, in medicine and clinical sciences.[65] Typical titles are:

- *Recent Advances in Cardiology*
- *Recent Advances in Gastroenterology*
- *Recent Advances in Histopathology.*

Systematic reviews

A new form of review document has emerged as a response to the requirement for evidence-based practice: the systematic review. This is an analysis of relevant literature, carried out according to a predefined and explicit protocol, weighting the evidence according to its perceived value – e.g. giving more credence to a randomized clinical trial than to a series of unrelated case reports – with a view to producing guidance as to good practice on the basis of the best available evidence. The systematic review is the basis of most evidence-based guidance and practice. Producing such reviews is an activity to which health information professionals can make a great contribution, particularly if they have skills in information analysis as well as information retrieval (McKibbon, 2006).

The resulting evidence-based guidance – other than strictly local protocols, such as approved drug lists for a hospital, which may be communicated on paper or through an intranet – is typically made available by health services through the web, in a variety of formats. UK examples are:

- the various forms of guidance, e.g. clinical guidance, technology appraisals, and public health guidelines, from NICE[66]
- Clinical Knowledge Summaries, aimed at providing quick, evidence-based answers for healthcare workers[67]
- Specialist Libraries within the NHS Evidence Resources area, giving access to systematic reviews, guidelines and other evidence in more than 30 areas[68]
- Map of Medicine, a series of evidence-based guides to the 'pathways' of

diagnosis and treatment of a variety of health problems. Although intended for health professionals, this has now been made available to consumers, with the invitation 'see what your doctor can see'.[69]

Publishers have been quick to incorporate this sort of guidance into handbooks. Examples are:

- the Oxford Desk Reference series, intended for health practitioners, which aims to include 'the latest evidence base in one place'.[70] Typical titles in the series are:
  — *Oxford Desk Reference: Rheumatology*
  — *Oxford Desk Reference: Respiratory Medicine.*
- evidence-based handbooks published by the Royal Society of Medicine for practitioners,[71] e.g. *The Labour Ward Handbook.*
- the Oxford 'The Facts' series,[72] intended primarily for patients and carers, but also for healthcare practitioners wanting 'brief, practical reviews'. They are arranged around medical conditions and topics, with titles such as:
  — *Back Pain*
  — *Cosmetic Surgery*
  — *Falls*
  — *Lupus*
  — *Osteoarthritis.*

Consumer advice services

These are now so numerous and significant that they deserve a section to themselves. Invariably web based, they are provided by a range of organizations, including health services, charities, publishers and commercial information providers. They are usually at pains to try to establish the high-quality, reliability and unbiased nature of the information and advice which they provide. They differ from the popular health encyclopaedias, noted above, in being more focused on advice giving than on general information and in their selection of particularly significant issues, and can be more rapidly updated than printed sources.

Examples are:

- BestTreatments, from the UK *Guardian* newspaper, and incorporating *British Medical Journal* patient information[73]
- NetDoctor, a UK site edited by health professionals and funded by

advertising, offering health advice integrated with 'healthy living' issues and supporting a variety of forums and support groups[74]

- MedicineNet, a US site, similarly edited and funded, offering a wide range of consumer health and wellness information and health news items, as well as individual case stories and discussion forums; much information is in the form of slideshows, videos and podcasts[75]

- Children First for Health, maintained by Great Ormond Street children's hospital, UK, providing health and lifestyle information and advice for young people and parents, in a 'youth accessible' format.[76]

Abstracting and indexing (A & I) services

These are another long-standing tool for the management of healthcare information, dating back to the 19th century. All have now migrated from their original printed index format to a digital presence on the web, and some are also still produced in the form of CD-ROM. They are typically accessed through an aggregator online host system. Examples of such host systems, each of which offers a wide range of health-related databases are:

- Ovid[75]
- Dialog[76]
- National Library of Medicine Gateway[77]
- DIMDI[78] (German Institute of Medical Documentation and Information).

Although the databases offered may seem identical, and the interfaces similar, very different results can be obtained from simple searches on the same databases on different hosts, and it is necessary to be aware of how each host interface operates to get best results (Younger and Boddy, 2009).

Most of these databases are primarily sources of disciplinary information (medicine, chemistry, toxicology, pharmacy . . .), though some deal with a specific type of information (report literature, patents . . .). They are the epitome of secondary resources, giving pointers to the primary literature while at the same time providing substantive information in their abstracts and summaries, and are organized through high-quality intellectual indexing and classification.

There are numerous databases of this kind which may be of relevance to health sciences and healthcare; a scan of the host system database listings will show the range. The pharmaceutical industry, in particular, has a wide variety of such sources, covering all stages of drug discovery and development and emphasizing competitor intelligence (Bawden and Robinson, 2010).

A selection of the more significant and long-standing A&I databases are listed here as exemplars:

- Medline (formerly Index Medicus): healthcare and health sciences[79]
- EMBASE (formerly Excerpta Medica): healthcare and health sciences[80]
- CINAHL (Cumulative Index to Nursing and Allied Health Literature): nursing and allied health research and practice[81]
- AMED (Allied and Complementary Medicine): allied health and complementary healthcare practice[82]
- Cochrane Library: systematic reviews and other information resources supporting evidence-based practice[83]
- Biosis: life sciences[84]
- CA Search: chemistry, including clinical chemistry and pharmaceuticals[85]
- Toxline: toxicity and hazardous effects[86]
- Derwent Drug File: drug discovery and development[87]
- PsychInfo: psychology and related areas[88]
- Pharmline: medicines management and prescribing[89]
- Web of Science/Web of Knowledge: academic journal literature from all subject areas[90]
- ASSIA (Applied Social Sciences Index and Abstracts): includes health and social services.[91]

Databanks and statistical compilations

Research and practice in healthcare, and research in the medical sciences supporting it, generate copious amounts of data, numerical and factual. This is often presented in the form of reports or summarized in monographs, reference works and journal articles, but in some cases the whole dataset may be presented. In the past, this was achieved through multi-volume printed databooks, but is now invariably presented in digital form. Among the major producers of such data is medical science research, which generates extensive data compilations, particularly in fields such as genomics and proteonomics, which yield sequence databases (Tennant and Lyon, 2007). Epidemiology and public health monitoring give rise to many statistical compilations, both the healthcare industries and the health services rely on marketing and other financial data sources. These resources are particularly numerous and rapidly changing. Those with a marketing emphasis are usually produced commercially, and accessible only a high cost. Examples are:

- electronic Medicines Compendium (eMC): commercially produced database, freely accessible, with detailed information about all medicines licensed for use in the UK, including full text of patient information leaflets[92]
- Registry of Toxic Effects of Chemical Substances (RTECS): compilation of literature data on harmful effects of chemicals[93]
- Entrez: integrated set of genomic, nucleotide, protein sequence and protein structure data collections[94]
- US National Center for Health Statistics: variety of datasets of health statistics and surveys and epidemiology data[95]
- World Health Organization Statistical Information System (WHOSIS): core health statistics for 193 countries.[96]

Terminologies and classifications

Vocabularies in a subject area – terminologies, classifications, taxonomies and so on – are counted as secondary resources in their own right because they present organized knowledge of their subject. As well as being useful aids to finding information, through their use in indexing and classification they can be sources of information in themselves. 'Reading' a classification or a glossary can give good insight into the concepts of the subject area and how they relate to one another. All of the vocabularies mentioned in Chapter 4, and other examples of their kind, may be used in this way. So may the numerous taxonomies and nomenclatures of the health sciences, devised for scientific, rather than information retrieval, purposes (Bowker and Star, 2000; Bowker, 2005).

Searching features and strategies

It is usually with secondary sources that subject-specific and format-specific retrieval tools have been developed, and optimal searching strategies investigated. Most healthcare information sources require only 'conventional' text searching, web search or numeric data retrieval techniques. Some exceptions are noted below. The healthcare area has, however, been the stage over many years for studies aimed at optimizing search strategies, in both printed and electronic resources, in order to find the best information for some particular purpose. This reflects the importance for practice of finding high-quality information, and also comprehensive information, for topics such as harmful effects of substances. It also reflects the wide range of sources available in healthcare and the range of vocabularies used for indexing, and the consequent need for comparisons of effectiveness. An additional recent factor has been the need for finding the best evidence for systematic reviews.

There are very many examples of this sort of study: to get a feel for their scope, see Bawden and Brock (1982), Sayers, Joice and Bawden (1990), Robinson, McIlwaine, Copestake, and Anderson (2000), Brettle and Long (2001), Glanville, Lefebvre, Miles, and Camosso-Stefinovic (2006), DeLuca, Mullins, Lyles, Crepaz, Kay and Thadiparthi (2008), Golder and Loke (2009) and McKibbon, Wilczynski and Haynes (2009).

These studies have yielded a great deal of specific advice, much of it relevant to searching in subjects other than healthcare. The main points can be summarized as:

- always use a number of complementary sources
- if it is necessary to be comprehensive, use as many complementary sources as possible
- remember that not all useful information is digital
- be aware of, and take advantage of, the unique access points of each source
- be familiar with, and take advantage of, the indexing policies of each source
- use controlled vocabulary and free text in a complementary manner.

Specialized searching features for healthcare sources are mainly limited to searching of particular categories of information, in medical science research, and for pharmaceutical and toxicological information. Specific searching systems are needed for the searching of chemical structures and substructures, and for identifying similar chemical substances (Willett, 2008). Many of these systems were pioneered in pharmaceutical research, and in the identification of potentially harmful substances. Matching techniques are required for the sequence databases (genomic, nucleotide and protein), to identify similarity in genetic structure, etc. (Rapp and Wheeler, 2005; O'Grady, 2007).

Medicines information sources utilize a number of unique search facilities (Snow, 2008; Bawden and Robinson, 2010). These include:

- searching features allowing for the multiple nomenclatures and terminologies used for medicinal substances
- identification and distinction of medicines with names which either look or sound similar
- identification of unknown medicines, in capsule or tablet form, by searching on shape, colour, markings, etc.

Because of the number and diversity of its sources, and the sophisticated terminologies and codings available, healthcare information has been an attractive area for experimentation with new forms of retrieval system and features; an example is a study of an 'expert assistant' for searching for drug information (Oakes and Taylor, 1998).

Tertiary sources

These are a large set of rather diverse sources, whose main purpose is to list or aid the use of primary and secondary information resources, and sometimes other tertiary resources. While some are subject specific, many are not; database host systems, for example, may well list a variety of resources, some relevant to health and some not. Typically they do not carry substantive subject information, although it may be possible to use them to answer reference queries. A medical directory, for example, may show what qualifications a particular doctor has; a list of library services can be used to identify libraries for nurses in a particular region; and a listing of curricula can show which subjects are prominent at a particular medical school. But on the whole, resources of this type are used first to identify and then to utilize primary and secondary resources. They are presented here in three categories:

- resource lists and guides to sources
- lists of people and organizations
- retrieval tools.

Resource lists and guides to sources

This category, with two main and overlapping sub-divisions, includes some rather traditional forms of tools – which take new forms and formats in a digital environment – for pointing to resources.

Resource lists

Listings of this sort have developed from traditional bibliographies and reading lists (generally referring to printed materials) to lists of resources in all media. Lists of web resources have proliferated, and have been joined by listings on media sharing sites such as Delicious, LibraryThing, CiteULike,

RefWorks and Google Docs. Lists of communications forums, such as newsgroups, e-mail lists and Facebook groups are also significant, largely replacing their equivalents of the print-on-paper era, such as lists of addresses for paper mailing. In the area of education, lists of courses, syllabi and teaching and training materials retain their importance.

In library/information context, important types of list include availability and location/access details for journals, and listings of abstracting and indexing services. Recommended or 'core' resources listings, of the types mentioned in earlier sections, are growing in importance as the number of available resources increases and budgets to purchase them do not.

Resources of this sort are very numerous and typically short-lived. Here are a few examples, just to give the flavour of the category:

- NLM resource lists and bibliographies: selection of bibliographies on biomedical topics of popular interest at the time of compilation, mainly prepared in support of a conference[97]
- open access health science journals available through Biomed Central[98]
- health and medical mailing lists from the UK Joint Information Systems Committee (JISC) host[99]
- health and social care courses from the UK Open University[100]
- History of Medicine: Online Syllabus Archive.[101]

Guides to sources

These encompass annotated descriptions of printed and – more generally nowadays – digital resources. The classic example was the printed 'guide to sources' in a particular subject area. The healthcare information domain has become too massive, too diverse and too dynamic for any detailed resource guides to the whole topic to have been attempted since the early 1990s. Substantial guides now fall into two categories. There are those which deal in detail with information resources in a specific part of the domain: Snow's (2008) book on drug information sources is a good example. And there are those which deal with particular ways of accessing domain information, such guides to finding information in support of evidence-based practice; for a good example of the latter, see De Brún and Pearse-Smith (2009).

Guides may appear in shorter format, typically as journal articles. The *Journal of the Medical Library Association* has published an extensive series of articles on 'mapping the literature' of specific subjects, reporting bibliometric analysis to identify the size of the information base of that subject, with recommendations of important books, journals and databases. As an example, see Delwiche and Hall (2007).

Lists of people and organizations

This is another 'traditional' type of information source which has largely moved into the digital environment, such listings now generally being on the web. This gives them a much greater chance of being kept up to date than were the annual directory volumes and the irregularly updated printed lists of organizations which preceded them. Some of these are official (indeed some, such as lists of medical practitioners, have a legal status) and others are commercial.

Lists of libraries and information services

Such lists are of obvious value and application. Examples with specific healthcare relevance are:

- Health Library and Information Services Directory (UK and Ireland)[102]
- Find a Library (medical libraries in the USA and Canada)[103]
- Medical and Health Science Libraries on the Web (largely US institutions).[104]

Lists of healthcare organizations, academic departments and research institutes

These are as numerous as the organizations which they list. As examples, see:

- List of medical associations and societies, from the Royal Society of Medicine, UK[105]
- List of Australian health associations and organizations, from the Australian Healthcare and Hospitals Association[106]
- Directory of the American Association of Medical Colleges (AAMC), including American and Canadian medical schools, teaching hospitals and academic and professional societies[107]
- Constituent institutes of US National Institutes of Health[108]
- Binley's Directory of NHS Management. Comprehensive directory to

organizations and individuals involved in managing the British health service. Published as a print volume three times per year.[109]

Lists of individuals

Lists of all kinds in healthcare fields are numerous. Most common are those which list licensed practitioners, members of a professional association, or those who are in some respect specialists or experts. Examples are:

- The Medical Register, the official listing of doctors entitled to practice in the UK, from the General Medical Council[110]
- Specialistinfo, a commercial directory of doctors with their specialities in the UK and Ireland[111]
- American College of Obstetricians and Gynecologists, Physician Directory.[112]

Retrieval tools

These tools, which would in the past have included card catalogues, printed indexes and so on, are now virtually all digital.

Internet search engines

Search engines, both general and special purpose, are an important means of access to health information for both professionals and consumers. Google predominates as a search tool, and Google Scholar in particular can be seen as an alternative to more traditional databases (Freeman, Lauderdale, Kendrach and Woolley, 2009).

Online host systems

Host systems, arguably the more traditional alternative to the search engine, offer collections of databases, a search interface, documentation, training, etc. Four such hosts noted above – Dialog, DIMDI, Ovid and NLM – are of particular relevance to health information.

Internet subject gateways

These offer collections of 'quality assured' resources, categorized and indexed, sometimes with a common search interface. Examples are:

- the Intute gateway service, maintained by the UK higher education community, with sections for medicine and dentistry, nursing, midwifery and allied health, and biological sciences (these sections were formerly known as the OMNI and BIOME gateways)[113]
- the Health on the Net Foundation, which offers a selection of reliable medical websites, with separate listings for health professionals, patients and publishers.[114]

Library catalogues

Library catalogues, the epitome of the tertiary source, are now increasingly to be found embedded in information portals, essentially entry points to a mixed set of resources: databases, tools and links, with social networking media increasingly likely to be included. In an institutional environment, where the resources are for internal use, this may take the form of an intranet. For public use, portals may take many different forms, depending on the user group.

Health service portals

Portals maintained by national government agencies provide a wide range of information resources for patient information and education and for promoting their own services. These portals are often focused on resources produced within the services which maintain them and are therefore somewhat analogous to intranets. A detailed description of the development of the US NLM's MedlinePlus portal is given by Miller, Tyler and Backus (2004), and of a French language equivalent, CISMeF-patient, by Darmoni, Thirion, Platel, Douyere, Mouraga and Leroy (2002).

An advantage of portals of all kinds is that, being based on existing digital resources, they can be created from scratch very rapidly to meet new needs. This was seen in mid-2009, when several portals or sections within existing portals were created – both by health services and by commercial providers – to provide focused information on pandemic swine flu. Examples of health service portals are:

- The UK NHS Choices portal offers copious information about national and local health services, health problems and treatments, access to medical advice through the NHS Direct service, health news, information for carers, and a variety of consumer blogs and comments on services. Apart from a link to the NHS's own Map of Medicine – mentioned above – it does not link to professional resources, nor to a wide range of other web resources outside the NHS.[115]
- The US NLM's MedlinePlus portal offers a wide range of consumer health information (including interactive tutorials and various reference tools) and directories of local and national health services, as well as news updates. There is little emphasis on patient experience and feedback, but there is access to a range of professional databases and other secondary information sources (largely from NLM itself, or other US government agencies), to healthcare libraries and to equivalent health service sites internationally.[116]
- The site for French-language patient information resources, modelled on MedlinePlus, is maintained at Rouen University Hospital.[117]

Consumer health portals

These portals typically integrate a wide range of patient information and advice with what would usually be regarded as 'professional' resources. Although aimed at the public, they are often used by health professionals, who value their convenient integration of a mass of information.

A good example is Patient UK (www.patient.co.uk), maintained by health professionals and supported by advertising. This offers a very wide range of consumer advice and information services, including directories of healthcare providers, recommended books, links to many other web resources, and hosting of support groups and patient forums. It also provides access to information resources including clinical guidelines, databases (such as Medline and the Cochrane library), online textbooks, collections of medical images, and evidence-based medicine resources.

An equivalent American example is WebMD (www/webmd.com), maintained and supported in a similar way and providing a similar range of consumer health information, directories and news services. Professional links include Medline access, information on medical conferences, and medical education resources.

Health professional portals

These portals are fewer in number, since most services for professionals have tended to separate formal and informal media, although this demarcation is becoming increasingly blurred by social networking developments.

An example is the US commercial Medscape site (www.medscap.com), aimed at health professionals and arranged by speciality, including nursing, pharmacy and student areas, as well as medical specialism. It offers articles, commentaries and reviews, educational resources, health news feeds, access to e-journals, e-books and databases, conference reports, 'ask the expert' interactions, and informal interaction through discussion forums and links to blogs.

Quaternary sources

This is by far the most sparsely populated of the four levels. It comprises resources which point to tertiary resources, and sometimes to other quaternaries. In essence, these are 'lists of lists', 'bibliographies of bibliographies', 'directories of directories' and the like. In pre-web days, these were few and far between. Now, however, 'lists of lists' are a common web phenomenon. Most are rather general in nature, but some are subject specific. Also included in this category are listings of subject guides, of portals and gateways, and so on. The value of this kind of resource is in the early stage of information seeking, particularly if a comprehensive approach is required, especially in an unfamiliar subject area. Some examples of the relatively few such sources that are wholly devoted to healthcare, or that at least have a strong healthcare component, are given below.

Hardin MD is the best known. It was established in 1996, at quite an early stage in the development of the internet, and gave its *raison d'etre* as being a source of the best lists of directories in health and medicine. It is maintained at the Hardin Health Science Library, University of Iowa, USA; the name indicates 'Hardin Meta Directory' since it was conceived explicitly as a 'directory of directories'.[118]

Other 'list of lists' sites of relevance to health include:

- Children's disability list of lists, presenting lists of support groups for families of children with disabilities or special needs[119]
- List of nursing resources lists, from the UN Economic Commission for Africa[120]
- The Knowledgerush popular encyclopaedia, with a list of lists including

over 20 medical and health lists[121]
- MedlinePlus 'directory of directories', listing directories of health professionals and facilities in the USA, from NLM.[122]

As examples of directories of subject gateways, we can mention:

- Pinakes, a directory of internet subject gateways which includes gateways listing resources in health and life sciences, chemistry, psychology, and reproductive health[123]
- the World Wide Web Virtual Library section for Medicine and Health, which includes 10 categories, such as 'pharmacy' and 'public health', leading to lists of relevant resources.[124]

Conclusion

The healthcare domain has a very rich and very diverse set of information resources. The area has often been a pioneer in the adoption of new forms of communication, and this continues to be true. The main factors promoting the development of new types of resources are the burgeoning field of consumer health and the increasing influence of evidence-based healthcare practice, both of which have interacted with the availability of new forms of technology to promote communication.

Nonetheless, the inertia noted in earlier chapters remains a factor. While new media and new types of resource continually appear, they tend to coexist with the familiar preceding formats, which rarely disappear. Possible exceptions to this are some types of printed reference tool, which have largely been superseded by digital equivalents, and social networking, where newsgroups and web-rings have been largely replaced by services like Facebook, blogs and Twitter. Social networking has also promoted one of the other notable changes to be noted: the breaking down of the hitherto fairly rigid barrier between professional and public, formal and informal, information; this is to be seen particularly in the newly developed kinds of portal.

Understanding the relative merits of this disparate range of resources is a daunting task, and it is not surprising that many people, not excluding information specialists, prefer to rely on a few familiar sources. The framework used in this chapter should help to position resources conceptually, and aid users to understand – and hence use – them better.

Notes

1   www.mssm.edu/library/brandon-hill.
2   www.ovid.com/site/catalog/Catalog_Journal.jsp.
3   www.medscape.com.
4   www.fade.nhs.uk.
5   www.kingsfund.org.uk/what_we_do/services_for_researchers.
6   www.who.int/en/publications.
7   www.bioportfolio.com/cgi-bin/acatalog/sitemap.html.
8   www.iom.edu/CMS/4683.aspx.
9   www.rheumatoid.org.uk/download.php?asset_id=615&link=true.
10 www.commonwealthfund.org/~/media/Files/Publications/
Fund%20Report/2009/May/International%20Comparison/1241_
Halfon_intl_comparison_early_child_init_svcs_to_sys_FINAL.pdf.
11 www.isdscotland.org/isd/3401.html.
12 www.who.int/whr.
13 www.med.yale.edu/library/about/annualreport08.pdf.
14 www.bbc.co.uk/health.
15 www.nhs.uk/News/Pages/NewsIndex.aspx.
16 www.healthnewsreview.org.
17 www.nlm.nih.gov/medlineplus/newsbydate.html.
18 www.pulsetoday.co.uk.
19 www.reutershealth.com.
20 www.scripnews.com.
21 http://library.nhs.uk/guidelinesFinder/AboutUs.aspx/.
22 www.library.nhs.uk/GUIDELINESFINDER.
23 www.emea.europa.eu/htms/human/raguidelines/dossier_format.htm.
24 www.fda.gov/ScienceResearch/SpecialTopics/RunningClinicalTrials.
25 www.nmc-uk.org/aArticle.aspx?ArticleID=34.
26 http://wellcomelibrary.blogspot.com/.
27 http://blogs.usask.ca/medical_education.
28 http://bmacymruwales.blogspot.com.
29 www.cdnaonline.org/index.php?option=com_content&task=
blogsection&id=3&Itemid=57.
30 http://jmlacasestudies.blogspot.com/.
31 http://trusttheevidence.net.
32 http://fadelibrary.wordpress.com.
33 http://friendfeed.com/medlibs.
34 https://www.jiscmail.ac.uk/cgi-bin/webadmin?A0=lis-medical.
35 https://www.jiscmail.ac.uk/cgi-bin/webadmin?A0=MIUA.

36   https://www.jiscmail.ac.uk/cgi-bin/webadmin?A0=NURSE-
      PHILOSOPHY.
37   www.healthtalkonline.org.
38   http://ocw.mit.edu/OcwWeb/Health-Sciences-and-Technology.
39   http://pathmicro.med.sc.edu/book/welcome.htm.
40   http://people.eku.edu/ritchisong/301syl.html.
41   www.lab.anhb.uwa.edu.au/mb140/.
42   www.nlm.nih.gov/medlineplus/tutorial.html.
43   http://uk.youbube.com/sgulcso.
44   http://medicaleducation.wetpaint.com/page/Interactive+
      Medical+Animations.
45   www.examdoctor.co.uk.
46   http://toxtown.nlm.nih.gov.
47   www.nlm.nih.gov/research/visible/visible_human.html.
48   https://www.countway.harvard.edu/menuNavigation/
      historicalResources/warrenAnatomicalMuseum.html.
49   http://images.wellcome.ac.uk/.
50   www.lib.unc.edu/dc/mackinney/about.html.
51   www.rcseng.ac.uk/museums/wellcome-museum-of-anatomy-and-
      pathology.
52   http://hlwiki.slais.ubc.ca/index.php/Podcasts_and_Videocasts.
53   www.roysocmed.ac.uk/librar/libcat_coll.php.
54   http://digital.library.mcgill.ca/osler/index.php.
55   www.kew.org/collections/herbcol.html.
56   www.mssm.edu/library/brandon-hill.
57   www.doody.com/dct.
58   www.nhs.uk/Conditions.
59   www.nlm.nih.gov/medlineplus/encyclopedia.html.
60   www.umm.edu/medref.
61   www.radiologywiki.org; http://wikisurgery.com; www.medpedia.com.
62   www.mims.co.uk.
63   www.merckbooks.com/mindex.
64   http://ukcatalogue.oup.com/category/academic/series/medicine/
      oxhmed.do.
65   www.rsmpress.co.uk/catra.htm.
66   http://guidance.nice.org.uk.
67   www.cks.nhs.uk.
68   www.library.nhs.uk/specialistcollections.
69   www.connectingforhealth.nhs.uk/systemsandservices/mapmed.
70   http://ukcatalogue.oup.com/category/academic/series/medicine/drs.do.

71 www.rsmpress.co.uk.
72 http://ukcatalogue.oup.com/category/academic/series/medicine/facts.do.
73 www.guardian.co.uk/lifeandstyle/besttreatments.
74 www.netdoctor.co.uk.
75 www.medicinenet.com.
76 www.childrenfirst.nhs.uk.
75 www.ovid.com.
76 www.dialog.com/products/guide/science.shtml.
77 www.nlm.nih.gov/databases/index.html.
78 www.dimdi.de/static/en.
79 www.nlm.nih.gov/pubs/factsheets/medline.html.
80 http://info.embase.com/about/what.shtml.
81 www.ebscohost.com/cinahl.
82 www.bl.uk/reshelp/findhelpsubject/scitectenv/medicinehealth/amed/amed.html.
83 http://www3.interscience.wiley.com/cgi-bin/mrwhome/106568753/AboutCochrane.html.
84 http://thomsonreuters.com/content/PDF/scientific/BIOSIS_Factsheet.pdf.
85 www.cas.org.
86 www.nlm.nih.gov/pubs/factsheets/toxlinfs.html.
87 http://thomsonreuters.com/products_services/science/science_products/life_sciences/discovery_research_development/derwent_drug_file.
88 www.apa.org/psycinfo.
89 www.pharm-line.nhs.uk.
90 http://thomsonreuters.com/content/PDF/scientific/Web_of_Knowledge_factsheet.pdf.
91 www.csa.com/factsheets/assia-set-c.php.
92 http://emc.medicines.org.uk.
93 www.cdc.gov/niosh/rtecs.
94 www.ncbi.nlm.nih.gov/Database.
95 www.cdc.gov/nchs.
96 www.who.int/whosis/en.
97 www.nlm.nih.gov/pubs/resources.html.
98 www.biomedcentral.com/browse/journals/.
99 www.jiscmail.ac.uk/mailinglists/category/Medicine_&_Health.htm.

100 www3.open.ac.uk/study/undergraduate/health-and-social-care/courses/index.htm.
101 www.nlm.nih.gov/hmd/collections/digital/syllabi/index.html.
102 www.hlisd.org.
103 www.nlm.nih.gov/medlineplus/libraries.html.
104 www.lib.uiowa.edu/hardin/hslibs.html.
105 www.rsm.ac.uk/welcom/linksocs.php.
106 www.aushealthcare.com.au/links/index.asp.
107 www.aamc.org/about/membership.htm.
108 www.nih.gov/icd/index.html.
109 www.binleys.com.
110 www.gmc-uk.org/register.
111 www.specialistinfo.com.
112 www.acog.org/member%2Dlookup.
113 www.intute.ac.uk.
114 www.hon.ch.
115 www.nhs.uk.
116 http://medlineplus.gov.
117 www.chu-rouen.fr/cismefp.
118 www.lib.uiowa.edu/hardin/md.
119 www.comeunity.com/disability/speclists.html.
120 www.uneca.org/itca/healthport/nursing.htm.
121 www.knowledgerush.com/kr/encyclopedia/List_of_lists.
122 www.nlm.nih.gov/medlineplus/directories.html.
123 www.hw.ac.uk/libwww/irn/pinakes/pinakes.html.
124 www.vlib.org.uk/Medicine.

References

Ayatollahi, H., Bath, P. A. and Goodacre, S. (2009) Paper-based Versus Computer-based Records in the Emergency Department: staff preferences, expectations and concerns, *Health Informatics Journal*, 15 (3), 199–211.

Baker, L. M. and Gollop, C. J. (2004) Medical Textbooks: can lay people read and understand them?, *Library Trends*, 53 (2), 336–47.

Barbour, V., Clark, J., Peiperl, L., Veitch, E., Wong, M. and Yamey, G. (2008) False Hopes, Unwarranted Fears: the trouble with medical news stories, *PLOS Medicine*, 5 (5), 681–3, available from

www.plosmedicine.org/article/info%3Adoi%2F10.1371%2Fjournal.pmed.
0050118.

Bawden, D. and Brock, A. M. (1982) Chemical Toxicology Searching: a
collaborative evaluation, comparing information resources and searching
techniques, *Journal of Information Science*, **5** (1), 3–18.

Bawden, D. and Robinson, L. (2010) Pharmaceutical Information: a 30-year
perspective on the literature, *Annual Reviews of Information Science and
Technology*, in press.

Beard, L., Wilson, K., Morra, D. and Keelan, J. (2009) A Survey of Health-
related Activities in Second Life, *Journal of Medical Internet Research*, **11** (2),
e17, available from www.jimr.org/2009/2/e17/HTML.

Bhatia, K., Rao, N. M. and Saiyed, H. N. (2006) Research Trends in a
Premier Institute Based on Annual Reports, *Annals of Library and
Information Studies*, **53** (2), 61–4.

Bowker, G. C. (2005) *Memory Practices in the Sciences*, MIT Press.

Bowker, G. C. and Star, S. L. (2000) *Sorting Things Out: classification and its
consequences*, MIT Press.

Brazier, M. and Cave, E. (2007) *Medicine, Patients and the Law*, Penguin.

Brettle, A. J. and Long, A. F. (2001) Comparison of Bibliographic Databases
for Information on the Rehabilitation of People with Severe Mental
Illness, *Bulletin of the Medical Library Association*, **89** (40), 353–62.

Buckland, M. (1997) What is a 'Document'?, *Journal of the American Society
for Information Science*, **48** (9), 804–9.

Caporizzo, M. (2008) Digitizing and Securing Archived Laboratory
Notebooks, *Computers in Libraries*, **28** (9), 26–30.

Carey, J. C. (2006) Significance of Case Reports in the Advancement of
Medical Knowledge, *American Journal of Medical Genetics part A*, **140A**
(19), 2131–4.

Ciesielka, D. (2008) Using a Wiki to Meet Graduate Nursing Education
Competencies in Collaboration and Community Health, *Journal of Nursing
Education*, **47** (10), 473–76.

Clauson, K. A., Polen, H. H., Boulos, M. N. K. and Dzenowagis, J. H.
(2008) Scope, Completeness and Accuracy of Drug Information in
Wikipedia, *Annals of Pharmacotherapy*, **42** (12), 1814–21.

Cobus, L. (2009) Using Blogs and Wikis in a Graduate Public Health
Course, *Medical Reference Services Quarterly*, **28** (1), 22–32.

Coleman, J., Olsen, S. J., Sauter, P. K., Baker, D., Hodgin, M. B., Stanfield,
C., Emerling, A., Hruban, R. H. and Nolan, M. T. (2005) The Effect of a
Frequently Asked Questions Module on a Pancreatic Cancer Web Site
Patient/family Chat Room, *Cancer Nursing*, **28** (6), 460–8.

Cuddy, C. (2006) Delivery of Electronic Journal Content to Personal Digital Assistants (PDAs): seven free options for health care professionals, *Journal of Electronic Resources in Medical Libraries*, **3** (4), 77–85.

Cuddy, C. (2009) Twittering in Health Science Libraries, *Journal of Electronic Resources in Medical Libraries*, **6** (2), 169–74.

Cunningham, K. (2005) Health and Medical News on the Web: comparing the results of news-providing web resources, *Medical References Services Quarterly*, **24** (4), 17–40.

Darmoni, S., Thirion, B., Platel, S., Douyere, M., Mouraga, P. and Leroy, J. P. (2002) CISMeF-patient: a French counterpart to MedlinePlus, *Journal of the Medical Library Association*, **90** (2), 248–53.

David, R. (ed.) (2008) *Egyptian Mummies and Modern Science*, Cambridge University Press.

De Brún, C. and Pearce-Smith, N. (2009) *Searching Skills Toolkit: finding the evidence*, Wiley/Blackwell.

DeLuca, J. B., Mullins, M. M., Lyles, C. M., Crepaz, N., Kay, L. and Thadiparthi, S. (2008) Developing a Comprehensive Search Strategy for Evidence Based Systematic Reviews, *Evidence Based Library and Information Practice*, **3** (1), 3–32.

Delwiche, F. A. and Hall, E. F. (2007) Mapping the Literature of Athletic Training, *Journal of the Medical Library Association*, **95** (2), 195–201.

Dentzer, S. (2009) Communicating Medical News – Pitfalls Of Health Care Journalism, *New England Journal of Medicine*, **360** (1), 1–3.

Dorrington, L. (2006) Health Libraries as Joint Use Libraries: serving medical practitioners and students, *Library Trends*, **54** (4), 596–606.

Duckitt, P. (1991) Biologicals and Biomedical Information. In Pickering, W. R. (ed.), *Information Sources in Pharmaceuticals*, Bowker Saur, 70–96.

Eldredge, J. D. (1998) The Vital Few Meet the Trivial Many; unexpected use patterns in a monographs collection, *Bulletin of the Medical Library Association*, **86** (4), 496–503.

Ellero, N. P. (2009) Crossing Over: health sciences librarians contributing and collaborating on electronic medical record (EMR) implementation, *Journal of Hospital Librarianship*, **9** (1), 89–107.

Ewing, B. T., Kruse, J. B. and Thompson, M. A. (2005) Comparing the Impact of News: a tale of three health care sectors. *Journal of Business Finance and Accounting*, **32** (7/8), 1587–611.

Ewing, L. M. (2007) Electronic Health Records: new tasks ahead for health info pros, *Searcher*, **15** (5), 49–51.

Farmer, A. D., Bruckner Holt, C. E. M., Cook, M. J. and Hearing, S. D. (2009) Social Networking Sites: a novel portal for communication,

Postgraduate Medical Journal, **85** (1007), 455–9.

Feldschreiber, P. (ed.) (2008) *The Law and Regulation of Medicines*, Oxford University Press.

Fisher, G. (2006) Time to Change the Healthcare Record on Document Management? *Records Management Bulletin*, 134, 17–18.

Freeman, M. K., Lauderdale, S. A., Kendrach, M. G. and Woolley, T. W. (2009) Google Scholar Versus PubMed in Locating Primary Literature to Answer Drug-related Questions, *Annals of Pharmacotherapy*, **43** (3), 478–84.

Frohmann, B. (2009) Revisiting 'What is a Document?', *Journal of Documentation*, **65** (2), 291–303.

Glanville, J. M., Lefebvre, C., Miles, J. N. V. and Camosso-Stefinovic, J. (2006) How to Identify Randomized Controlled Trials in MEDLINE: ten years on, *Journal of the Medical Library Association*, **94** (2), 130–6.

Golder, S. and Loke, Y. (2009) Search Strategies to Identify Information on Adverse Effects; a systematic review, *Journal of the Medical Library Association*, **97** (2), 84–92.

Graham, S. C., Bawden, D. and Nicholas, D. (1997) Health Information Provision in Men and Women's Magazines, *Aslib Proceedings*, **49** (5), 117–48.

Grant, M. J. and Booth, A. (2009) A Typology of Reviews: an analysis of 14 review types and associated methodologies, *Health Information and Libraries Journal*, **26** (2), 91–108.

Guillaume, L. and Bath, P. A. (2008) A Content Analysis of Mass Media Sources in Relation to the MMR Vaccine Scare, *Health Informatics Journal*, **14** (4), 323–34.

Guyatt, G., Rennie, D., Meade, M. O. and Cook, D. J. (2008) *Users' Guides to the Medical Literature: a manual for evidence-based clinical practice*, 2nd edn, McGraw-Hill Medical.

Hague, H. R. (1992) Standard Reference Sources. In Morton, L. and Godbolt, S. (eds), *Information Sources in the medical sciences*, 4th edn, Bowker Saur, 67–86.

Harrabin, R., Coote, A. and Allen, J. (2003) *Health in the News: risk, reporting and media influence*, King's Fund.

Hogan, K. and Scarborough, R. (1996) Patents for Medical Libraries, *Medical Reference Services Quarterly*, **15** (2), 23–31.

Illig, J. (2008) Archiving 'Event Knowledge': bringing 'dark data' to light, *Journal of the Medical Library Association*, **96** (3), 189–91.

Jhetam, I. (2009) Libraries of the Future, *British Medical Journal*, **339**, b4065 (online).

Jones, M. (2004) Learning the Lessons of History? Electronic records in the United Kingdom acute hospitals, 1988, 2002, *Health informatics Journal*, 10 (4), 253–63.

Kelly, J. A. (1998) Scientific Meeting Abstracts: significance, access and trends, *Bulletin of the Medical Library Association*, 86 (1), 68–76.

King, C. (2009) images.MD – the Online Encyclopaedia of Medical Images, *Journal of Electronic Resources in Medical Libraries*, 6 (2), 163–8.

Lambert-Zazulak, P. I., Rutherford, P. and David, R. (2003) The International Ancient Egyptian Mummy Tissue Bank at Manchester Museum as a Resource for the Palaeoepidemiological Study of Schistosomiasis, *World Archaeology*, 35 (2), 223–40.

Laurent, M. R. and Vickers, J. T. (2009) Seeking Health Information Online: does Wikipedia matter?, *Journal of the American Medical Informatics Association*, 16 (4), 471–9.

Li, M., Chapman, S., Agho, K. and Eastman, C. J. (2008) Can Even Minimal News Coverage Influence Consumer Health-related Behaviour? A case study of iodized salt sales, Australia, *Health Education Research*, 23 (3), 543–8.

Lingle, V. A. (2004) FAQs and Tips about Electronic Journals on Library Websites: what information are we Sharing with our Users, *Journals of Electronic Resources in Medical Libraries*, 193, 57-64.

Lombardo, N. T., Mower, A. and McFarland, M. M. (2008) Putting wikis to work in libraries, *Medical Reference Services Quarterly*, 27 (2), 129–45.

MacCall, S. L. (2006) Online Medical Books: their availability and an assessment of how health science libraries provide access on their public websites, *Journal of the Medical Library Association*, 94 (1), 75–80.

McKibbon, K. A. (2006) Systematic Reviews and Librarians, *Library Trends*, 55 (1), 2020–215.

McKibbon, K. A., Wilczynski, N. L. and Haynes, R. B. (2009) Retrieving Randomized Controlled Trials from MEDLINE: a comparison of 38 published search filters, *Health Information and Libraries Journal*, 26 (3), 187–202.

MacMillan, D. (2005) Patently Obvious: the place for patents in information literacy in the sciences, *Research Strategies*, 20 (3), 149–61.

Manheimer, E. and Anderson, D. (2002) Survey of Public Information About Ongoing Clinical Trials Funded by Industry: evaluation of completeness and accessibility, *British Medical Journal*, 325 (7363), 528–31.

Mantzoukas, S. (2009) The Research Evidence Published in High Impact Nursing Journals Between 2000 and 2006: a quantitative content analysis, *International Journal of Nursing Studies*, 46 (4), 479–89.

Miller, N., Tyler, R. J. and Backus, J. E. B. (2004) MedlinePlus: the National Library of Medicine brings quality information to health consumers, *Library Trends*, 53 (2), 375–88.

Morton, L. (1974) *Use of Medical Literature*, Butterworth.

Morton, L. and Godbolt, S. (eds) (1992) *Information Sources in the Medical Sciences*, 4th edn, Bowker Saur.

Oakes, M. P. and Taylor, M. J. (1998) Automated Assistance in the Formulation of Search Statements for Bibliographic Databases, *Information Processing and Management*, 34 (6), 645–68.

Oermann, M. H., Nordstrom, C. K., Wilmes, N. A., Denison, D., Webb, S. A., Featherstone, D. E., Bednarz, H., Striz, P., Blair, D. A. and Kowalewski, K. (2008) Dissemination of Research in Clinical Nursing Journals, *Journal of Clinical Nursing*, 17 (2), 149–56.

O'Grady, T. (2007) *Entrez* and BLAST: precision and recall in searches of NCBI databases, *Issues in Science and Technology Libraries*, 52 (Fall), paper 2, available from www.istl.org/07-fall/refereed2.html.

O'Neill, D. (2009) Electronic Patient Records within NHS Trusts and Strategic Health Authorities – when one size doesn't fit all, *Records Management Bulletin*, 149, 14–15.

O'Sullivan, D. (2009) *Wikipedia: a new community of practice?*, Ashgate.

Pinfield, S. (2009) Journals and Repositories: an evolving relationship?, *Learned Publishing*, 22 (3), 165–75.

Piorun, M. and Palmer, L. A. (2008) Digitizing Dissertations for an Institutional Repository: a process and cost analysis, *Journal of the Medical Library Association*, 96 (3), 223–9.

Pon, J. J., Nahm, M., Wakim, P., Cushing, C., Poole, L. Tai, B. and Pieper, C. F. (2009) A Centralized Informatics Infrastructure for the National Institute on Drug Abuse Clinical Trials Network, *Clinical Trials*, 6 (1), 67–75.

Pribble, J. M., Goldstein, K. M., Fowler, E. F. and Greenberg, M. J. (2006) Medical News for the Public to Use? What's on local TV, *American Journal of Managed Care*, 12 (3), 170–6.

Randell, B. (2007) A Computer Scientist's Reactions to NPfIT, *Journal of Information Technology*, 22 (3), 222–34.

Rapp, B. A. and Wheeler, D. L. (2005) Bioinformatics Resources from the National Center for Biotechnology Information: an integrated foundation for discovery, *Journal of the American Society for Information Science and Technology*, 56 (5), 538–50.

Robinson, L. (2000) A Strategic Approach to Research using Internet Tools and Resources, *Aslib Proceedings*, **52** (1), 11–19.

Robinson, L., McIlwaine, I., Copestake, P. and Anderson, C. (2000) Comparative Evaluation of the Performance of Online Databases in Answering Toxicology Queries, *International Journal of Information Management*, **20** (1), 79–87.

Sambunjak, D., Huic, M., Hren, D., Katic, M., Marusic, A. and Marusic, D. (2009) National vs. International Journals: views of medical professionals in Croatia, *Learned Publishing*, **22** (1), 57–70.

Sankofa, J. and Johnson-Taylor, W. L. (2007) News Coverage of Diet-related Health Disparities Experienced by Black Americans: a steady diet of misinformation, *Journal of Nutrition Education and Behavior*, **39** (2S), S41–S44.

Sayers, M., Joice, J. and Bawden, D. (1990) Retrieval of Biomedical Reviews: a comparative evaluation of online databases for reviews of drug therapy, *Journal of Information Science*, **16** (5), 321–5.

Scherer, R. R., Langenberg, P. and von Elm, E. (2007) Full Publication of Results Initially Presented in Abstracts, *Cochrane Database of Systematic Reviews*, Issue 2, Article MR000005, available from www.mrw.interscience.wiley.com/cochrane/clsysrev/articles/MR000005/frame.html.

Schmidt, C. M. and Eckerman, N. L. (2001) Circulation of Core Collection Monographs in an Academic Medical Library, *Bulletin of the Medical Library Association*, **89** (2), 165–9.

Siess, J. (2008) What Role Does and Should the Medical Library Play in Patient Education?, *One-person Library*, **24** (12), 7–9.

Smith, R. (2006) *The Trouble with Medical Journals*, Royal Society of Medicine Press.

Snow, B. (2008) *Drug Information: a guide to current resources*, 3rd edn, Medical Library Association Guides, Neal-Schumann.

Starr, S. and Williams, J. (2008) The Long Tail: a usage analysis of pre-1993 print biomedical journal literature, *Journal of the Medical Library Association*, **96** (1), 20–7.

Streeter, J. L., Lu, M. T. and Rybicki, F. J. (2007) RadiologyWiki.org: the free radiology resource that anyone can edit, *Radiographics*, **27** (4), 1193–1200.

Suarez, A. V. and Tsutsui, N. D. (2004) The Value of Museum Collections for Research and Society, *Bioscience*, **54** (1), 66–74.

Taylor, P. (2006) Reading and Writing Patient Records, In Taylor, P. *From Patient Data to Medical Knowledge: the principles and practice of health informatics*, Blackwell/BMJ, 15–31.

Tennant, M. R. and Lyon, J. A. (2007) *Entrez* Gene: a gene-centred 'Information Hub', *Journal of Electronic Resources in Medical Libraries*, 4 (3), 53–78.

Turner, M. B., Vader, A. M. and Walters, S. T. (2008) An Analysis of Cardiovascular Health Information in Popular Young Women's Magazines: what messages are women receiving?, *American Journal of Health Promotion*, 22 (3), 183–6.

Ugaz, A. G. and Resnick, T. (2008) Assessing Print and Electronic Use of Reference/core Medical Textbooks, *Journal of the Medical Library Association*, 92 (2), 145–7.

Uslu, A. M. and Stausberg, J. (2008) Value of the Electronic Patient Record: an analysis of the literature, *Journal of Biomedical Informatics*, 41 (4), 675–82.

Wang, Z. and Ganz, W. (2007) Health Content in Local Television News, *Health Communication*, 21 (3), 213–21.

Weitkamp, E. (2003) British Newspapers Privilege Health and Medicine Over other Science News, *Public Relations Review*, 29 (3), 321–33.

Willett, P. (2008) From Chemical Documentation to Chemoinformatics: 50 years of chemical information science, *Journal of Information Science*, 34 (4), 477–500.

Williams, F. and Boren, S. A. (2008) The Role of the Electronic Medical Record in Care Delivery in Developing Countries, *International Journal of Information Management*, 28 (6), 503–7.

Younger, P. and Boddy, K. (2009) When is a Search not a Search? A comparison of searching the AMED complementary health database via EBSCOhost, OVID and DIALOG, *Health Information and Libraries Journal*, 26 (2), 126–35.

Further reading

Searching for resources for evidence-based practice

De Brún, C. and Pearce-Smith, N. (2009) *Searching Skills Toolkit: finding the evidence*, Wiley/Blackwell.

Guyatt, G., Rennie, D., Meade, M. O. and Cook, D. J. (2008) *Users' Guides to the Medical Literature: a manual for evidence-based clinical practice*, 2nd edn, McGraw-Hill Medical.

Pharmaceutical information sources

In information terms, the most intensive and innovative part of the domain.

Barbour, V., Clark, J., Peiperl, L., Veitch, E., Wong, M. and Yamey, G. (2008) False Hopes, Unwarranted Fears: the trouble with medical news stories, *PLOS Medicine*, 5 (5), 681–3, available from www.plosmedicine.org/article/info%3Adoi%2F10.1371%2Fjournal.pmed.0050118.

Bawden, D. and Robinson, L. (2010) Pharmaceutical Information: a 30-year perspective on the literature, *Annual Reviews of Information Science and Technology*, in press.

Health News – A paper including links to related articles, and to several health news rating services.

Snow, B. (2008) *Drug Information: a guide to current resources*, 3rd edn, Medical Library Association Guides, Neal-Schumann.

Willett, P. (2008) From Chemical Documentation to Chemoinformatics: 50 years of chemical information science, *Journal of Information Science*, 34 (4), 477–500.

Medical journals

A controversial critique:

Smith, R. (2006) *The trouble with medical journals*, Royal Society of Medicine Press.

6

Healthcare information and knowledge management

Introduction

This chapter considers some issues of the management of information and knowledge, including the management of collections, records and archives as they specifically affect healthcare information. These topics have a very large, general literature which will not be reviewed here. The focus will be on the areas where the problems and solutions are specific to the healthcare domain, or at least particularly pressing, or where the healthcare domain has been an innovator and a leader for the rest of the information sector. As we shall see, this has very often been the case, most especially for the well-resourced and information-intensive pharmaceutical sector (Bawden and Robinson, 2010). For overviews of a large literature on information management in the healthcare sector, see Berg (2004), Taylor (2006), Anagnostelis (2008), Bath (2008), Jha, Doolan, Grandt, Scott and Bates (2008), Cleveland and Cleveland (2008), Burke and Weill (2008), and Goldzweig, Towfigh, Maglione and Shekelle (2009).

The health sector has always been in the forefront of the adoption of new technologies for communicating information. Examples since the 1960s include the application of the digital computer, and later the PC; microforms; magnetic tape services and CD-ROMs; online databases; the web; intranets and portals; and mobile devices.

This chapter provides an overview of this scenario, with literature references as appropriate, picking out significant aspects and examples, and is structured into four sections:

- healthcare libraries and information services, looking at the contributions of various types and sectors of library/information services and networks of services within the health domain
- managing healthcare information, including the management of collections, records and archives, and knowledge
- providing healthcare information, covering aspects of information services which are particularly significant for healthcare
- standards, evaluation and impact, dealing with ways health information specialists have evaluated their own services and the information they provide, and their impact on the life and work of their users.

Two previous books have dealt thoroughly with some of these issues and should be consulted for the situation up to their dates of publication (Booth and Walton, 2000; Walton and Booth, 2004). A British Library Research Report from 1997 offers a review of many initiatives and research projects which formed the basis for current practice (Merry, 1997). Wood (2007a) gives a wide-ranging account of health sciences librarianship, particularly from a US perspective.

Healthcare libraries and information services

The extent and diversity of the use of information and knowledge in the healthcare domain has meant that a wide variety of information service providers have a role. Of all domains, it is the one in which all the sectors of the library/information world are most involved and in which there is a particularly wide variety of 'special libraries' and specialist information services. For many of these services, providing healthcare information is their sole *raison d'etre*; for others, it is a part of a wider role. Some may provide their services to general public, but most are geared to serving a 'closed' user group, typically, employees of a health service or industrial organization, or staff and students of an educational institution. Within this setting, services may also be provided for a specific user group, typically, doctors, nurses, or students.

This means that users of healthcare information may have a choice of provider. Doctors in practice who are studying for higher qualifications, for example, may be entitled to services from a number of sources, including the hospital or other health service organization where they work, the educational institution where they study, and their professional association. This complex situation may cause problems for both users and providers in terms of working out who is entitled to use which services,; and may be particularly tricky when it comes to providing access to electronic resources. Fortunately, the 'walls' around services for particular professions or roles are breaking down as multidisciplinary working becomes the norm and as the whole domain becomes more information conscious. In the past, formal information services were provided only for the healthcare professions, and particularly for doctors. For the story of the development of libraries for nurses in the UK, see Wakeham (2002). Libraries are now likely to be actively promoted to the wider healthcare workforce, as well as to patients and other consumers.

We will now consider, in outline and with examples, the contributions of various types and sectors of library/information services, and networks of such services, within the healthcare domain. This follows from the introductory remarks on this topic in the first chapter.

Size and scope of the sector

Examples of the many kinds of healthcare information service have been given in Chapter 1, and throughout in the book. To give an indication of the scale of UK health libraries and information services, a 2002 survey (Ryder, 2002) identified over 660 such services. This is certainly an underestimate, since the survey relied on self-completed questionnaires. Of these services, 51% were in clinical settings (mainly hospitals) in the health services, 20% were in academic institutions, 14% served health management and promotion, 7% were in professional institutions and 4% each in scientific institutes (including a small number of pharmaceutical companies) and charities/patient groups. The British Library represented the national library sector, and two public library services were mentioned. The commercial and charitable sectors are certainly underestimated, because the nature of the survey emphasized formal libraries and health service settings. Nonetheless, it gives an indication of the size and complexity of the sector.

Note that these do not include the very many small and informally organized collections of information maintained by individuals, and a variety of organizations such as doctors' practices, academic departments and so on. This is not because of lack of importance – these local collections are often the first line of recourse of information; however, we are dealing here with formally constituted information services.

National and academic libraries

On the largest scale, excluding some international networks, which will be mentioned later, is the national library sector. For healthcare, this takes two forms. There are national medical or health libraries, often associated with or an off-shoot of the main national library. The best known example is the US National Library of Medicine (www.nlm.hih.gov). Such libraries may also be associated with major academic or public libraries. The Finnish National Library of Health Science is an example of an institution based in a research university , while the German National Library of Medicine is based in the University and City Library of Cologne.[1]

The academic library is most evidently represented by the library/information services of medical schools. Some, particularly those of Harvard and Yale, have already been mentioned as exemplars of large healthcare collections. Other academic library services will be found in the colleges of nursing and of other healthcare professions. Most numerous are the collections and services within universities and colleges that run courses in healthcare disciplines and the biomedical sciences. These, to a greater or lesser extent, provide separate services for their health-related users, distinct from the wider user community. Some larger schools for older pupils, particularly where there is a vocational curriculum, also provide significant collections and services for health-related topics.

Public libraries

The public library sector is not always thought of as being among healthcare information providers, but this situation is changing. Most obviously, collections of health-related material are expanding to meet the needs of a user population that is increasingly interested in health and wellness. Governments and health services are also looking more to the public library sector to support health promotion campaigns and to meet their goal for patients and carers to be better informed and take a more active part in planning their treatment. For an example of provision of this sort, see the health-related services of the Chicago Public Library (USA) and of Westminster Public Libraries (UK).[2]

Public libraries may play an even more direct role. The term 'bibliotherapy', or 'books on prescription', has been used to describe the use of materials (written and audio-visual), usually through a public library, to help the recovery of people suffering from both physical and mental illness (Brewster, 2008; Fanner and Urquhart, 2008). There is increasing evidence that such services can have measurable positive effects, and various public library based initiatives in the UK have resulted (Hicks, 2009).

Special library and information services

It is, however, the special library and information service sector which predominates in the provision of healthcare information. This sector has many and diverse forms of service, aimed at different user groups and providing different forms of services. The most significant of these are reviewed below.

Health service information services

These are among the most numerous services of this kind. They may operate on a national level (the British NHS Evidence service being a good example), but more typically at a local or regional level, providing services in hospitals, clinics, health centres, healthcare training centres and similar locations. They are typically organized to reflect the local organization of healthcare generally; in the UK, for example, they reflect the structure of NHS Trusts.

Most services are provided for clinical staff, but there are also services in support of health service management and of public health and health promotion. Highly specialist services, such as those providing quick-response information on poisons and poisoning, are also included here, as are those whose main duty is to provide statistical and financial summaries. Most such services meet the needs of defined groups of health professionals. However, as noted earlier, there is a developing tendency for cross-disciplinary provision, and for also provision to patients and consumers (Kennedy, 2007).

Professional associations

Some of these have been exemplified above as major health information providers. Associations for doctors, nurses and other healthcare providers (often quite specialized in nature, so that a practitioner may well belong to more than one) typically offer library services, including digital provision, plus a more or less extensive range of specialized services and collections. The more long-established associations often have historically valuable archives and other collections. Provided for their membership, they usually offer only limited access to 'outsiders'. Although not such a significant force, associations of professional and commercial organizations in the healthcare area also provide information services of various kinds.

Services in research centres and institutes

These are quite varied in nature. Research institutes in the biomedical and clinical sciences will offer largely scientific information services, often with access to specialized databanks and informatics capabilities. Those centres focusing on service provision and management – the UK King's Fund is a good example – will provide collections and services in those areas. Access to services from such sources is variable and often depends on whether their funding is largely public or private. Some offer full public access as part of their mission, others offer access only in a limited way, or as part of consultancy.

Industrial information services

These also comprise a very varied part of the sector. Best known are the various kinds of information service within the pharmaceutical industry. 'Outward facing' medical information units provide services to healthcare professionals (most usually doctors and pharmacists); research information units have the companies' research workers as their user group; commercial information units serve management and marketing functions; and records management and archiving functions safeguard information and data needed for legal and regulatory purposes. There may be overlaps and different relationships between these types of unit, based on the structure of their parent company.

Other companies within the healthcare industry also offer information services, though not to the same extent as the pharmaceutical sector, which has been recognized for many years as the epitome of an 'information intensive' industry (Haygarth-Jackson, 1987; Bawden and Robinson, 2010).

Commercial healthcare providers and funders

These include the operators of private medical services, hospitals, care homes, etc., as well as funders of healthcare, such as insurance companies. Their role and significance varies greatly, internationally, according to the healthcare systems in place in each country. They provide information services to their own staff, and increasingly to potential and actual users of their services.

Consumer health providers and patient groups

Another large and disparate group, this encompasses a wide variety of commercial providers, health service organizations, charities and self-help groups. While some offer well-resourced and sophisticated services, many are run informally and by individuals. Some are based on rather traditional library/information services, collections and advice functions, offering, for example, information largely as printed leaflets and guides. Many, however, are now largely digital and focused around a social networking approach.

Networking groups

As if this plethora of services of different types were not sufficient, there is also a strong tradition of information groupings and networks in this area. Health information specialists are sociable creatures, and very fond of creating networks and groups. These have been, and still are, very productive in making the best use of resources by collaboration and in sharing ideas for good practice. Such groups and networks are to be found at local, regional, national and international levels.

Managing healthcare information

In this section we will deal with three aspects of information management of great importance in the healthcare domain: the management of collections; the management of records and archives; and the management of knowledge.

Managing collections

The collection – an organized set of information-bearing items chosen for a particular purpose in a particular context or environment, and usually unique to that situation – is at the heart of any library, information service, records centre or archive.

Collection management is usually understood as comprising all the processes are involved in the creation and maintenance of a collection: selection, acquisition, processing of material for integration into the collection, preservation, provision of access, evaluation of use and weeding/disposal. It may be necessary to provide special cataloguing or resource description procedures, or to allow for particular access points and interfaces, for a collection. Similarly, it may be necessary to establish policies for preservation and control of use for the items within a collection; the latter being 'positive', to promote wide usage, or 'negative', to restrict access in some way (see Clayton and Gorman, 2001 for a detailed account of these issues, and Kovacs, 2009 for an account of electronic collections in particular).

Health information collections have to be created and maintained in situations where there is usually a large number of potential sources, with an identifiable 'core' set of resources but a scatter across many sources; hence the enthusiasm for various core lists. We looked at a number of these, designed for smaller library services, in Chapter 5. On a larger scale, the UK health service has negotiated (through the National Library for Health, succeeded by NHS Evidence) a number of variants of a national core content collection, encompassing several bibliographic databases, thousands of e-journals and hundreds of e-books, as well as collections of medical images, accessible, in principle, to all staff of the English health services (some hundreds of thousands of potential users).

Optimizing collections

A number of methods have been developed for optimizing collections, generally based on some combination of expert assessment, comparison of usage figures, and bibliometric analysis. Examples include:

- creation of a book collection, based on expert assessment and comparison with published core lists, to meet the needs of physicians' assistants (Grodzinski, 2001)
- creation of a journal collection for orthopaedics, based on usage of current stock, interlibrary loan requests and journal impact factors and half-lives (Bardyn, Resnick, Mazo and Egol, 2009)
- identification of a core journal collection for user groups in medical sub-specialities, combining bibliometric factors, usage statistics and user opinion (McAphee, Vucovich and Lorbeer, 2008)
- identification of a core journal list for a medical school by analysing the overlap of journals held by institutions and on published core lists, and

comparing this with usage and interlibrary loan data (Shearer and Nagy, 2003); data on use of the list generated in this way was later used to compare alternative e-journal bundles (Shearer, Klatt and Nagy, 2009).

A closely associated process, using the same sorts of tools, is the assessment of an existing collection as a basis for planning future collection development. An example is the analysis of the book and journal collections of an academic health science library for the adequacy of their coverage of the literature of drug resistance. This used a variety of methods, including checking against bibliographies and other library collections, and bibliometric analysis (Bergen and Nemee, 1999).

Digital collections

The trend towards a digital information environment has implications for the nature of the collection itself, as well as the practicalities of managing it. Again, this applies, in principle, to the healthcare domain no more and no less than to others. The healthcare sector has, however, been in the lead, first in the integration of digital materials into printed collections, and then in the creation of fully digital collections. Libraries in the healthcare area, like others, have seen use of printed collections fall dramatically, while electronic resources have correspondingly increased (Martell, 2008).

The move to digital collections generally means a move from 'ownership' and 'location' to 'access'. The collection takes on a virtual, dynamic and impermanent nature. The lifecycles of such collections can vary much more than with traditional physical collections: they may be stable over time or grow steadily, in the manner of a physical collection, or they may be created and dispersed very rapidly. We noted in Chapter 5 that one advantage of digital resources is that virtual special collections can be created very rapidly, for example, in response to the swine flu pandemic of 2009.

Any digital resource, perceived as a single entity by its users, may in fact be a composite or aggregate of distributed sources: a collection composed of such entities is even more an aggregate. Given that the resources of which it is composed will often link to other resources, it becomes very difficult to place a 'boundary' around the collection, clearly distinguishing what is inside it. Furthermore, a single digital resource may be simultaneously in several digital collections, which could not happen in the pre-digital world.

Collections of digital resources can no longer be thought of as a set of physical items in a particular location, or even as a collection of digital items on a particular computer. Rather, they provide a means of selecting items from the universe of knowledge. The collection may be defined as 'a set of criteria for selecting resources from the broader information space', with collection membership defined 'through criteria rather than containment' (Lagoze and Fielding, 1998).

The move to a largely digital collection, of course, raises questions about what the physical space of a library or information service is for, and the continued role for a 'library place'. For ruminations on this from a health information perspective, see Littleton and Rethlefsen (2008), and for a broader view see Pomerantz and Marchionini (2007).

As with all other aspects of the move to a largely digital environment, the collection manager must adapt to a wider range of forms of material – not merely the digital equivalents of well-understood printed materials, but also newer formats. The effect of this in health environments has been described for formats such as e-books (Armstrong and Lonsdale, 2005) and podcasts (Kraft, 2007). Traditional materials are often presented in unfamiliar ways, which require change in collection processes; for an example of the changes to cataloguing required in health libraries, see Perkins (2009). Kovacs (2009) gives detailed examples of the creation and maintenance of digital collections in a health sciences library and a partnership between a health sciences library and a public library.

It is not, by the way, only digital materials that pose problems for collections managers. Healthcare libraries collections, by virtue of the breadth of interests and perspectives within the domain, often include materials which it is problematic to integrate; an example is works of fiction which, though they may be appropriate and important, are difficult to fit into academic health sciences collections (Dali and Dilevko, 2006).

Journals, rather than being acquired by subscription to individual titles, are commonly obtained as part of an e-journal 'bundle', greatly widening the pool of available information, at the expense of the careful selection of components of the collection. Several studies in health libraries have shown that reliance on bundles, publishers' portfolios, core collections and the like is not entirely satisfactory. The purchaser may be paying for many unwanted journals, while missing much-needed specialist titles (see, for example, Murphy (2007 and Kelson, 2008).

With the move towards Web 2.0 facility, the nature of the collection alters again, since the spirit of Web 2.0 suggests that the users of the collection should contribute to its content, perhaps by creating wikis and similar knowledge sharing tools. This is a troubling prospect to many collection managers. However, in the healthcare area, particularly for collections used mainly by healthcare professionals, this may be a very appropriate approach.

Finally, as a counterpart to the predominant issue of the move to digital collections, we might note that sometimes there is an opportunity to create a historical collection of printed material. A description of the issues involved in such a project for the pharmacy area is given by Flannery (2001).

Managing records and archives

'The medical record', wrote Nicholson and Walker in 1995, 'is the most important tool for healthcare information storage retrieval and analysis. It is the repository of all information concerning the patient's history and health, diseases, health risks, diagnoses, prognoses, tests and examinations, treatment and follow up. It is also a main source of information for health management; quality assurance, health statistics, service utilization analysis among other activities. Information support of healthcare therefore centres on and begins with the medical record system.'

Patient and treatment records

This quotation emphasizes the importance of the individual medical record. Taylor (2006, chapter 2) gives a detailed overview of the issues. The management of medical records is a major task for national health services (which must necessarily seek to maintain an accurate and up-to-date record for each member of their populations) and their transition to digital form is typically accompanied by many difficulties. This last has certainly been so in the UK experience. Systems differ greatly internationally, according to local circumstances, but the basic importance of such records, and the records management challenges which they create, are universal. These include the perennial issue of how long records must be kept and in what format, and to what extent disposal of some material relating to patient care is justifiable after some determined period (Corn, 2009).

Although the patient's medical record is of obvious importance, it is by no means the only form of record relating to episodes of healthcare. There are, for example, records systems specifically for nursing care (Currell and Urquhart, 2005). There will also usually be some form of patient administration system in a hospital, clinic or practice, keeping other forms of data. Typically; these and other forms of record of care are not integrated either with each other or with the individual patient record. When care is provided by different parts of a health service, the transfer of essential information is usually not a trivial matter.

This very large amount of data, from varied sources, is ultimately consolidated into the form of health service statistics, which may be used to assess the effectiveness of the service, identify problems, and so on. An example from the UK is the Hospital Episodes Statistics (HES) system, a 'data warehouse' for hospital treatment in England.[3] This has been used not only for numerous studies of the effectiveness of treatments for particular conditions, but – more controversially – for the comparison of different payment regimes (Farrar, Yi, Sutton, Chalkley, Sussex and Scott, 2009) and for comparison of the performance of individual doctors (Croft, Williams, Mann, Cohen and Phillips, 2007).

Library/information specialists have typically had little role in this massive records management task. Organization of tasks within health services – based largely on historical factors – typically places the management of medical records in a different part of the structure from the management of other forms of information and knowledge. This is far from ideal in terms of managing the whole of healthcare information in an integrated way.

Taylor (2006, chapter 2) sets out three challenges for the management of such records in the future:

- the integration of information across different healthcare organizations
- the use of routinely collected data as the basis for medical records
- the development of software that can respond to the content of a patient's history.

The first of these has been noted above. The second seeks to address the problem of inconsistency in records, due to the freedom that healthcare staff have in deciding what should be entered into the records on any particular occasion. The third invokes a long-standing wish to have a system that could 'look through' the masses of data available, and act as an aide memoire to practitioners.

Other healthcare-related records

We have concentrated here on the kinds of records which are of direct relevance to healthcare provision. But, as Fisher (2006) points out, health services hold many other kinds of records: drug ordering, and building construction and maintenance, for example. All of these need to be managed appropriately and efficiently.

While acknowledging the great importance of health records of this kind, and the data compilations derived from them, we should note that the management of records is of great importance in other health contexts. Any biomedical or clinical research activity must keep appropriate records to meet the requirements of regulations such as Good Clinical Practice and Good Laboratory Practice. The pharmaceutical industry, in particular, has for many years been required to adopt elaborate records management programmes throughout the processes of drug discovery and development, in order to meet the requirements of regulators (Bawden and Robinson, 2010). For specific examples, see Stamatoplos (2005), Chalmers (2001), Goodman (1994), Rammell (1997), and Samuel (1998).

Healthcare has, as has been emphasized, a very long history of recorded documentation, which means that archives of historical material are of importance in many settings, and are important for the history of healthcare in particular and of society generally. There are many examples, in varied settings, from the records of the pharmaceutical industry (Stevenson, 1997) to the archives of specific health centres and services (Hall, 2001), and those of long-established professional associations. The Royal Society of Medicine in London is a good example of the last category.[4]

Archiving is, of course, a discipline and profession in its own right. However, there will be occasions when health information specialists without archive training may become involved in such work, perhaps with local collections; Sokolow (2004) gives advice for this eventuality.

Managing knowledge

The idea of knowledge management (KM) came to prominence in the 1990s. It became a much-promoted business concept, stimulated in particular by Nonaka and Takeuchi's influential 1995 book *The knowledge-creating company*, and a great deal of effort was devoted to it. It rapidly gained a great deal of publicity as an important new discipline or practice for the information sciences, even though there was not − and still is not − any agreed understanding of exactly what it is. It was dismissed by some as a fad or a gimmick, and one eminent commentator went so far as to call it a 'nonsense' (Wilson, 2002). It has generated a large literature of its own: for general overviews, see Jashapara (2004), Tsoukas (2005), Srikantaiah and Koenig (2008) and Martin (2008).

One reason for the disagreement as to the nature of KM is that it has been 'claimed' by three different professional groups – computing and IT, human resources (HR), and information science – all whom have reasons to say that KM is a natural part of their territory. To compound the confusion, the relation of KM to the rest of information science has been understood to two very different ways.

One perspective takes KM to be a kind of umbrella concept, including everything to do with the management of information. This idea is expressed nicely for healthcare by Wyatt (2001), for clinical knowledge management, which he regards as 'the collection, processing, visualization, storage, preservation, and retrieval of health related data and information, whether it be on an individual or collection of subjects'.

More common, however, and the perspective which we will take here, is that KM is a particular aspect of information management: that which is concerned with the knowledge possessed by individual people (so-called tacit knowledge) rather than the explicit knowledge written down in formal documents, and with how the sharing of this tacit knowledge can be promoted. This view, of KM as a 'sub-speciality' within information science which may be of particular value for improving both clinical care and practice management, is expressed clearly by Orzano et al. (2008). This concept builds on the importance of the 'practical craft knowledge' in the healthcare domain, which was discussed in Chapter 1.

Two main approaches to the practice of KM have been adopted. One, seeing it as an extension of conventional information management, focuses on creating 'know how databases', to which expert practitioners are encouraged to contribute their practical knowledge. The second, considering that personal and tacit knowledge, by its nature, cannot be captured in this explicit way, focuses on putting people in touch with one another through tools such as 'indexes of expertise' or 'corporate yellow pages'.

Regardless of which approach is favoured, knowledge management always involves some element of change of organization culture so as to encourage the sharing of knowledge, which rarely happens naturally. This is why HR people sometimes like to claim KM as their speciality. An increasingly common example is the 'community of practice': a group of practitioners who come together voluntarily, typically outside any formal organizational groupings, to share knowledge and experience (see, for example, Urquhart, Yeoman and Sharp, 2002; Booth, 2004a; and Adams, Blandford, Budd and Bailey, 2005). This kind of informal or organizational learning is usually regarded as a key part of the benefit of KM (Jashapara, 2004), and has been recognized as such in healthcare settings for many years (see, for example, Confessore, 1997).

Technology, providing the means by which knowledge is shared, is also invariably important. Web 2.0 applications have had a great influence on the technology side, largely replacing the 'group working' IT solutions previously used.

Knowledge management programmes

There are usually three elements to a knowledge management programme, though one often predominates, according to circumstances:

- content: the type of knowledge to be shared, and the way in which it is represented
- technology: the means by which it is shared
- culture, promoting the sharing of knowledge.

This means that there can be no 'one size fits all' best solution for healthcare knowledge management. Booth (2001) gives a helpful list of ten 'building blocks' for KM in healthcare settings, encompassing all three elements:

- conducting a knowledge audit
- knowledge mapping
- providing a knowledge-sharing network
- compiling a database of expertise
- scanning the environment
- creating communities of practice
- measuring knowledge capital
- organizing and classifying knowledge
- creating a chief knowledge officer
- conducting entry and exit debriefings.

This approach has been implemented in the Knowledge Management section of the UK NHS Evidence service, which shows the implementation of several of these activities .[5] It is also present in an overview of KM in the public health area, which emphasizes discussion forums, social networking, online communities, people locator systems and team strengthening activities (Liebowitz, Schieber and Andreadis (2009).

Published examples of KM activities in various aspects of healthcare include: Booth and Brice (2004), who give a clear account of the rationale for a variety of approaches in UK health services; Orzano et al. (2009), for primary care; and Ghosh and Scott (2007), for hospital nurses.

It seems clear that KM will remain a very significant part of information management practices in the health information domain, given the importance of informal tacit 'practice knowledge', and also the potential of KM to assist organizational learning. Information specialists from the healthcare library/information community would seem to be a good position to promote this, to a greater extent than has happened up to the present time.

Providing healthcare information

The detailed activities within services which provide health information are, in many respects, similar to those in other domains. We will not therefore look in any detail at topics such as the layout of physical libraries, the marketing and promotion of library services, planning and project management, preservation and conservation, operation of library management systems, budgeting, people management and the many other aspects of the operation of library information services. These are well described in numerous sources; good starting points are the books by Chowdhury, Burton, McMenemy and Poulter (2008), and by Evans, Layzell Ward and Rugaas (2000). A specific 'healthcare take' on these issues will be found in the books edited by Booth and Walton (2000) and by Walton and Booth (2004).

There are certain aspects of information provision that directly reflect the nature of the healthcare information domain. These are services which are unique to healthcare, or are particularly strongly represented in the health environment, or in which the sector has been a pioneer. These will be considered in five sections:

- reference services
- document supply
- supporting learning
- facilitating users
- proactive services.

Reference services

Reference services are one of the fundamental forms of information service, and have been offered through healthcare libraries since they acquired their modern form. With the move to greater user access to digital resources there is a trend for provision of this kind of service to be replaced by advice and facilitation, as will be discussed later, but provision of reference service is still common, if not universal, in health settings.

Processes and frameworks for dealing with reference queries are given by Cassell and Hiremath (2009) and, for the specific situation of a pharmaceutical industry information department, by Davies (2001). Spatz (2008) gives a detailed account for librarians who have to answer reference queries on medical topics from the public.

Reference services are usually provided locally, although digital materials and electronic communication now go a long way towards mitigating the limitations of local collections of reference material. Support for local reference has been provided for many years by central and national centres (see, for example, Burke, Greenberg and Ahmed, 2007 for NLM reference services).

There is a specific and difficult issue arising in healthcare reference work when it is carried out on behalf of the general public. Information specialists performing this work have a duty to provide appropriate information, but may not – except in the unusual circumstances where they are qualified healthcare professionals – give medical advice. This may pose tricky ethical dilemmas in some circumstances. Medical information service staff in pharmaceutical companies, for example, are severely restricted in the nature of the information and advice which they are permitted to give to enquirers other than healthcare workers.

Most reference service is provided through the usual medium of a selection of quality factual sources – mainly resources of the tertiary level noted above, with secondary sources for more specialized enquiries. Boorkman, Huber, and Blackwell (2008) give an extensive listing. Small sets of reference sources of the kind which might be found in general collections, particularly in public libraries, are given for British users by Duckett, Walker and Donnelly (2008) and for American users by Cassell and Hiremath (2009). Both list a range of dictionaries, directories, encyclopaedias, handbooks, statistical sources and such. While are common to both, it is interesting to note that most are specific to the national setting. Health concepts and health sciences are international; the specific information needed, by the general public in particular, is national and local.

Many reference sources are now, of course, in digital form, though some persist in print, typically as pocket books or annual updates of references sources, as we saw in Chapter 5. Reference services have had to adapt to meet this change and to accommodate the newer forms of communication available; Wood (2007b) gives an overview of this from a health library perspective. One consequence is that reference services increasingly take the form of technical support, as enquiries are less about the information itself than about the technicalities of accessing digital resources (Bardyn and Young, 2007).

Health libraries have been in the lead in providing digital and mobile reference services, by means such as instant messaging and virtual chat services (Kipnis and Kaplan, 2008; Lapidus and Bond, 2009; Tao, McCarthy, Krieger and Webb, 2009).

Document supply

As we have seen, the healthcare domain has a large and wide selection of sources, and information on any particular topic is scattered among them. This means that, despite the best efforts of information providers to provide optimal collections, and core lists of the most important titles, there will always be required material that is not present in even the largest collections. Health information services, more than those in most other areas, therefore require means to obtain material which they do not hold.

There are variations within the health sector. The pharmaceutical industry has always been a major user of, and innovator in, document supply services, often developing such systems on a global basis to supply multinational organizations through a single system. The industry also pioneered the use of systems for digital document provision, rather than relying on paper documents arriving in the post (for examples of industry systems developing over the years, see Haygarth-Jackson, 1987; Delaney, 2003; Kasarab, 2006).

In academic and clinical settings the need for document supply is usually met by inter-library loan services, using the document supply services of national libraries and commercial organizations operating regionally, nationally or internationally (see, for examples, Lacroix and Collins, 2007; Flake and Poznaka, 2007; Gavel and Hedlund, 2008; Glover, Addison, Gleghorn, Aalai and Annis, 2009; and Hill and Roth, 2009).

There is also a reliance on the various networks which proliferate in the health information environment. An example of this form of self-help is the mailing lists operated by JISC in the UK for British healthcare librarians.[6] These are widely used to request loan of documents and provision of photocopies, for announcements of duplicated journal holdings, and so on.

Supporting learning

Virtually all healthcare information services have some remit with regard to the support of learning, including formal education and training. For some services, this is their main function; the libraries of medical schools and academic health science libraries are the obvious example. Libraries and information services in clinical settings, hospital libraries for example, will often support their users who are undertaking formal courses. Others will support individual informal learning and the organization learning processes noted earlier in the context of knowledge management. For an overview of these various aspects, see Peacock, Walton and Booth (2004).

Health libraries have been in the forefront of using new technologies for learning, and in the integration of information provision into e-learning, blended learning and mobile learning (Booth, Carroll, Papaioannou, Sutton and Wang, 2009; Walton, Childs and Blenkinsopp, 2005).

Facilitating users

As is the case in other domains, the move to an increasingly digital information environment has meant that health information specialists are increasingly involved in the facilitation of direct use of information sources by users. This is in contrast to the previous main roles of the information professional, as custodian and as intermediary.

This requirement for user facilitation is amplified in the healthcare setting by the increasingly strong requirements for healthcare professionals to be competent in their dealings with information. For example, the UK General Medical Council's *Tomorrow's Doctors* report (2009) states that doctors should be able to:

- access information sources and use the information in relation to patient care, health promotion, giving advice and information to patients, and research and education
- access reliable information about medicines
- make effective use of computers and other information systems, including storing and retrieving information.

An equivalent report on desirable competencies in undergraduate medical education Europe-wide (Cumming and Ross, 2008) suggests that doctors should be able to:

- use information and information technology effectively in a medical context

- define and carry out an appropriate literature search
- access information sources.

These, and similar requirements for doctors in other countries and for other healthcare professions, place an added emphasis on the need for information specialists to provide various ways of assisting health workers to make good use of the domain's knowledge base. This is done in a number of ways, of which two are of particular importance.

The creation of portals, at local or wider level, giving access to selected resources, often with guidance as to selection and use, is a commonly used method of assisting users. This is often associated with training of users in the use of specific information sources. Pioneered in the pharmaceutical industry (Goodman and Boyce, 2001), this has become a significant task for many health information specialists in recent years (Hicks, 2000); for some specific examples, see Lapidus (2007) for pharmacy students, Ayre (2006) for primary and community healthcare staff, and Whipple, Richwine, Kaneshiro and Brahmi (2009) for new medical students. Attempts have been made to assess the effectiveness of this training in terms both of improved skills and confidence in using information sources, and of impact on professional practice (see, for example, Brettle, 2007; Trinder, Fleet and Gray, 2007).

This kind of user training has some overlap with the promotion of learning mentioned above, particularly for information services in academic institutions, but emphasizes training in information skills, rather than simply providing materials. An increasingly common trend is for information skills training to be seen as part of a move to promote 'information literacy' to healthcare students, or indeed to the whole workforce of a healthcare organization. Information literacy, and some very similar concepts, are known by a number of different names, including digital literacy, media literacy and information fluency (Bawden, 2001, 2008a). In general, they all relate to an ability to understand the nature of information and information resources in one's subject area, and resulting competencies in selecting and using appropriate resources.

Promoting this idea for the whole healthcare workforce is a new and challenging concept. Traditionally, information services have targeted the professionally qualified groups – doctors and nurses in particular – who may be assumed to have some prior level of understanding of these issues. While the importance of serving these groups has not diminished, there is now a perceived need to reach out to those groups in the workforce who do not have such high levels of general and professional education. This may mean that information services may become involved in the promotion of basic literacy and numeracy, at one end of the information literacy spectrum.

Information literacy programmes have been described, for example, for nursing students (Craig and Corrall, 2007; Schulte, 2008), for doctors in practice (Petrak, Markulin and Matic, 2008), and for research scientists in a pharmaceutical company (Bawden and Robinson, 2002a), and recommended for the education of public health workers (Cobus, 2008). Craig (2009) describes a programme intended for the whole of the healthcare workforce in Scotland.

In order to provide such training and promotion, and support for learners in all respects, health information specialists may themselves need training both in information literacy concepts and in training methods. Robinson, Hilger-Ellis, Osborne, Rowlands, Smith, Weist, Whetherly and Phillips (2005) review the skills and competencies needed by library/information staff doing this kind of work, and the ways in which they may be gained. Andretta (2008) describes training of this kind provided to health librarians in London. The term 'health literacy' or 'health information literacy', is sometimes used when referring to patients' ability to use information so as to make decisions about their health and to follow instructions for their treatment (Bankson, 2009; Marge, Baker and Wilson, 2009). This is a particular concern for those working in consumer health information services, public libraries and those health service libraries which offer services to patients and carers. Important in all environments, it may be particularly significant in developing countries (Ogunsola, 2009).

Proactive services

The traditional, and no doubt unfair, image of the librarian is of a rather passive figure, curating a collection and waiting to be asked to provide information. This image, if ever truly accurate, has given way to a different reality as library/information services have taken on more proactive roles. Again, healthcare services have been among the first in this, and some of the new forms of service are unique to the healthcare domain.

The first and most widespread of these proactive roles was that of the subject specialist librarian or information officer who, by virtue of their subject knowledge, was able to provide current awareness services, advocacy for new resources, creation of search strategies, detailed subject-oriented training on the use of resources and similar services. It was, and remains, more usual for health information specialists to have a strong subject orientation than is the case for information specialists in other subject areas. This is particularly so in areas like pharmaceutical industry information services, or in medicines information services in the health services, where it would be difficult to perform the role without subject knowledge. In academic health science libraries, and in posts in health service libraries, an initial subject background, while helpful, is not essential, but some means of gaining an understanding of health terminology and concepts is certainly needed (Petrinic and Urquhart, 2007; Watson, 2008).

The natural extension of the subject specialist role has been the 'embedding' of information specialists into research or clinical departments or teams so that they can be physically close to their users, appreciating their needs better and providing a proactive service with the ability to see and evaluate the results immediately. This kind of role was pioneered in scientific research institutions, and particularly in the pharmaceutical industry (Sze, 1985).

Clinical librarians and 'informationists'

In health services, this role has been taken by the 'clinical librarian', established in the USA and UK as long ago as the 1970s (Childs, 2004). The clinical librarian supports one or more teams of health workers, usually in a hospital setting, attending ward rounds and clinical meetings, with the intention of providing quality information at the point of need. The development of this role was strongly linked with increasing emphasis on the need for good information for evidence-based practice. Because clinical librarians can get to know their users well and follow up on the value of the information provided, this should enable a very good standard of information service. However, evidence is limited as to whether this approach is cost-effective or effective at all, given the new range of digital services available to clinicians.

The clinical librarian role has not been adopted very widely, many services having been experimental or temporary (for overviews and examples, see Childs, 2004; Tod, Bond, Leonard, Gilsenan and Palfreyman, 2007; Urquhart, Turner, Durbin and Ryan, 2007; and Brookman, Lovell, Henwood and Lehmann, 2006).

A further extension of the embedding role has come, in the USA particularly, in the form of the 'informationist'. This is a person with a good understanding of both the scientific or clinical speciality and the library/information aspects, and accredited as such. Informationists are an integral part of a scientific, clinical or public health team, rather than on secondment from a central library or information service. Again the emphasis is on immediate information support for evidence-based practice. Although there has been interest in this role, it remains to be seen to what extent it will be adopted (see, for background, Rankin, Grefsheim and Canto, 2008; Whitmore, Grefsheim and Rankin, 2008; Oliver, Dalrymple, Lehmann, McClennan, Robinson and Twose, 2008). The idea is not entirely new: the 'scientific informationist', as distinct from the information scientist, was recognized some decades ago (Bawden, 2008b).)

The clinical librarian and informationist roles assume that the information specialist will work in close contact with groups of users in the same setting – typically a hospital or research institute – over a extended period of time. This has evident advantages in allowing understanding of needs to be gained, relationships to be developed, and follow-up actions for information provided, to be the norm. There will also be considerable similarity of needs, interests and behaviour in the groups being served, making service provision easier to plan.

Outreach services

An arguably more challenging form of proactive service is the 'outreach' service to groups of users who are not in one place, nor in convenient contact with conventional library/information services. The most obvious example is frontline community healthcare workers – family doctors, community nurses, social care and health promotion workers and so on – who typically work from small clinics and offices and spend much of their time in the field. They may feel isolated, in information terms as well as otherwise, and lack confidence in being up-to-date with best practice. For a study of these issues with community-based physiotherapists in the UK, see Bourne, Dziedzic, Morris, Jones and Sim (2007).

Providing effective services to these groups presents problems of continuity of contact, in addition to the great diversity of needs and interests. A proactive approach is needed to overcome the isolation factor, and this is typically provided by a specialist outreach service, operated on a full-time or part-time basis by an information specialist from a central service. For examples of such services in the UK, and evaluations of their effectiveness, see Dowse and Sen (2007) and Robinson and Bawden (2007).

Standards, evaluation and impact

In this section, we will consider the ways in which health information specialists have evaluated their services, set standards and benchmarks for services and tried to show their impact on the life and work of their users; and also how they have evaluated the information which they provide. The two aspects of evaluation are closely connected.

Evaluating information

Concern for the quality of health information is not at all a new thing. As we saw in Chapter 2, health has always been a popular topic for authors and publishers, and much that is published has been inaccurate, biased, out of date, or just plain weird. Librarians have always had a concern to provide reliable and up-to-date materials. The concerns have become much greater since the internet became a major source of health information. For one thing, the older form of the information chain had built-in quality mechanisms, imperfect though these may have been. Books were produced through reputable publishers, whose editors tended to commission them from qualified authors and provided quality assurance in the publication process. Journal articles appeared, for the most part, only after peer review and editorial approval. Though these processes did not prevent some poor-quality material appearing, and sometimes may have held up the appearance of innovative work, they did maintain a generally high level of reliability of information.

With the advent of the internet, and specifically the web, such measures could be by-passed, with websites created by anyone who wished. The 'homogenizing' effect of the web is another factor. Through a web browser, all information looks pretty much the same; we have lost the visual and tactile clues which distinguish the textbook from the letter, the academic journal from the newspaper, and the photocopied advertisement from the encyclopaedia article. Anonymity, and even misrepresentation of authorship, is much more easily achieved on the web than in the older information environment. And, particularly with the use of the web for consumer health information and advice to patients, the role of the doctor and nurse as advisers has to a degree been circumvented.

All these factors have contributed to a desire, from quite an early stage of the web's use for communicating health information, to have some form of objective assessment of the quality of health information on the internet. This was, and is, usually done through some form of 'checklist' attributes of the source of information. These lists are many and they all differ slightly, but typically include factors such as:

- authorship: who provides the information?
- authority: what qualifications do they have to do so?
- bias: is any particular point of view stressed, is the source 'sponsored'?
- content: what is included?
- completeness: is the information intended to be comprehensive?
- coverage: what are the limits – time coverage, geographic scope, etc.?
- audience: for whom is information intended – professionals, students, public?
- accuracy: is detailed 'hard' information given, and is it correct?
- reliability: can the information be relied upon?
- links: what links or references are given to back up the information provided, or to give access to more details?
- currency: how up-to-date is the material?
- language: in what language/s is the information presented (this may mean professional/laypersons' language, as well as English, French, etc.)?

Cullen (2006) and Javier (2004) give comparisons of several such lists, and discuss the issues in their construction and use.

The results of this kind of assessment have appeared in various resources. Sources judged as good quality have appeared in core lists, been made available through portals and so on. Internet subject gateways, such as the healthcare and biomedical sections of Intute (noted in Chapter 5), have used such assessments to choose sources and have usually made their quality criteria public (Bawden and Robinson, 1999, 2002b). And various organizations have promulgated quality labelling, or 'kitemarking', of health resources which pass a quality threshold. The best known and longest established of the latter is the HONcode labelling of the independent Health on the Net Foundation (www.hon.ch). This does not attempt to assess quality, but simply to ensure that the source and purpose of the information are clearly stated, and that its presentation conforms to some basic standards, stating sources of funding, privacy policy and so on (Boyer, Selby, Scherrer, and Appel, 1998).

Evaluating services

The evaluation of performance and effectiveness of health information services of all kinds has been an important issue for many years. Not the least of the reasons for this is that these services wish to be seen to be evidence based, like the health professionals they serve. For the most part, the same general approaches are used as for all library/information services. For general overviews, see Matthews (2007), Brophy (2006) and the classic text of Lancaster (1993), and for evaluation in the health sector specifically, see the book by Dudden (2007), and reviews by Booth (2000, 2004b) and Banwell (2000).

The most important methods of evaluation, which may well be used in combination, are audits and maps; performance indicators; and user satisfaction surveys.

Information audits and maps

Information audits are a form of 'whole service' evaluation, aiming to assess the resources available. At their simplest, they enumerate systems, services and resources. More complex audits will assess the cost, and sometimes attempt to assess the use and the value, of the items identified (Buchanan and Gibb, 2007, 2008). Information audits have mainly been carried out in commercial and government information services and records centres. Library services have relied more on use of performance indicators.

Information maps are a form of audit focusing on how information flows within an organization or a part of it. They may use various graphical means to display this. For an overview of the value of information auditing and mapping in a variety of settings, including healthcare organizations, see Ellis, Barker, Potter and Pridgeon (1993).

Performance indicators

The use of standardized sets of performance indicators is a main tool for service quality evaluation in library services. An International Standards Organization (ISO) standard – ISO 11620 *Information and documentation: library performance indicators* (2008) – lists 45 indicators meant for all types of library. An IFLA handbook (Poll and te Boekhorst, 2007) lists 40 indicators, with examples of results. Many national sets of indicators have also been devised, though they are increasingly being replaced by the international standards. These indicators are quantitative measures of service, such as:

- number of visits
- number of loans
- occupancy of seats in reading rooms
- number of accesses to e-resources

- document use rate
- availability of required items
- speed of inter-library loan
- cost per loan
- rate of satisfactorily answered reference requests
- accuracy of book shelving.

The advantages of such indicators are that they should be available from a library's management information with a minimum of extra work, and that they are readily comparable with similar libraries and, year-on-year, within one library. Drawbacks are that they are rather oriented towards traditional, paper-based libraries and they give little qualitative insight into the reasons for the adequacy or otherwise of the service. The data also needs to be interpreted with sensitivity to user needs: the relative importance of the speed of an inter-library loan and of its cost, for example, may be very different for a medical library serving a critical care department and for an academic departmental library serving mainly humanities research students.

It is obviously advantageous if the same set of measures is used across a sector, so that, for example, a medical school library can compare itself directly with similar services: Funk (2008) gives examples for medical libraries. A number of such initiatives have been put into practice. The US Association of Academic Health Sciences Libraries, for example, has carried out annual surveys since 1975, which include performance measures (Shedlock and Byrd, 2003; Byrd and Shedlock, 2003). The US Medical Library Association developed a set of benchmarks, initially for hospital libraries and later also for other health libraries outside academic institutions (Dudden, Corcoran, Kaplan, Magouirk, Rand and Smith, 2006).

Other forms of benchmarking may be used for services other than in libraries. The pharmaceutical industry, for example, has used a variety of performance methods for evaluating the quality of its information services to health professionals and the public. These cover such aspects as the number of enquiries, timeliness of response, amount of information provided, expressed enquirer satisfaction and so on (Robson and Riggens, 2001; Curran, Sundar and Westhe, 2003)

User satisfaction surveys

User satisfaction surveys, a very common method, evaluate a system or service by focusing on the behaviour and opinions of its users, applying a variety of survey methods, both quantitative and qualitative. Inevitably they only give a partial picture, since they cannot include those who could use the service but do not. Most are small-scale and ad hoc, geared to a particular context. Turtle (2005) gives an example of a survey of this kind, in a newly merged service, which attempted to include those who did not currently use the service.

To get the 'bigger picture', user satisfaction figures, in a rather limited quantitative fashion, are included in library performance statistics, using a standard format for comparability. This is particularly common within academic libraries, including academic health science libraries and medical school libraries. In the UK, for example, the Society of College, National and University Libraries (SCONUL) recommends and promotes such surveys through its 'Performance Portal'.[7] Shedlock and Walton (2004) give an example of the standard LibQUAL+ survey tool in an academic medical library, and Robbins and Daniels (2001) give an example of the SERVPERF survey tool used to evaluate reference services in academic health science libraries.

Assessing the impact of services

The ideal evaluation of an information service will show a direct effect or impact. For example, a hospital library will show that its services have improved the survival rates of patients, shortened recovery times, enabled out-patient treatment rather than hospitalization and so on. An academic health science library, or medical school library, will show improved student progression rates and better grades, greater success for staff in gaining research grants and achieving publication. Information units in the pharmaceutical industry will point to shorter development time for products, innovations and patents, higher rates of prescribing of the company's products and so on. In all circumstances, demonstrating a direct contribution to cutting costs and making better use of resources is desirable.

The health sector has been at the forefront of attempts to demonstrate this kind of direct impact, but it is notoriously difficult to do so. While the desirable outcomes are easily measured, relating them to the activities of library/information services in a convincing way has proved problematic. Attempts to find relationships between, for example, spending on information services and desired outcomes have proved disappointing. Either no such relation can be found, or it is confused with other aspects; organizations which spend a lot on information services, for example, are likely to have good training facilities and high-quality equipment, so it is difficult to identify the specific 'information contribution'. An example of a study of this sort is an examination of the effect on prescribing patterns of information provided by a pharmaceutical company (Albano and Santhouse, 2003). Another is a study of the link between clinical librarian input and decreased length of stay in hospital (Banks, Shi, Timm, Christopher, Duggar, Comegys, and McLarty, 2007).

Most of the attempts to demonstrate impact have therefore used some form of critical incident analysis based on interviews with users, examination of records, etc. to identify specific cases where information provision has made an unambiguous change to an outcome. Guidance for the process, based on previous experience, is provided by Weightman, Urquhart, Spink and Thomas (2009), and by Marshall (2007).

Conclusion

The healthcare information domain, as we have seen, has to operate within a rapidly changing environment, with consequently changing user needs. It has to manage a large and diverse knowledge base, with massive records management issues. Its activities may a make direct and significant impact on the health of individuals and populations. It is therefore not surprising that, as we have seen in this chapter, the health sector has been at the forefront of developments in the management of information and knowledge. In several aspects, described above, it has been a leader for the whole library/information profession.

Notes

1 www.terkko.helsinki.fi/english; www.zbmed.de/info.html?&lang=en.
2 www.chipublib.org/cplbooksmovies/poptopics/health.php;
   www.westminster.gov.uk/services/libraries/special/health.
3 www.hesonline.nhs.uk.
4 www.roysocmed.ac.uk/librar/archivess.php.
5 www.library.nhs.uk/knowledgemanagement.
6 See for example, LIS-MEDICAL, LIS-MEDJOURNAL-DUPLICATES
   and LIS-ILL at http://www,jiscmail.ac.uk.
7 http://vamp.diglib.shrivenham.cranfield.ac.uk.

References

Adams, A., Blandford, A., Budd, D. and Bailey, N. (2005) Organisational Communication and Awareness: a novel solution for health informatics, *Health Informatics Journal*, **11** (3), 163–78.

Albano, D. and Santhouse, A. (2003) Evaluation of Wyeth Medical Communications Written Responses and the Impact on Prescribing, *Drug Information Journal*, **37** (4), 445–50.

Anagnostelis, B. (2008) Information Technology: retrospective, *Health Information and Libraries Journal*, **25** (supplement 1), 32–4.

Andretta, S. (2008) Promoting Reflective Information Literacy Practice through Facilitating Information Literacy Education (FILE), *Health Information and Libraries Journal*, **25** (2), 150–3.

Armstrong, C. and Lonsdale, R. (2005) Challenges in Managing e-Books Collections in UK Academic Libraries, *Library Collections, Acquisitions and Technical Services*, **29** (1), 33–50.

Ayre, S. (2006) Workplace Information Skills Outreach Training to Primary Care Staff, *Health Information and Libraries Journal*, **23** (supplement 1), 50–4.

Banks, D. E., Shi, R., Timm, D. F., Christopher, K. A., Duggar, D. C., Comegys, M. and McLarty, J. (2007) Decreased Hospital Length of Stay Associated with Presentation of Cases at Morning Report with Librarian Support, *Journal of the Medical Library Association*, **95** (4), 381–7.

Bankson, H. L. (2009) Health Literacy: an exploratory bibliometric analysis, 1997–2007, *Journal of the Medical Library Association*, **97** (2), 148–50.

Banwell, L. (2000) Evaluating Information Services. In Booth, A. and Walton, G. (eds), *Managing Knowledge in Health Services*, Library Association Publishing, 173–81.

Bardyn, T. P. and Young, C. S. (2007) Migration to an Electronic Journal Collection in a Hospital Library: implications for reference service, *Medical Reference Services Quarterly*, **26** (4), 27–44.

Bardyn, T., Resnick, T., Mazo, R. and Egol, K. A. (2009) Building Orthopedic Journal Collections: analyzing use and bibliometrics in a teaching hospital library, *Journal of Hospital Librarianship*, **9** (2), 123–38.

Bath, P. A. (2008) Health Informatics: current issues and challenges, *Journal of Information Science*, **34** (4), 501–18.

Bawden, D. (2001) Information and Digital Literacies; a review of concepts, *Journal of Documentation*, **57** (2), 218–59.

Bawden, D. (2008a) Origins and Concepts of Digital Literacy. In Lankshear, C. and Knobel, M. (eds), *Digital Literacies: concepts, policies and paradoxes*, Peter Lang, 17–32.

Bawden, D. (2008b) Smoother Pebbles and the Shoulders of Giants: the developing foundations of information science, *Journal of Information Science*, 34 (4), 415–26.

Bawden, D. and Robinson, L. (1999) Internet Subject Gateways, *International Journal of Information Management*, 19 (6), 511–22.

Bawden, D. and Robinson, L. (2002a) Promoting Literacy in a Digital Age: approaches to training for information literacy, *Learned Publishing*, 15 (4), 297–301.

Bawden, D. and Robinson, L. (2002b) Internet Subject Gateways Revisited, *International Journal of Information Management*, 22 (2), 157–62.

Bawden, D. and Robinson, L. (2010) Pharmaceutical Information; a 30-year perspective on the literature, *Annual Reviews of Information Science and Technology*, in press.

Berg, M. (2004) *Health Information Management: integrating information technology in health care work*, Routledge.

Bergen, P. L. and Nemee, D. (1999) An Assessment of Collections at the University of Wisconsin Madison Health Sciences Library: drug resistance, *Bulletin of the Medical Library Association*, 87 (1), 37–42.

Boorkman, J. A., Huber, J. T. and Blackwell, J. (2008) *Introduction to Reference Sources in the Health Sciences*, 5th edn, Neal-Schuman.

Booth, A. (2000) Identifying Users' Needs. In Booth, A. and Walton, G. (eds), *Managing Knowledge in Health Services*, Library Association Publishing, 101–11.

Booth, A. (2001) Managing Knowledge for Clinical Excellence: ten building blocks, *Journal of Clinical Excellence*, 3 (4), 187–94.

Booth, A. (2004a) In Pursuit of e-Quality: the role of 'communities of practice' when evaluating electronic information services, *Journal of Electronic Resources in Medical Libraries*, 1 (3), 25–42.

Booth, A. (2004b) Evaluating Your Performance. In Booth, A. and Brice, A. (eds), *Evidence-based Practice for Information Professionals*, Facet Publishing, 124–37.

Booth, A. and Brice, A. (eds) (2004) Evidence-based Practice for Information Professionals, Facet Publishing.

Booth, A. and Walton, G. (eds) (2000) *Managing Knowledge in Health Services*, Library Association Publishing.

Booth, A., Carroll, C., Papaioannou, D., Sutton, A. and Wang, R. (2009) Applying Findings from a Systematic Review of Workplace-based e-Learning: implications for health information professionals, *Health Information and Libraries Journal*, 26 (1), 4–21.

Bourne, J. A., Dziedzic, K., Morris, S. J., Jones, P. W. and Sim, J. (2007)

Survey of the Perceived Professional, Education and Personal Needs of Physiotherapists in Primary Care and Community Settings, *Health and Social Care in the Community*, **15** (3), 231–7.

Boyer, C., Selby, M., Scherrer, J. R. and Appel, R. D. (1998) The Health on the Net Code of Conduct for Medical and Health Websites, *Computers in Biology and Medicine*, **28** (5), 603–10.

Brettle, A. (2007) Evaluating Information Skills Training in Health Libraries: a systematic review, *Health Information and Libraries Journal*, **24** (1), 18–37.

Brewster, L. (2008) The Reading Remedy, *Public Library Journal*, **23** (3), 2–5.

Brookman, A., Lovell, A., Henwood, F. and Lehmann, J. (2006) What do Clinicians Want from Us? An evaluation of Brighton and Sussex University Hospitals NHS Trust clinical librarian service and its implications for developing future working patterns, *Health Information and Libraries Journal*, **23** (1), 10–21.

Brophy, P. (2006) *Measuring Library Performance: principles and techniques*, Facet Publishing.

Buchanan, S. and Gibb, F. (2007) The Information Audit: role and scope, *International Journal of Information Management*, **27** (3), 19–172.

Buchanan, S. and Gibb, F. (2008) The Information Audit: methodology selection, *International Journal of Information Management*, 2891), 3–11.

Burke, L. and Weill, B. (2008) *Information Technology for the Health Professions*, 3rd edn, Upper Prentice Hall.

Burke, C., Greenberg, S. and Ahmed, T. (2007) Serving our Colleagues: reference and history of medicine services from the National Library of Medicine, *Medical Reference Services Quarterly*, **26** (1), 73–80.

Byrd, G. D. and Shedlock, J. (2003) The Association of Academic Health Science Libraries Annual Statistics: an exploratory twenty-five-year trend analysis, *Journal of the Medical Library Association*, **91** (2), 186–202.

Cassell, K. A. and Hiremath, U. (2009) *Reference Information Services in the 21st Century: an introduction*, 2nd edn, Neal-Schuman.

Chalmers, S. (2001) Developments in Records and Document Management. In Robson, A. S., Bawden, D. and Judd, A. (eds), *Pharmaceutical and Medicines Information Management: principles and practice*, Churchill Livingstone, 199–217.

Childs, S. (2004) Clinical librarianship. In Walton, G. and Booth, A. (eds), *Exploiting Knowledge in Health Services*, Facet Publishing, 89–98.

Chowdhury, G. G., Burton, P. F., McMenemy, D. and Poulter, A. (2008) *Librarianship: an introduction*, Facet Publishing.

Clayton, P. and Gorman, G. E. (2001) *Managing Information Resources in*

Libraries: collection management in theory and practice, Library Association Publishing.

Cleveland, A. D. and Cleveland, D. B. (2008) *Health Informatics for Medical Librarians*, Neal-Schuman.

Cobus, L. (2008) Integrating Information Literacy into the Education of Public Health Professionals: roles for librarians and the library, *Journal of the Medical Library Association*, 96 (1), 28–33.

Confessore, S. J. (1997) Building a Learning Organization: communities of practice, self-directed learning and continuing medical education, *Journal of Continuing Education in the Health Professions*, 17 (1), 5–11.

Corn, M. (2009) Archiving the Phenome: clinical records deserve long-term preservation, *Journal of the American Medical Informatics Association*, 16 (1), 1–6.

Craig, A. and Corrall, S. (2007) Making a Difference? Measuring the impact of an information literacy programme for pre-registration nursing students in the UK, *Health Information and Libraries Journal*, 24 (2), 118–27.

Craig, E. (2009) Learning and Teaching in Action, *Health Information and Libraries Journal*, 26 (1), 77–80.

Croft, G. P., Williams, J. G., Mann, R. Y., Cohen, D. and Phillips, C. J. (2007) Can Hospital Episode Statistics Support Appraisal and Revalidation? Randomised study of physician attitudes, *Clinical Medicine*, 7 (4), 332–8.

Cullen, R. (2006) *Health Information on the Internet; a study of providers, quality and users*, Praeger.

Cumming, A. D. and Ross, M. T. (2008) The Tuning project (medicine) – learning outcomes/competences for undergraduate medical education in Europe, University of Edinburgh, available from www.tuning-medicine.com.

Curran, C. F., Sundar, M. N. and Westhe, D. R. (2003) A Same-day Standard for Responding to Drug Information Requests by a Pharmaceutical Company, *Drug Information Journal*, 37 (2), 241–9.

Currell, R. and Urquhart, C. (2005) Reviewing the Evidence on Nursing Record Systems, *Health Informatics Journal*, 11 (1), 33–44.

Dali, K. and Dilevko, J. (2006) Towards Improved Collections in Medical Humanities: fiction in academic health sciences libraries, *Journal of Academic Librarianship*, 32 (3), 259–73.

Davies, J. (2001) Providing Information. In Robson, A. S., Bawden, D. and Judd, A. (eds), *Pharmaceutical and Medicines Information Management*, Churchill Livingstone, 60–74.

Delaney, E. L. (2003) GlaxoSmithKline Pharmaceuticals Research and Development: document delivery in a global corporate environment, *Interlending and Document Supply*, **31** (1), 15–20.

Dowse, F. M. and Sen, B. (2007) Community Outreach Library Services in the UK: a case study of Wirral Hospital NHS Trust (WHNT), *Health Information and Libraries Journal*, **24** (3), 177–87.

Duckett, B., Walker, P. and Donnelly, C. (2008) *Know It All; Find It Fast*, 3rd edn, Facet Publishing.

Dudden, R. F. (2007) *Using Benchmarking, Needs Assessment, Quality Improvement, Outcome Measurement, and Library Standards: a how-to-do-it manual*, Neal-Schuman.

Dudden, R. F., Corcoran, K., Kaplan, J., Magouirk, J., Rand, D. C. and Smith, B. T. (2006) The Medical Library Association Benchmarking Network: development and implementation, *Journal of the Medical Library Association*, **94** (2), 107–17.

Ellis, D., Barker, R., Potter, S. and Pridgeon, C. (1993) Information Audits, Communication Audits and Information Mapping: a review and survey, *International Journal of Information Management*, **13** (2), 134–52.

Evans, G. E., Layzell Ward, P. and Rugaas, B. (2000) *Management Basics for Information Professionals*, Neal-Schuman.

Fanner, D. and Urquhart, C. (2008) Bibliotherapy for Mental Health Service Users. Part 1: a systematic review, *Health Information and Libraries Journal*, **25** (4), 237–52.

Farrar, S., Yi, D., Sutton, M., Chalkley, M., Sussex, J. and Scott, A. (2009) Has payment by results affected the way that English hospitals provide care? Difference-in-difference analysis, *British Medical Journal*, **339**, b3047 (online).

Fisher, G. (2006) Time to Change the Healthcare Record on Document Management?, *Records Management Bulletin*, **134**, 17–18.

Flake, D. and Poznaka, V. (2007), An Innovative Interlibrary Loan Program Linking Eastern Europe's Latvia with US and Canadian Medical Libraries, *Journal of Interlibrary Loan, Document Supply and Electronic Reserve*, **17** (3), 9–14.

Flannery, M. A. (2001) Building a Retrospective Collection in Pharmacy: a brief history of the literature with some considerations for US health sciences library professionals, *Bulletin of the Medical Library Association*, **89** (2), 212–21.

Funk, C. J. (2008) Using Standards to Make Your Case: examples from the medical library community, *New Library World*, **109** (5/6), 251–7.

Gavel, Y. and Hedlund, L. O. A. (2008) Managing Document Supply: a

SAGA come true in Sweden [Karolinska Institute medical library], *Interlending and Document Supply*, **36** (1), 30–6.

General Medical Council (2009) *Tomorrow's Doctors*, General Medical Council, available from
www.gmc-uk.org/education/undergraduate/undergraduate_policy/
tomorrows_doctors.asp.

Ghosh, B. and Scott, J. E. (2007) Effective Knowledge Management Systems for a Clinical Nursing Setting, *Information Systems Management*, **24** (1), 73–84.

Glover, S. W., Addison, J., Gleghorn, C., Aalai, E. and Annis, S. (2009) Interlending and Document Supply Trends in NHS North West Health Libraries 2003/2004 to 2006/2007, *Health Information and Libraries Journal*, **26** (1), 32–8.

Goldzweig, C. L., Towfigh, A., Maglione, M. and Shekelle, P. G. (2009) Costs and Benefits of Health Information Technology: new trends from the literature, *Health Affairs*, **28** (2), 282–93.

Goodman, E. and Boyce, G. (2001) End-user Support and Training. In Robson, A. S., Bawden, D. and Judd, A. (eds), *Pharmaceutical and Medicines Information Management: principles and practice*, Churchill Livingstone, 218–33.

Goodman, E. C. (1994) Records Management as an Information Management Discipline – case study from SmithKline Beecham Pharmaceuticals, *International Journal of Information Management*, **14** (2), 134–43.

Grodzinski, A. (2001) A Medical Book Collection for Physician Assistants, *Bulletin of the Medical Library Association*, **89** (3), 277–86.

Hall, L. A. (2001) The Archives of the Pioneer Health Centre, Peckham, in the Wellcome Library, *Social History of Medicine*, **14** (3), 525–38.

Haygarth-Jackson, A. R. (1987) Journal Holdings and Interlibrary Lending Policies in the Pharmaceuticals Industry: a survey of ICI Pharmaceuticals Division, *Interlending and Document Supply*, **15** (1), 3–6.

Hicks, A. (2000) Training the Users. In Booth, A. and Walton, G. (eds) (2000) *Managing Knowledge in Health Services*, Facet Publishing, 182–94.

Hicks, D. (2009) Reading is Good for You, *Library and Information Update*, **8** (10), October, 46–8.

Hill, T. W. and Roth, K. L. (2009) Electronic Document Delivery: a six-year study to benchmark the shift to electronic interlibrary loan in two hospital libraries, *Journal of the Medical Library Association*, **97** (1), 54–7.

Jashapara, A. (2004) *Knowledge Management; an integrated approach*, Financial Times/Prentice Hall.

Javier, C. (2004) Training the Health Information Seeker: quality issues in health information, *Library Trends*, **53** (2), 360–74.

Jha, A. K., Doolan, D., Grandt, D., Scott, T. and Bates, D. W. (2008) The Use of Health Information Technology in Seven Nations, *International Journal of Medical Informatics*, 77 (12), 848–54.

Kasarab, H. V. (2006) The Impact of e-Resources on Document Supply in a Corporate Pharmaceutical Library: the experience of Novo Nordisk, *Interlending and Document Supply*, **34** (3), 105–8.

Kelson, J. (2008) Local Purchasing of Journals is Required in Addition to a Nationally Purchased Collection to Meet the Information Needs of NHS Staff, *Evidence-based Library and Information Practice*, 3 (1), 68–71.

Kennedy, J. (2007) Providing Consumer Health Services Without a Circulating Collection, *Journal of Hospital Librarianship*, 7 (3), 43–8.

Kipnis, D. G. and Kaplan, G. E. (2008) Analysis and Lessons Learned Instituting an Instant Messaging Reference Service at an Academic Health Sciences Library: the first year, *Medical Reference Services Quarterly*, 27 (1), 33–51.

Kovacs, D. K. (2009) *The Kovacs Guide to Electronic Library Collection Development*, 2nd edn, Neal-Schuman.

Kraft, M. (2007) Integrating and Promoting Medical Podcasts into the Library Collection, *Medical Reference Services Quarterly*, 26 (1), 27–35.

Lacroix, E. M. and Collins, M. E. (2007), Interlibrary Loan in US and Canadian Health Sciences Libraries 2005: update on journal article use, *Journal of the Medical Library Association*, **95** (2), 189–94.

Lagoze, C. and Fielding, D. (1998) Defining Collections in Distributed Digital Libraries, *D-Lib Magazine*, paper 11 (online), available from www.dlib.org/dlib/november98/lagoze/11lagoze.html.

Lancaster, F. W. (1993) *If you Want to Evaluate Your Library*, 2nd edn, Library Association Publishing.

Lapidus, M. (2007) Educating Student Pharmacists About Herbal Medicines: faculty–librarian cooperation, *Health Information and Libraries Journal*, 24 (4), 267–73.

Lapidus, M. and Bond, I. (2009) Virtual Reference: chat with us!, *Medical Reference Services Quarterly*, 28 (2), 133–42.

Liebowitz, J., Schieber, R. A. and Andreadis, J. (eds) (2009) *Knowledge Management in Public Health*, CRC Press.

Littleton, D. and Rethlefsen, M. (2008) Library Learning Space – empirical research and perspective, *Medical Reference Services Quarterly*, 27 (3), 313–21.

McAphee, S., Vucovich, L. and Lorbeer, E. R. (2008) Beyond Core Journal

Lists: identifying the best journals for your collection, *Journal of Electronic Resources in Medical Libraries*, **5** (4), 373–7.

Marge, K., Baker, L. M. and Wilson, F. L. (2009) *The Medical Library Association Guide to Health Literacy*, Neal-Schuman.

Marshall, J. G. (2007) Measuring the Value and Impact of Health Library and Information Services: past reflections, future possibilities, *Health Libraries and Information Journal*, **24** (1), 4–17.

Martell, C. (2008) The Absent User: physical use of academic library collections and services continues to decline 1995–2006, *Journal of Academic Librarianship*, **34** (5), 400–7.

Martin, B. (2008) Knowledge Management, *Annual Review of Information Science and Technology*, **42**, 371–424.

Matthews, J. R. (2007) *The Evaluation and Measurement of Library Services*, Libraries Unlimited.

Merry, P. (1997) *Effective Use of Health Care Information: a review of recent research*, British Library Research and Innovation Report 48, Bowker Saur.

Murphy, S. A. (2007) The Effects of Portfolio Purchasing on a Specialized Subject Collection, *Journal of the Medical Library Association*, **95** (1), 9–13.

Nicholson, L. and Walker, H. (1995) Health Records. In Sheaff, R. and Peel, V. (eds), *Managing health Service Information Systems: an introduction*, Open University Press, 120-32.

Nonaka, I. and Takeuchi, H. (1995) *The Knowledge-creating Company*, Oxford University Press.

Ogunsola, L. A. (2009) Health Information Literacy: a road map for poverty alleviation in the developing countries, *Journal of Hospital Librarianship*, **9** (1), 59–72.

Oliver, K. B., Dalrymple, P., Lehmann, H. R., McClennan, D. A., Robinson, K. A. and Twose, C. (2008) Bringing Evidence to Practice: a team approach to teaching skills required for an informationist role in evidence-based clinical and public health practice, *Journal of the Medical Library Association*, **96** (1), 50–7.

Orzano, A. J., McInerney, C. R., Scharf, D., Tallia, A. F. and Crabtree, B. F. (2008) A Knowledge Management Model: implications for enhancing quality in health care, *Journal of the American Society for Information Science and Technology*, **59** (3), 489–505.

Orzano, A. J., McInerney, C. R., McDaniel, R. R., Meese, A., Alajmi, B., Mohr, S. M. and Tallia, A. F. (2009) A Medical Home: value and implications of knowledge management, *Health Care Management Review*, **34** (3), 224–33.

Peacock, D., Walton, G. and Booth, A. (2004) The Role of LIS in

Supporting Learning. In Walton, G. and Booth, A. (eds) *Exploiting knowledge in health services*, Facet Publishing, 97–112.

Perkins, H. (2009) The Effect that Electronic Collections has on Cataloguing, *Journal of Hospital Librarianship*, **9** (2), 218–20.

Petrak, J., Markulin, H. and Matic, T. (2008) Information Literacy in Continuing Professional Development of Medical Practitioners: a Croatian example, *Health Information and Libraries Journal*, **25** (1), 46–9.

Petrinic, T. and Urquhart, C. (2007) The Education and Training Needs of Health Librarians – the generalist versus specialist dilemma, *Health Information and Libraries Journal*, **24** (3), 167–76.

Poll, R. and te Boekhorst, P. (2007) *Measuring Quality: performance measurement in libraries*, 2nd edn, IFLA Publications no. 127, K. G. Saur.

Pomerantz, J. and Marchionini, G. (2007) The Digital Library as Place, *Journal of Documentation*, **63** (4), 505–33.

Rammell, E. (1997) The Trials of Clinical Records Management: making sense of GCP, *Records Management Bulletin*, 81, 3–5.

Rankin, J. A., Grefsheim, S. F. and Canto, C. C. (2008) The Emerging Informationist Speciality: a systematic review of the literature, *Journal of the Medical Library Association*, **96** (3), 194–206.

Robbins, K. and Daniels, K. (2001) Benchmarking Reference Desk Service in Academic Health Science Libraries: a preliminary survey, *College and Research Libraries*, **62** (4), 348–53.

Robinson, L. and Bawden, D. (2007) Evaluation of Outreach Services for Primary Care and Mental Health; assessing the impact, *Health Information and Libraries Journal*, **24** (1), 57–66.

Robinson, L., Hilger-Ellis, J., Osborne, L., Rowlands, J., Smith, J. M., Weist, A., Whetherly, J. and Phillips, R. (2005) Healthcare Librarians and Learner Support: a review of competencies and methods, *Health Libraries and Information Journal*, **22** (4), supplement 2, 42–50.

Robson, A. S. and Riggens, J. L. (2001) Medical Information in the Pharmaceutical Industry. In Robson, A. S., Bawden, D. and Judd, A. (eds), *Pharmaceutical and Medicines Information Management: principles and practice*, Churchill Livingstone, 124–43.

Ryder, J. (2002) *Directory of Health Library and Information Services in the UK and the Republic of Ireland 2002–03*, 11th edn, Library Association Publishing.

Samuel, J. (1998) The Intellectual Infrastructure Underpinning Records Management within Pfizer Central Research, *Records Management Journal*, **8** (1), 11–23.

Schulte, S. J. (2008) Integrating Information Literacy into an Online

Undergraduate Nursing Informatics Course: the librarian's role in the design and teaching of the course, *Medical Reference Services Quarterly*, 27 (2), 158–72.

Shearer, B. S. and Nagy, S. P. (2003) Developing an academic Medical Library Core Journal Collection in the (almost) Post-print Era: the Florida State University College of Medicine Medical Library experience, *Journal of the Medical Library Association*, 91 (3), 292–302.

Shearer, B. S., Klatt, C. and Nagy, S. P. (2009) Development of a New Academic Digital Library: a study of usage data of a core medical electronic journal collection, *Journal of the Medical Library Association*, 97 (2), 93–101.

Shedlock, J. and Byrd, G. D. (2003) The Association of Academic Health Science Libraries Annual Statistics: a thematic history, *Journal of the Medical Library Association*, 91 (2), 178–85.

Shedlock, J. and Walton, L. (2004) An Academic Medical Library Using LibQUAL+: the experience of the Gaiter Health Sciences Library, Northwestern University, *Journal of Library Administration*, 40 (3/4), 99–110.

Sokolow, D. (2004) You want me to do what? Medical Librarians and the Management of Archival Collections, *Journal of Hospital Librarianship*, 4 (4), 31–50.

Spatz, M. (2008) *Answering Consumer Health Questions: the Medical Library Association guide for reference librarians*, Neal-Schuman.

Srikantaiah, T. K. and Koenig, M. E. D. (eds) (2008) *Knowledge Management in Practice: connections and context*, ASIST Monograph Series, Information Today.

Stamatoplos, A. (2005) Digital Archiving in the Pharmaceutical Industry, *Records Management Journal*, 39 (4), 54–9.

Stevenson, J. (1997) The Business Archives Council Survey of the Historical Records of the Pharmaceutical Industry, *Records Management Bulletin*, 81, 15 and 23.

Streeter, J. L., Lu, M. T. and Rybicki, F. J. (2007) RadiologyWiki.org: the free radiology resource that anyone can edit, *Radiographics*, 27 (4), (July), 1193-1200.

Sze, M. C. (1985) The Departmental Information Professional: a role of increasing importance, *Online Information Review*, 9 (6), 467–70.

Tao, D., McCarthy, P. G., Krieger, M. M. and Webb, A. B. (2009) The Mobile Reference Service: a case study of an onsite reference service program at the School of Public Health, *Journal of the Medical Library Association*, 97 (1), 34–40.

Taylor, P. (2006) *From Patient Data to Medical Knowledge: the principles and practice of health informatics*, Blackwell/BMJ.

Tod, A. M., Bond, B., Leonard, N., Gilsenan, I. J. and Palfreyman, S. (2007) Exploring the Contribution of the Clinical Librarian to Facilitating Evidence-based Nursing, *Journal of Clinical Nursing*, 16 (4), 621–9.

Trinder, V. M., Fleet, G. E. and Gray, A. E. (2007) Evaluating the Impact of Library User Training Programmes Across Thames Valley Strategic Health Authority in the UK, *Health Information and Libraries Journal*, 24 (1), 34–40.

Tsoukas, H. (2005) *Complex Knowledge: studies in organizational epistemology*, Oxford University Press.

Turtle, K. M. (2005) A Survey of Users and Non-users of a UK Teaching Hospital Library and Information Service, *Health Information and Libraries Journal*, 22 (4), 267–75.

Urquhart, C., Yeoman, A. and Sharp, S. (2002) *NeLH {National electronic Library for Health} Communities of Practice Evaluation Report*, University of Aberystwyth, available from http://users.aber.ac.uk/cju/.

Urquhart, C., Turner, J., Durbin, J. and Ryan, J. (2007) Changes in Information Behaviour in Clinical Teams After Introduction of a Clinical Librarian Service, *Journal of the Medical Library Association*, 95 (1), 14–22.

Wakeham, M. (2002) From Locked Cupboard to University Library: libraries for nurses in the UK after 1955, *Library History*, 18 (1), 39–60.

Walton, G. and Booth, A. (eds) (2004) *Exploiting Knowledge in Health Services*, Facet Publishing.

Walton, G., Childs, S. and Blenkinsopp, E. (2005) Using Mobile Technologies to Give Health Students Access to Learning Resources in the UK Community Setting, *Health Information and Libraries Journal*, 22 (4), supplement 2, 51–65.

Watson, E. M. (2008) The Role of Subject Knowledge in Academic Health Sciences Libraries: an online survey of librarians working in the United States, *Journal of the Canadian Health Libraries Association*, 29 (1), 3–11.

Weightman, A., Urquhart, C., Spink, S. and Thomas, R. (2009) The Value and Impact of Information Provided through Library Services for Patient Care: developing guidance for best practice, *Health Libraries and Information Journal*, 26 (1), 63–71.

Wilson, T. D. (2002) The Nonsense of Knowledge Management, *Information Research*, 8 (1), paper 144, available from www.informationr.net/ir/8–1/paper144.html.

Whipple, E. C., Richwine, M. W., Kaneshiro, K. N. and Brahmi, F. A. (2009) Teaching First-year Medical Students Where to go First:

connecting information needs to e-resources, *Medical Reference Services Quarterly*, **28** (2), 180–6.

Whitmore, S. C., Grefsheim, S. F. and Rankin, J. A. (2008) Informationist Programme in Support of Biomedical Research: a programme description and preliminary findings of an evaluation, *Health Information and Libraries Journal*, **25** (2), 135–41.

Wood, M. S. (ed.) (2007a), *Introduction to health Sciences Librarianship*, Routledge.

Wood, M. S. (ed.) (2007b), *Medical Librarian 2.0: use of Web 2.0 technologies in reference services*, Haworth Press.

Wyatt, J. C. (2001) *Clinical Knowledge and Practice in the Information Age: a handbook for health professionals*, RSM Press.

Further reading

Dudden, R. F. (2007) *Using Benchmarking, Needs Assessment, Quality Improvement, Outcome Measurement, and Library Standards: a how-to-do-it manual*, Neal-Schuman.

General Medical Council (2009) *Tomorrow's Doctors*, General Medical Council, available from www.gmc-uk.org/education/undergraduate/undergraduate_policy/tomorrows_doctors.asp.

Lankshear, C. and Knobel, M. (eds), *Digital Literacies: concepts, policies and paradoxes*, Peter Lang.

Pomerantz, J. and Marchionini, G. (2007) The Digital Library as Place, *Journal of Documentation*, **63** (4), 505–33.

Spatz, M. (2008) *Answering Consumer Health Questions: the Medical Library Association guide for reference librarians*, Neal-Schuman.

Afterword

This book has been written with the aim of providing an overview of the whole area of healthcare information so that readers can gain an understanding of the way in which health information and knowledge are created, communicated and used. It is, as we have seen, a particularly information-intensive domain, with an information-rich environment, in terms of the number and diversity of its information resources and communication pathways. It is also an area which is quite introspective in information terms, as we can see from the many journals, articles, and web resources devoted to health information, and the services which provide it.

This extensive health information literature is obviously a great advantage to the writer of a book such as this, as it means that the reader can be directed to it for detailed coverage of specific aspects. To have reproduced even a part of this material would have resulted in an impossibly long book, while to have ignored it would have made the book seriously incomplete.

To include links to a significant part of the health information literature, and to provide a reasonable range of examples of resources and services, runs the risk of producing a disorganized compilation, which would be difficult for the reader to comprehend fully. Some structuring is necessary if an explanation of this complex area is to be effective. In this book, this has been provided by the conjunction of three frameworks: domain analysis; communication chain; and the categorization of resources into levels. The author's hope is that this conjunction of frameworks has provided a helpful basis for the reader to gain a real understanding of the topic.

Keeping up to date

Healthcare information never remains static. At the time of writing, in the UK current issues included the absorption of the main NHS information provider, formerly the National Library for Health, into a new NHS Evidence service, with unclear consequences for many of its services. Controversy about the feasibility of the troubled implementation of an electronic medical record system intensified as a result of the problems caused by the economic downturn. Plans to allow patients greater choice of family doctor services were announced, leading to issues of need for information about doctors, and about transferability of medical records. And the health service was considering some form of quality assurance for healthcare websites. Internationally, there was concern about the provision of 'swine flu portals' by commercial providers, and whether these gave information consistent with health policies in different countries. The World Health Organization was compiling the first-ever comprehensive directory of medical libraries.

By the time this book appears in print, these issues, problems and possibilities will no doubt have been succeeded by others. A book, even if it runs into many editions, can never be a fully adequate tool for giving an up-to-date picture of a dynamic domain such as this. While the general understanding of the domain which it promotes should stay valid for many years, readers with a strong interest in the topic will need to find ways of keeping in touch with new developments.

Journal literature

One way of doing this is through the journal literature. As will be clear from the many different journals cited in this book, the literature of healthcare information, like that of healthcare itself, is scattered over numerous journals: on health information specifically, but also on library and information science, on health informatics, and on the healthcare disciplines. Of these, however, two are at present particularly helpful and informative:

- *Journal of the Medical Library Association*
- *Health Information and Libraries Journal.*

Other useful health information journals include:

- *Drug Information Journal*
- *Journal of Hospital Librarianship*

- *Medical Reference Services Quarterly*
- *Journal of Electronic Resources in Medical Libraries*
- *Health Informatics Journal*
- *Journal of the American Medical Informatics Association.*

Of 'general' journals of librarianship and information science, those which most commonly publish material on health information issues include:

- *Journal of Information Science*
- *Journal of Documentation*
- *Information Processing and Management*
- *Library Trends*
- *Journal of the American Society for Information Science and Technology*
- *Aslib Proceedings.*

Professional groups

Membership of the numerous local, national and international groups dealing with health information, mentioned with web links in Chapter 1, is also a good way of keeping in touch. National examples are the US Medical Libraries Association and the UK Health Libraries Group of CILIP. International examples are the European EAHIL and the health and bioscience section of IFLA. If a particular information individual or organization can be identified, subscribing to a blog, taking RSS feeds from their websites, or following them on Twitter, are all ways of keeping in touch.

Our blog

Finally, this book offers its own 'updating service', via its accompanying blog.[1] While the framework for understanding healthcare information should remain substantially unchanged, at least until a new edition of this book, there will inevitably be frequent new developments and sources, changes to web addresses, and so on. These will be announced on the book's blog, categorized by chapter and section. We welcome comments from readers. Comment on what is written in the book will be gratefully received, as will – particularly – news of new sources, publications, etc. These will be included in the blog where appropriate, and contributors will, of course, be acknowledged in any future editions of the book.

Note

1 http://understandinghealthcareinformation.com.

Index